D1156916

Fifty Years of Serial Thrills

by ROY KINNARD

The Scarecrow Press, Inc.
Metuchen, N.J., and London
1983

Library of Congress Cataloging in Publication Data

Kinnard, Roy, 1952–
   Fifty years of serial thrills.

   Includes indexes.
   1. Moving-picture serials. I. Title.
PN1995.9.S3K5 1983   791.43'05   83–13950
ISBN 0-8108-1644-X

The following individuals have generously donated materials, as well as their time, to this project: Buster Crabbe, Jean Rogers, Stephen Sally, Vito Stasiunaitus, Rich Vitone, Al Bielski, and Mike Saenz.

TABLE OF CONTENTS

INTRODUCTION--THE SERIAL QUAGMIRE

When they are seen today by audiences, at revival theatres, on television, or on videotape, the old movie serials are almost always misunderstood--viewed either as cheap, shoddy relics of the past that are hopelessly inadequate as entertainment, or denigrated as inept "camp" good only for a condescending laugh. But criticizing a film made in the thirties or forties by applying the standards of a half-century later is hardly an objective approach; and the facile, ultimately meaningless concept of "camp," usually defined as something that is so bad or outrageous that it is "good" (that is, amusing), has always been one of the more decadent and offensive of pseudo-intellectual conceits.

Every age has, or had, its share of inept, worthless entertainment, but there is a huge difference between dated acting styles and directorial techniques and simple lack of talent. But modern audiences (often led on by irresponsible "critics" who see nothing wrong in clubbing old movies to death with the "camp" truncheon) often fail to make the distinction, with the sorry result that audiences at revival theatres, ignorant of what they are watching, will deride an excellent feature deserving far more respect as vehemently as they mock a cheap Republic serial. But they are wrong in both cases, and that is the greatest flaw in the "camp" sensibility--its alliance with callous philistinism. In all fairness, there are certain allowances that should be made when watching old movies--allowances for the times in which they were made and for the circumstances under which they were produced. Most movie serials were made for children, which makes it rather pointless to adopt a tone of superiority by laughing at them, and prompts one to speculate on the future nature of "camp," the followers of which will probably be laughing at kinescopes of Captain Kangaroo TV shows.

Most present-day moviegoers are too young even to

A typical serial predicament: Virginia Lindley bound and gagged in The Black Widow (Republic, 1947).

remember what a movie serial was, aside from the obvious knowledge that these films were presented in continuing weekly installments. The last American movie serial, a feeble effort called Blazing the Overland Trail, was released by Columbia Pictures over a quarter of a century ago in 1956. Actually, it is surprising that Columbia was still in the game at that late date. Seriously ailing since the end of World War II, serials were finally killed off by a combination of social and economic factors, and by the time Blazing the Overland Trail appeared Columbia was the only studio still actively involved in serial production. The independent producers had called it quits long before; Republic Pictures had released their last serial in 1955, and Universal Pictures had shut down their serial unit in 1946, shrewdly preferring to rely on a backlog of re-issues to exploit what they correctly perceived to be a dwindling market.

The reasons were simple enough: the Hollywood of old was quite different from its modern counterpart. In those days there were five major production companies, Metro-Goldwyn-Mayer, Warner Brothers, 20th Century-Fox, Paramount, and RKO; two lesser contenders, Universal and Columbia; plus a scattering of independent and "poverty row" firms. Each of the seven large studios managed the seemingly impossible task of releasing one feature film every ten days, year in and year out, in addition to a variety of short subjects, cartoons, newsreels, and serial chapters. A typical Columbia Pictures campaign booklet sent to exhibitors during the 1940-41 season announced, in addition to the company's schedule of 35 or so features, 104 one-reel short subjects, 26 two-reel comedies, and four serials, each running 15 two-reel chapters. This prodigious output was possible only within the old studio contract system, under which producers, directors, writers, actors, and technical people of every description were all signed to long-term contracts at the studios, paid whether they were currently working on a project or not, and ready to apply their diverse talents to the demands of the Hollywood dream machine. But chinks finally began to appear in the studios' armor as labor unions, gaining increasing power, demanded and received higher wages, which of course inflated production costs. As those production costs rose, the serials, always low man on the totem pole at the Hollywood movie factories to begin with, were forced to slash their already distressingly low budgets, and as corners were mercilessly trimmed the films naturally lost more and more of their audience following, producing less income, which of course necessitated further budget cuts, and so on. The last serials were certainly pretty dismal, many of them hastily and desperately produced around stock footage from earlier releases. As an example, in 1955 die-hard Columbia released a witless hodgepodge called Captain Africa, starring John Hart, and eked out its minuscule budget through the simple expedient of raiding studio vaults for stock footage from another serial, The Phantom, released twelve years before. The Phantom, based on the popular newspaper comic strip by Lee Falk, had starred Tom Tyler in the title role, and for Captain Africa Columbia merely attired star John Hart in a similar costume and intercut scenes from the two films, matching the old footage with the new--or at least attempting to. There are many similar and equally depressing tales from the dying days of the serials.

The relentless and inescapable downward economic spiral probably would have been enough in itself to finish the serials, but then there was television to compound the problem. What 12-year-old would pay to see Captain Africa when George Reeves was waiting at home in The Adventures of Superman--for free? And so the serials died. Not that very many people cared, or should have, for that matter, for the serial had contributed almost nothing to motion-picture art, and the audience had been primarily juvenile and unsophisticated from the beginning of the sound era. Cheaply and hastily produced, with their ludicrous plots, wooden heroes and cardboard sets, the serials were held in contempt by nearly everyone. They were the dumping ground for has-beens, the last refuge of the hack, the lowest common denominator in the studio equation. But serials also frequently introduced new talent, like John Wayne, or tackled subjects considered too outlandish for features. Buck Rogers took its audience to other planets more than a decade before the innovative Destination Moon was released, and the current success of blockbuster features like Star Wars, The Empire Strikes Back, and Raiders of the Lost Ark, all of which owe a great deal to the chapter plays of yesteryear, suggests that the serials deserve, if not respect, then at least a backward glance.

This book does not pretend to offer an in-depth examination of its subject; what it does attempt to do is place the serial in its proper perspective by examining the more interesting and memorable films produced in a largely reviled genre that, by all rights, should have vanished with the arrival of the microphone in Hollywood. This survey of films is broken down by studio, with the more outstanding efforts of each company examined in some detail, followed by an index of the other releases in chronological order, indicating title, year of release, number of episodes, re-issue and feature version titles, director(s), and principal casts. With the exception of Universal and Mascot, both of which have a steady continuity of production from the silent into the sound period, the majority of the silent serials (and the early sound films from the small independent producers as well) are listed chronologically but are not broken down by studio, for during the silent era many short-lived production firms cluttered the market, inevitably floundering and dying out with the arrival of sound. Together, the indexes provided here form a catalogue of every motion-picture serial released in the United States from 1912 to 1956, totalling 500 different titles.

There are a few surprises and facts of note to be found in this listing. More than half of all the serials produced in America were made during the silent period (of these 269 productions, fewer than two dozen, in complete or partial form, survive today). Universal Pictures emerges as the serial leader (in terms of quantity at least); that studio produced a total of 145 serials, 69 of them in the sound era. The longest serial was The Hazards of Helen, a 1919 Helen Holmes vehicle released by Kalem, offering a stupefying 119 episodes! During the silent days, major (or soon-to-be major) production companies like Paramount and Warner Brothers briefly entered (and promptly left) the serial field, with the 15-episode A Dangerous Adventure (Warner Brothers, 1922) directed by Sam and Jack Warner themselves. Many fine actors, such as Walter Brennan and Boris Karloff, found themselves marking time in early serials before they achieved fame and, needless to say, once they left they never returned. There were also those who never left; William Desmond (who surely appeared in more serials than any other actor) and Francis Ford (director John Ford's brother), once two of the more popular names of the silents, slid down the cast lists as the years went by, until finally they were humble bit players.

Also included is a cross-reference listing indicating the feature version and re-issue titles of various serials. Over the years, many serials were re-edited into feature versions for the purpose of earning further profits from those exhibitors who were not interested in booking the individual chapters, or, much later, for television distribution. The feature version titles listed are only for those films carrying titles different from those of the original serials from which they were edited. The re-issue titles are titles applied to rereleases of complete serials. This was done (often rather deceitfully) to create the impression of a new film or to imply a non-existent sequel. Thus The Tiger Woman became Perils of the Darkest Jungle on re-issue; Captain America became The Return of Captain America, and so on. This abundance of duplicitous titles is understandably confusing to many movie fans, and this information is presented here in an effort to clarify the situation.

The classic silent serial: Pearl White (center) in <u>Perils of Pauline</u> (Pathé, 1914).

THE SILENT YEARS

The motion-picture serial had its beginnings in the silent era, and was originally conceived as a lowly sales gimmick. The first serial, entitled What Happened to Mary? and starring Mary Fuller, was a joint effort between the Thomas Edison studios and a now-forgotten publication called McClure's Ladies' World. The concept was basic, but valid; a continuing fiction story was first published in McClure's, and as each installment appeared a corresponding chapter of the Edison serial would be released to theaters, cannily exploiting what was, in effect, an early incarnation of the movie "tie-in." As a film, What Happened to Mary? was nothing special, even by the standards of its day, and it was not even really a true serial as the genre would later be defined; the installments were not incomplete "cliffhangers" in the usual sense, each episode ending on a resolved, upbeat note and being a complete short subject in itself. The same was also true of The Adventures of Kathlyn, released by Selig the following year and starring Kathlyn Williams.

The Adventures of Kathlyn was more action-oriented than its predecessor, but it was with The Perils of Pauline, starring Pearl White and released by Pathé in 1914 that the silent serial really hit its stride. Directed by Louis Gaznier and Donald MacKenzie, The Perils of Pauline, especially considering its classic status, was a surprisingly crude and often inept production, with frenzied, overwrought acting and amateurish direction. Even the narrative title cards were often plagued by sub-literate misspellings, but despite its awkwardness The Perils of Pauline was exciting, quickly-paced entertainment to the audiences of the period; each chapter's tense cliffhanger ending kept them coming back for more, and made a star of Pearl White in the process. All flaws aside, The Perils of Pauline remains noteworthy in a historical sense, if only because it firmly established the serial as an important and economically viable commodity.

Interestingly, the silent serials were dominated by women performers, with Helen Holmes and Ruth Roland emerging as Pearl White's most serious rivals (Roland was probably the best actress of them all, and her performances stand the test of time fairly well). What was most important about the silent serials, though, was the fact that these films were readily accepted by an adult audience as a respectable form of entertainment. It was certainly no disgrace for a performer to appear in serials during the silent days, and even a celebrity like magician Harry Houdini turned up in a little opus called The Master Mystery in 1919.

The silent serials continued to flourish until the mid-twenties, when Jazz-Age audiences, growing more and more sophisticated in the aftermath of World War I, finally began to tire of them. The hectic, fast-paced age of the flapper, personified on movie screens by Clara Bow, had arrived, and perhaps the serials should have changed with the times, experimenting with new formats and subject matter. But with their audience deserting them in greater and greater numbers, they continued to decline in the late twenties, and really hit a snag during the chaotic transitional period between silents and talkies. With the chapter plays appealing to a decimated audience, studio executives probably had serious doubts about continuing with serial production at all, and with the coming of sound the genre had lapsed into a sorry state indeed, dismissed by critics and relegated to the stagnant backwaters of the cinema, where the films played only during matinees at second- and third-run neighborhood theaters. By the sound era, serials were produced only by the two smaller major studios, Columbia and Universal, and a tiny group of feeble independents; it was accepted that serials were for children and the most unsophisticated of adults, and if an actor appeared in one he was either a newcomer who had not yet achieved respectability, an outright incompetent, or a tragic has-been desperately clutching at straws on the way downhill to obscurity. To put it simply, the sound serial was the comic book of the screen, and when movie audiences of the time watched them (usually in impatient anticipation of the feature that would immediately follow the chapter), they did so with lowered expectations.

SILENT SERIAL INDEX

WHAT HAPPENED TO MARY? (1912--Edison), 12 episodes. Cast: Mary Fuller, Ben Wilson, Marc MacDermott, Charles Ogle, Barry O'Moore, William Wadsworth.

The ADVENTURES OF KATHLYN (1913--Selig), 13 episodes. Directed by F. J. Grandon. Cast: Kathlyn Williams, Tom Santschi, Charles Clary, William Carpenter, Goldie Coldwell, Hurri Taingh.

WHO WILL MARRY MARY? (1913--Edison), 6 episodes. Cast: Mary Fuller.

The ACTIVE LIFE OF DOLLY OF THE DAILIES (1914--Edison), 12 episodes. Directed by Walter Edwin. Cast: Mary Fuller, Yale Boss, Charles Ogle, Harry Beaumont, Gladys Hulette, William West, Edwin Clark, Richard Neil.

The PERILS OF PAULINE (1914--Pathé), 20 episodes. Directed by Louis Gaznier and Donald MacKenzie. Cast: Pearl White, Crane Wilbur, Paul Panzer, Edward Jose, Francis Carlyle, Eleanor Woodruff, Clifford Bruce, Sam Ryan, Donald MacKenzie.

The MILLION DOLLAR MYSTERY (1914--Thanhouser), 23 episodes. Directed by Howell Hansell. Cast: Florence LaBadie, Marguerite Snow, James Cruze, Frank Farrington, Sidney Bracy, Creighton Hale, Mitchell Lewis, Irving Cummings.

The MAN WHO DISAPPEARED (1914--Edison), 10 episodes. Directed by Charles Brabin. Cast: Marc MacDermott, Miriam Nesbitt, Barry O'Moore.

The BELOVED ADVENTURER (1914--Lubin), 15 episodes. Directed by Arthur V. Johnson. Cast: Arthur V. Johnson, Lottie Briscoe, Florence Hackett, Ruth Bryan, Howard M. Mitchell, J. Robinson Hall, Jeanette Hackett, Ed McLaughlin, Josephine Longworth, D. B. Bentley.

The EXPLOITS OF ELAINE (1914--Pathé), 14 episodes. Directed by Louis Gaznier and George B. Seitz. Cast: Pearl White, Creighton Hale, Arnold Daly, Sheldon Lewis, Floyd Buckley.

The HAZARDS OF HELEN (1914--Kalem), 119 episodes. Directed
by J. P. McGowan and James Davis. Cast: Helen Holmes, Helen
Gibson, Robyn Adair, Ethel Clisbee, Tom Trent, G. A. Williams,
Pearl Anibus, P. S. Pembroke, Roy Watson.

ZUDORA, THE TWENTY MILLION DOLLAR MYSTERY (1914--
Thanhouser), 20 episodes. Directed by Howell Hansell. Cast:
James Cruze, Marguerite Snow, Harry Benham, Sidney Bracey,
Mary Elizabeth Forbes, Frank Farrington.

RUNAWAY JUNE (1915--Reliance), 15 episodes. Directed by
Oscar Engle. Cast: Norma Phillips, Margaret Loveridge, J. W.
Johnston, Charles Mason, Rica Allen.

The FATES AND FLORA FOURFLUSH (1915--Vitagraph), 3 episodes. Directed by Wally Van. Cast: Clara Kimball Young, Charles
Brown, L. Rogers Lytton, Temple Saxe, George Stevens.

The GODDESS (1915--Vitagraph), 15 episodes. Directed by Ralph
Ince. Cast: Anita Stewart, Earle Williams, Paul Scardon, William
Dangman, Ned Finley.

The DIAMOND FROM THE SKY (1915--North American), 30 epi-
sodes. Directed by William Desmond Taylor and Jacques Jaccard.
Cast: Lottie Pickford, Irving Cummings, William Russell, Charlotte
Burton, Eugenie Ford, George Periolat, Orral Humphrey, W. J.
Tedmarsh, Lillian Buckingham.

The ROAD OF STRIFE (1915--Lubin), 15 episodes. Directed by
John Ince. Cast: Crane Wilbur, Mary Charleston, Jack Standing,
Rosetta Brice, Charles Brandt, Howard M. Mitchell.

The GIRL AND THE GAME (1915--Signal), 15 episodes. Directed
by J. P. McGowan. Cast: Helen Holmes, J. P. McGowan, Leo
Maloney, George McDaniel.

NEAL OF THE NAVY (1915--Pathé), 14 episodes. Directed by
W. M. Harvey. Cast: Louise Lorraine, William Courtleigh, Jr. ,
Ed Brady, Henry Stanley, William Conklin.

The NEW EXPLOITS OF ELAINE (1915--Pathé), 10 episodes.
Directed by George B. Seitz. Cast: Pearl White, Creighton Hale,
Arnold Daly, Edwin Arden.

The RED CIRCLE (1915--Pathé), 14 episodes. Cast: Ruth Roland, Frank Mayo, Philo McCullough, Gordon Sackville.

The ROMANCE OF ELAINE (1915--Pathé), 12 episodes. Directed
by George B. Seitz. Cast: Pearl White, Creighton Hale, Arnold
Daly, Lionel Barrymore.

The VENTURES OF MARGUERITE (1915--Kalem), 16 episodes.
Directed by Hamilton Smith, John E. Mackin and Robert Ellis.

Cast: Marguerite Courtot, Richard Purdon, E. T. Roseman, Paula Sherman.

The STRANGE CASE OF MARY PAGE (1916--Essanay), 15 episodes. Directed by J. Charles Haydon. Cast: H. B. Walthall, Edna Mayo, Ernest Cossart, Sydney Ainsworth, Harry Dunkinson, Tom Cummerford.

The MYSTERIES OF MYRA (1916--Pathé), 15 episodes. Directed by Theodore Wharton and Leo Wharton. Cast: Jean Sothern, Howard Estabrook, Allen Murnane, M. W. Rale, Bessie Wharton.

The SECRET OF THE SUBMARINE (1916--American), 15 episodes. Directed by George Sargent. Cast: Juanita Hansen, Tom Chatterton, William Tedmarsh, Lamar Johnstone, Hylda Hollis, George Clancy, Harry Edmundson, George Webb, Hugh Bennet.

The IRON CLAW (1916--Pathé), 20 episodes. Directed by Edward Jose. Cast: Pearl White, Creighton Hale, Sheldon Lewis, Harry Fraser, J. E. Dunn.

BEATRICE FAIRFAX (1916--International), 15 episodes. Directed by Theodore Wharton and Leo Wharton. Cast: Harry Fox, Grace Darling, Robin Townley, Olive Thomas, Elaine Hammerstein, Nigel Barre, Mae Hopkins, Mary Cranston, Betty Howe.

The CRIMSON STAIN MYSTERY (1916--Consolidated), 16 episodes. Directed by T. Hayes Hunter. Cast: Maurice Costello, Ethel Grandin, Eugene Strong, Thomas J. McGrane.

GLORIA'S ROMANCE (1916--Kleine), 20 episodes. Directed by Walter Edwin. Cast: Billie Burke, David Powell, Frank McGlynn, Henry Kolker, William Roselle, William T. Carleton, Jule Power, Henry Weaver, Helen Hart.

The GRIP OF EVIL (1916--Pathé), 14 episodes. Directed by W. A. Douglas and Harry Harvey. Cast: Jackie Saunders, Roland Bottomley.

LASS OF THE LUMBERLANDS (1916--Signal), 15 episodes. Directed by J. P. McGowan and Paul C. Hurst. Cast: Helen Holmes, Thomas Lingham, L. D. Maloney, Ned Chapman, Paul C. Hurst, Katherine Goodrich, F. L. Hemphill.

PEARL OF THE ARMY (1916--Pathé), 15 episodes. Directed by Edward Jose. Cast: Pearl White, Ralph Kellard, Marie Wayne, Floyd Buckley, Theodore Friebus, W. T. Carleton.

PERILS OF OUR GIRL REPORTERS (1916--Niagara), 15 episodes. Directed by George W. Terwilliger. Cast: Helen Green, Earl Metcalfe, Zena Keefe, William Turner.

The SCARLET RUNNER (1916--Vitagraph), 12 episodes. Directed

by Wally Van and William P. S. Earle. Cast: Earle Williams,
Jean Stuart, Arthur Robinson, Billie Billings, Thomas R. Mills,
Alex Kyle, Zena Keefe, Walter McGrail, Josephine Earle, Harold
Forshay, Betty Howe, Nellie Anderson, Ray Walburn.

The SEQUEL TO THE DIAMOND FROM THE SKY (1916--Ameri-
can), 4 episodes. Directed by Edward Sloman. Cast: William
Russell, Charlotte Burton, Rhea Mitchell, William Tedmarsh, Orral
Humphrey.

The SHIELDING SHADOW (1916--Pathé), 15 episodes. Directed
by Louis Gasnier and Donald MacKenzie. Cast: Grace Darmond,
Leon Bary, Ralph Kellard, Madeline Traverse.

The YELLOW MENACE (1916--Serial Film Co.), 16 episodes.
Directed by William Steiner. Cast: Edwin Stevens, Florence Malone, Margaret Gale, Gerald Griffen, Marie Treador, Armand Cor-
tes, J. A. Hall.

The FIGHTING TRAIL (1917--Vitagraph), 15 episodes. Directed
by William Duncan. Cast: William Duncan, Carol Holloway, George
Holt, Joe Ryan, Walter Rodgers, Fred Burns.

The FATAL RING (1917--Pathé), 20 episodes. Directed by
George B. Seitz. Cast: Pearl White, Earle Fox, Warner Oland,
Floyd Buckley, Cesare Gravina, Ruby Hoffman, Henry G. Sell,
Mattie Ferguson.

The SECRET KINGDOM (1917--Vitagraph), 15 episodes. Directed
by Theodore Marston and Charles Brabin. Cast: Charles Richman,
Dorothy Kelly, Arline Pretty, Joseph Kilgour, Ned Finley, Charles
Wellesley, William Dunn.

PATRIA (1917--International), 15 episodes. Directed by Theodore
Wharton, Leo Wharton and Jacques Jaccard. Cast: Irene Castle,
Warner Oland, Milton Sills, Floyd Buckley, Marie Walcamp, George
Maharoni, Allen Murname, Dorothy Green.

The RAILROAD RAIDERS (1917--Signal), 15 episodes. Directed
by J. P. McGowan. Cast: Helen Holmes, Thomas Lingham, L. D.
Maloney, Paul C. Hurst, William Brunton, F. L. Hemphill, William
Behrens, J. P. McGowan, William Buhler, Marvin Martin.

The NEGLECTED WIFE (1917--Pathé), 15 episodes. Directed
by William Bertram. Cast: Ruth Roland, Roland Bottomley, Corrine Grant, Neil Hardin, Philo McCullough.

The GREAT SECRET (1917--Serial Producing Co.), 18 episodes.
Directed by Christy Cabanne. Cast: Francis X. Bushman, Beverly
Bayne, Belle Bruce, Fred R. Stanton, Tom Blake, Sue Balfour,
Charles Ripley, Ed Connelly, Helen Dunbar, Art Ortego, Charles
Fang, Tammany Young, Dorothy Haydel, W. J. Butler.

The MYSTERY OF THE DOUBLE CROSS (1917--Pathé), 15 episodes. Directed by William Parke. Cast: Mollie King, Leon Barry, Ralph Stuart, Gladden James, Theodore Friebus, Harry Fraser.

JIMMY DALE ALIAS THE GREY SEAL (1917--Monmouth), 16 episodes. Directed by Harry Webster. Cast: E. K. Lincoln, Doris Mitchell, Edna Hunter, Paul Panzer.

The HIDDEN HAND (1917--Pathé), 15 episodes. Cast: Doris Kenyon, Sheldon Lewis, Arline Pretty, Mahlon Hamilton.

The LOST EXPRESS (1917--Signal), 15 episodes. Directed by J. P. McGowan. Cast: Helen Holmes, Thomas Lingham, L. D. Maloney, John McKinnon, Ed Hearn, William Brunton.

The SEVEN PEARLS (1917--Pathé), 15 episodes. Directed by Donald MacKenzie. Cast: Mollie King, Creighton Hale, Floyd Buckley, Leon Bary, Henry G. Sell, John J. Dunn.

WHO IS NUMBER ONE? (1917--Paramount), 15 episodes. Directed by William Bertram. Cast: Kathleen Clifford, Cullen Landis.

VENGEANCE AND THE WOMAN (1917--Vitagraph), 15 episodes. Directed by William Duncan. Cast: William Duncan, Carol Holloway, George Holt, Tex Allen, Vincente Howard, Fred Burns, S. E. Jennings, Walter Rodgers.

A WOMAN IN THE WEB (1918--Vitagraph), 15 episodes. Directed by Paul C. Hurst and David Smith. Cast: Hedda Nova, J. Frank Glendon.

WOLVES OF KULTUR (1918--Pathé), 15 episodes. Directed by Joseph A. Golden. Cast: Leah Baird, Charles Hutchison, Sheldon Lewis.

The SILENT MYSTERY (1918--Burston), 15 episodes. Directed by Francis Ford. Cast: Francis Ford, Rosemary Theby, Mae Gaston, Elsie Van Name.

The IRON TEST (1918--Vitagraph), 15 episodes. Directed by R. N. Bradbury and Paul C. Hurst. Cast: Antonio Moreno and Carol Holloway.

The HOUSE OF HATE (1918--Pathé), 20 episodes. Directed by George B. Seitz. Cast: Pearl White, Antonio Moreno, Floyd Buckley, Peggy Shanor, Paul Dillon, John Gilmour.

HANDS UP (1918--Pathé), 15 episodes. Directed by James W. Horne. Cast: Ruth Roland, George Chesebro, George Larkin, Easter Walters.

A FIGHT FOR MILLIONS (1918--Vitagraph), 15 episodes. Directed by William Duncan. Cast: William Duncan, Edith Johnson, Joe Ryan, Walter Rodgers.

The EAGLE'S EYE (1918--Wharton), 20 episodes. Directed by George A. Lessey and Wellington Playter. Cast: King Baggot, Marguerite Snow, William N. Bailey, Florence Short, Bertram Marburgh, Paul Everton, John P. Wade, Fred Jones.

A DAUGHTER OF UNCLE SAM (1918--Jaxon), 12 episodes. Directed by James Morton. Cast: William Sorelle, Jane Vance, Henry Carleton, Lewis Dayton.

The ADVENTURES OF RUTH (1919--Pathé), 15 episodes. Directed by George Marshall. Cast: Ruth Roland, Herbert Hayes, Thomas Lingham, Charles Bennett, Helen Case, William Human, Helen Deliane.

The BLACK SECRET (1919--Pathé), 15 episodes. Directed by George B. Seitz. Cast: Pearl White, George B. Seitz, Walter McGrail, Wallace McCutcheon.

MAN OF MIGHT (1919--Vitagraph), 15 episodes. Directed by William Duncan. Cast: William Duncan, Edith Johnson, Joe Ryan.

The TERROR OF THE RANGE (1919--Pathé), 7 episodes. Directed by Stuart Paton. Cast: Betty Compson, George Larkin, H. P. Carpenter, Fred M. Malatesta, Ora Carew.

The PERILS OF THUNDER MOUNTAIN (1919), 15 episodes. Directed by R. N. Bradbury and W. J. Burman. Cast: Antonio Moreno, Carol Holloway, Kate Price.

The MASKED RIDER (1919--Arrow), 15 episodes. Directed by Aubrey M. Kennedy. Cast: Harry Myers, Ruth Stonehouse, Paul Panzer.

The LIGHTNING RAIDER (1919--Pathé), 15 episodes. Directed by George B. Seitz. Cast: Pearl White, Warner Oland, Henry G. Sell.

The GREAT GAMBLE (1919--Pathé), 15 episodes. Directed by Joseph A. Golden. Cast: Anne Luther, Charles Hutchison, Richard Neil, Billy Moran, William Cavanaugh, Warner Cook.

The CARTER CASE (1919--Oliver), 15 episodes. Directed by Donald MacKenzie. Cast: Herbert Rawlinson, Marguerite Marsh, Ethel Grey Terry, Kempton Green, William Pike, Coit Albertson, Joseph Marba, Don Hall, Louis Wolheim, Gene Baker, Leslie Stowe, Frank Wunderlee.

BOUND AND GAGGED (1919--Pathé), 10 episodes. Directed by George B. Seitz. Cast: Marguerite Courtot, George B. Seitz,

Frank Redman, Nellie Burt, Joe Cuny, Harry Semele, Harry Stone, Tom Goodwin, John Reinhard.

The FATAL FORTUNE (1919--SLK Serial Corp.), 15 episodes. Directed by Donald MacKenzie. Cast: Helen Holmes, Jack Levering, Leslie King, Bill Black, Frank Wunderlee, Floyd Buckley, Sidney Dalbrook, Nellie Lindrith.

LIGHTNING BRICE (1919--National), 15 episodes. Directed by Paul C. Hurst. Cast: Jack Hoxie, Ann Little, Steve Clemente, Ben Corbett, Walter Patterson, George Champion, Slim Lucas, George Hunter, Paul C. Hurst.

The LURKING PERIL (1919--Wistaria), 15 episodes. Directed by George Morgan. Cast: Anne Luther, George Larkin, Ruth Dwyer, William Betchel, Peggy Shanor.

The MASTER MYSTERY (1919--Octagon), 15 episodes. Directed by Burton King. Cast: Harry Houdini, Marguerite Marsh, Ruth Stonehouse, William Pike, Charles Graham, Edna Britton, Floyd Buckley.

The MYSTERY OF 13 (1919--Burston), 15 episodes. Directed by Francis Ford. Cast: Francis Ford, Rosemary Theby, Pete Girard, Mark Fenton, Phil Ford, Jack Saville, Doris Dare, Jack Lawton, V. Orilo, Ruth Maureice, Nigel De Brulier.

SMASHING BARRIERS (1919--Vitagraph), 15 episodes. Directed by William Duncan. Cast: William Duncan, Edith Johnson, Walter Rodgers, George Stanley, Fred Darnton, Slim Cole, William McCall.

TRAIL OF THE OCTOPUS (1919--Hallmark), 15 episodes. Directed by Duke Worne. Cast: Ben Wilson, Neva Gerber, William Dyer, Howard Crampton, William Carroll, Marie Pavis.

The TIGER'S TRAIL (1919--Pathé), episodes. Directed by Robert Ellis and Paul C. Hurst. Cast: Ruth Roland, George Larkin, Fred Kohler, Easter Walters, Harry G. Moody, George Field, Mark Strong.

The WHIRLWIND (1920--Allgood), 15 episodes. Directed by Joseph A. Golden. Cast: Charles Hutchinson, Edith Thornton, Richard Neil, Ben Walker.

A WOMAN IN GREY (1920--Serico), 15 episodes. Directed by James Vincent. Cast: Arline Pretty, Henry G. Sell, Fred Jones, Margaret Fielding, James A. Heenan, Ann Brodie, Violet de Bicari, Adelaine Fitzgallen.

VANISHING TRAILS (1920--Canyon), 15 episodes. Directed by Leon de la Mothe. Cast: Franklyn Farnum, Mary Anderson, L. M. Wells, Duke R. Lee, Harry Lonsdale, Vester Pegg, W. A. Orlamond, Pedro Leon.

VELVET FINGERS (1920--Pathé), 15 episodes. Directed by George B. Seitz. Cast: George B. Seitz, Marguerite Courtot, Tommy Carr, Harry Semels, Lucille Lennox, Frank Redman, Joe Cuny.

The VEILED MYSTERY (1920--Vitagraph), 15 episodes. Directed by Antonio Moreno, Webster Cullison and William J. Bowman. Cast: Antonio Moreno, Pauline Curley, H. A. Barrows, Nenette de Courey, W. L. Rogers, George Reed.

TRAILED BY THREE (1920--Pathé), 15 episodes. Directed by Perry Vekroff. Cast: Frances Mann, Stuart Holmes, John Webb Dillon, Wilfred Lytell, William Welsh, Ruby Hoffman, John Wheeler.

The TIGER BAND (1920--Holmes), 15 episodes. Directed by Gilbert F. Hamilton. Cast: Helen Holmes, Jack Mower, Dwight Crittenden, Omar Whitehead, Billy Brunton.

THUNDERBOLT JACK (1920--Berwilla), 10 episodes. Directed by Francis Ford and Mudock MacQuarrie. Cast: Jack Hoxie, Marin Sais, Chris Frank, Steve Clemente, Alton Hoxie, Edith Stayart.

The THIRD EYE (1920--Pathé), 15 episodes. Directed by James W. Horne. Cast: Eileen Percy, Warner Oland, Jack Mower, Olga Grey, Mark Strong.

SON OF TARZAN (1920--National), 15 episodes. Directed by Harry Revier and Arthur J. Flaven. Cast: P. Dempsey Tabler, Karla Scram, Manilla Martan, Gordon Griffith, Lucille Rubey, Kamuela C. Searle, De Sacia Saville, Kathleen May, Frank Morrell, Ray Thompson, Eugene Burr, Frank Earle, Mae Giraci.

The SILENT AVENGER (1920--Vitagraph), 15 episodes. Directed by William Duncan. Cast: William Duncan, Edith Johnson, Jack Richardson, Virginia Nightingale, Ernest Shields, Willis L. Robards, William S. Smith.

The SCREAMING SHADOW (1920--Hallmark), 15 episodes. Directed by Duke Worne. Cast: Ben Wilson, Neva Gerber, William Dyer, Howard Crampton, William Carroll, Fred Gamble, Joseph W. Girard, Francis Terry, Pansy Porter, Claire Mille, Joseph Manning.

RUTH OF THE ROCKIES (1920--Pathé), 15 episodes. Directed by George Marshall. Cast: Ruth Roland, Herbert Heyes, Thomas Lingham, Fred Burns, Norma Bichole, William Gilliss, Jack Rollens.

PIRATE GOLD (1920--Pathé), 10 episodes. Directed by George B. Seitz. Cast: Marguerite Courtot, George B. Seitz, Frank Redman, William Burt, Joe Cuny, Harry Stone, Harry Semels.

The PHANTOM FOE (1920--Pathé), 15 episodes. Directed by

Bertram Millhauser. Cast: Juanita Hansen, William N. Bailey, Warner Oland, Harry Semels, Wallace McCutcheon, Nina Cassavant, Tom Goodwin, Joe Cuny.

The $1,000,000 REWARD (1920--Grossman), 15 episodes. Directed by George A. Lessey. Cast: Lillian Walker, Coit Albertson, George A. Lessey, William Pike, Joseph Marba, Leora Spellman, Bernard Randall, Charles Middleton.

BRIDE 13 (1920--Fox), 15 episodes. Directed by Richard Stanton. Cast: Marguerite Clayton, John O'Brien, Greta Hartman, William Lawrence, Mary Christensen, Arthur Earle.

The EVIL EYE (1920--Hallmark), 15 episodes. Directed by J. Gordon Cooper and Wally Van. Cast: Benny Leonard, Stuart Holmes, Ruth Dwyer, Maria Shotwell, Madam Marstini, Bernard Randall.

DAREDEVIL JACK (1920--Pathé), 15 episodes. Directed by W. S. Van Dyke. Cast: Jack Dempsey, Josie Sedgwick, Lon Chaney, Spike Robinson, Ruth Langston, Hershall Mayall, Fred Starr, Frank Lanning, Albert Cody, Al Kaufman.

The BRANDED FOUR (1920--Select), 15 episodes. Directed by Duke Worne. Cast: Ben Wilson, Neva Gerber, Joseph Girard, William Dyer, Ashton Dearholt, Pansy Porter, William Carroll.

The MYSTERY MIND (1920--Supreme), 15 episodes. Directed by William Davis and Fred Sittenham. Cast: J. Robert Pauline, Peggy Shanor, Paul Panzer, Ed Rogers, Violet MacMillian, De Sacia Saville.

The LOST CITY (1920--Warner Brothers), 15 episodes. Directed by E. A. Martin. Cast: Juanita Hansen, George Chesebro, Frank Clark, Hector Dion.

The INVISIBLE RAY (1920--Frohman), 15 episodes. Directed by Harry Pollard. Cast: Jack Sherrill, Ruth Clifford, Sidney Bracy, Ed Davis, Corrine Uzzell, W. H. Tooker.

HIDDEN DANGERS (1920--Vitagraph), 15 episodes. Directed by William Bertram. Cast: Joe Ryan, Jean Page.

The HAWK'S TRAIL (1920--Burston), 15 episodes. Directed by W. S. Van Dyke. Cast: King Baggot, Rhea Mitchell, Grace Darmond, Harry Lorraine, Fred Windermere, Stanton Heck, George Siegmann.

The INVISIBLE HAND (1920--Vitagraph), 15 episodes. Directed by William J. Bowman. Cast: Antonio Moreno, Pauline Curley, Brinsley Shaw, Jay Morley, Sam Polo, George Mellcrest.

FANTOMAS (1920--Fox), 20 episodes. Directed by Edward Sedgwick. Cast: Edna Murphy, Ed Roseman, Eva Balfour, Johnny Walker, Lionel Adams, John Willard.

The FATAL SIGN (1920--Pathé), 14 episodes. Directed by Stuart
Paton. Cast: Claire Anderson, Harry Carter, Joseph W. Girard,
Boyd Irwin, Leo Maloney.

DOUBLE ADVENTURE (1921--Pathé), 15 episodes. Directed by
W. S. Van Dyke. Cast: Charles Hutchison, Josie Sedgwick, Ruth
Langston, Carl Stockdale, S. E. Jennings, Louis D'Or.

FIGHTING FATE (1921--Vitagraph), 15 episodes. Directed by
William Duncan. Cast: William Duncan, Edith Johnson, Larry
Richardson, Ford West, Frank Weed, William McCall.

The HOPE DIAMOND MYSTERY (1921--Kosmik), 15 episodes.
Directed by Stuart Paton. Cast: Grace Darmond, George Chesebro,
Harry Carter, William Marion, Boris Karloff, Carmen Phillips,
William Puckley, May Yohe.

MIRACLES OF THE JUNGLE (1921--Warner Brothers), 15 episodes. Directed by E. A. Martin and James Conway. Cast: Ben
Hagerty, Wilbur Higby, Irene Wallace, Genevieve Burte, Al Ferguson, Frederic Peters, John George.

The PURPLE RIDERS (1921--Vitagraph), 15 episodes. Directed
by William Bertram. Cast: Joe Ryan, Elinor Field, Joseph Rixon,
William Shields, Vincente Howard, Maude Emory.

The SKY RANGER (1921--Pathé), 15 episodes. Directed by George
B. Seitz. Cast: June Caprice, George B. Seitz, Harry Semels,
Peggy Shanor, Frank Redman, Joe Cuny.

The GREAT REWARD (1921--Burston), 15 episodes. Directed
by Francis Ford. Cast: Francis Ford, Ella Hall.

HURRICANE HUTCH (1921--Pathé), 15 episodes. Directed by
George B. Seitz. Cast: Charles Hutchison, Lucy Fox, Warner
Oland, Diana Deer, Ann Hastings, Harry Semels, Frank Redman.

The BLUE FOX (1921--Arrow), 15 episodes. Directed by Duke
Worne. Cast: Ann Little, J. Morris Foster, Joseph W. Girard,
Charles Mason, William LaRock, Hope Loring, Lon Seefield.

The AVENGING ARROW (1921--Pathé), 15 episodes. Directed
by William J. Bowman and W. S. Van Dyke. Cast: Ruth Roland,
Ed Hearn, Frank Lackteen, Virginia Ainsworth, Vera Sisson, Otto
Lederer.

The ADVENTURES OF TARZAN (1921--Weiss Brothers--Numa
Pictures), 15 episodes. Directed by Robert F. Hill. Cast: Elmo
Lincoln, Louise Lorraine, Percy Pembroke, Frank Whitson, James
Inslee, Lillian Worth, George Momberg, Frank Merrill, Joe Martin,
Charles Gay, Maceo Bruce Sheffield.

BREAKING THROUGH (1921--Vitagraph), 15 episodes. Directed

by Robert Ensminger.   Cast: Carmel Myers, Wallace MacDonald, Vincente Howard.

The MYSTERIOUS PEARL (1921--Photoplay Serials Co.), 15 episodes. Directed by Ben Wilson. Cast: Ben Wilson, Neva Gerber.

The YELLOW ARM (1921--Pathé), 15 episodes. Directed by Bertram Millhauser. Cast: Juanita Hansen, Marguerite Courtot, Warner Oland, William N. Bailey, Tom Keith, Stephan Carr.

CAPTAIN KIDD (1922--Star Serial Corp.), 15 episodes. Directed by J. P. McGowan. Cast: Eddie Polo, Katherine Myers, Leslie J. Casey, Sam Polo, Malveen Polo.

WHITE EAGLE (1922--Pathé), 15 episodes. Directed by W. S. Van Dyke and Fred Jackman. Cast: Ruth Roland, Earl Metcalfe, Otto Lederer, Harry Girard, Frank Lackteen, Virginia Ainsworth, Bud Osborne.

NAN OF THE NORTH (1922--Arrow), 15 episodes. Directed by Duke Worne. Cast: Ann Little, Leonard Clapham, Joseph W. Girard, Hal Wilson, Howard Crampton, J. Morris Foster, Edith Stayart.

GO GET 'EM HUTCH (1922--Pathé), 15 episodes. Cast: Charles Hutchison, Marguerite Clayton, Richard R. Neil, Frank Hagney, Pearl Shepard, Joe Cuny, Cecile Bonnel.

The JUNGLE GODDESS (1922--Export-Import Film Co.), 15 episodes. Directed by James Conway. Cast: Elinor Field, Truman Van Dyke, Vonda Phelps, Marie Pavis, Olin Francis, William Pratt, H. G. Wells, George Reed.

A DANGEROUS ADVENTURE (1922--Warner Brothers), 15 episodes. Directed by Sam Warner and Jack Warner. Cast: Grace Darmond, Philo McCullough, Jack Richardson, Robert Agnew, Derelys Perdue, Mabel Stark, Captain J. R. Riccarde.

SPEED (1922--Pathé), 15 episodes. Directed by George B. Seitz. Cast: Charles Hutchison, Lucy Fox, John Webb Dillon, Harry Semels, Cecile Bonnel, Winifred Verina, Joe Cuny, Tom Goodwin, Charles Raveda.

The TIMBER QUEEN (1922--Pathé), 15 episodes. Directed by Fred Jackman. Cast: Ruth Roland, Bruce Gordon, Val Paul, Leo Willis, Frank Lackteen, Bull Montana, Al Ferguson, Otto Freez, Chris Linton.

The FIGHTING SKIPPER (1923--Arrow), 15 episodes. Directed by Francis Ford. Cast: Peggy O'Day, Jack Perrin, Bill White.

HER DANGEROUS PATH (1923--Pathé), 10 episodes. Directed by Roy Clements. Cast: Edna Murphy.

The HAUNTED VALLEY (1923--Pathé), 15 episodes. Directed by George Marshall. Cast: Ruth Roland, Jack Daugherty, Larry Steers, Eulalie Jenson, Francis Ford, William Ryno, Edouard Trebeal.

The SANTA FE TRAIL (1923--Arrow), 15 episodes. Directed by Ashton Dearholt and Robert Dillon. Cast: Neva Gerber, Jack Perrin.

RUTH OF THE RANGE (1923--Pathé), 15 episodes. Directed by Ernest C. Warde. Cast: Ruth Roland, Bruce Gordon, Lorimer Johnston, Ernest C. Warde, Pat Harmon, Andre Peyre, Harry De Vere, V. Omar Whitehead.

PLUNDER (1923--Pathé), 15 episodes. Directed by George B. Seitz. Cast: Pearl White, Harry Semels, Warren Krech.

WAY OF A MAN (1924--Pathé), 10 episodes. Directed by George B. Seitz. Cast: Allene Ray, Harold Miller, Florence Lee, Bud Osborne, Whitehorse, Lillian Gale, Kathryn Appleton, Chet Ryan, Lillian Adrian.

TEN SCARS MAKE A MAN (1924--Pathé), 10 episodes. Directed by William Parke. Cast: Allene Ray, Jack Mower, Rose Burdick, Lillian Gale, Larry Steers, Leon Kent, Harry Woods.

RIDERS OF THE PLAINS (1924--Arrow), 15 episodes. Directed by Jacques Jaccard. Cast: Jack Perrin, Marilyn Mills, Ruth Royce, Charles Brinley, Kingsley Benedict.

DAYS OF '49 (1924--Arrow), 15 episodes. Feature version: California in '49. Directed by Jacques Jaccard and Ben Wilson. Cast: Neva Gerber, Edmund Cobb, Ruth Royce, Wilbur McGaugh, Yakima Canutt, Charles Brinley, Clark Coffey.

BATTLING BREWSTER (1924--Rayart), 15 episodes. Directed by Dell Henderson. Cast: Franklyn Farnum, Helen Holmes, George Wendell, Robert Walker, Roland Rand, Lafe McKee, Leon Holmes, Barbed Wire Ryan, Jerome Lacassee.

The FORTIETH DOOR (1924--Pathé), 10 episodes. Directed by George B. Seitz. Cast: Allene Ray, Bruce Gordon, Anna May Wong, Frank Lackteen, David Dunbar, Frances Mann, Lillian Gale, Bernard Siegel.

LEATHERSTOCKING (1924--Pathé), 10 episodes. Directed by George B. Seitz. Cast: Edna Murphy, Harold Miller, David Dunbar, Frank Lackteen, Whitehorse.

INTO THE NET (1924--Pathé), 10 episodes. Directed by George B. Seitz. Cast: Edna Murphy, Jack Mulhall, Constance Bennett, Harry Semels, Bradley Barker, Frank Lackteen, Frances Landau, Tom Goodwin, Paul Porter.

GALLOPING HOOFS (1924--Pathé), 10 episodes. Cast: Allene Ray, Johnnie Walker, J. Barney Sherry, Ernest Hilliard, Armand Cortez, William Nally, George Nardelli, Albert Roccardi.

WILD WEST (1925--Pathé), 10 episodes. Directed by Robert F. Hill. Cast: Jack Mulhall, Helen Ferguson, Eddie Phillips, George Burton, Milla Davenport, Virginia Warwick, Gus Saville.

The POWER GOD (1925--Vital), 15 episodes. Directed by Ben Wilson. Cast: Ben Wilson, Neva Gerber, Mary Brooklyn, Mary Crane, John Battaglia.

SUNKEN SILVER (1925--Pathé), 10 episodes. Directed by George B. Seitz. Cast: Allene Ray, Walter Miller, Frank Lackteen, Ivan Linlow, Charlie Fang.

SECRET SERVICE SAUNDERS (1925--Rayart), 15 episodes. Directed by Duke Worne. Cast: Richard Holt, Ann Little.

PLAY BALL (1925--Pathé), 10 episodes. Directed by Spencer Bennet. Cast: Allene Ray, Walter Miller, J. Barney Sherry, Harry Semels, Mary Milnor, Wally Oettel.

IDAHO (1925--Pathé), 10 episodes. Directed by Robert F. Hill.

The FLAME FIGHTER (1925--Rayart), 10 episodes. Directed by Robert Dillon. Cast: Herbert Rawlinson, Brenda Lane, Jerome Legasse, Edward Fetherstone, Purnell Pratt, Leigh Willard, Richard Gordon.

The MYSTERY BOX (1925--Vital), 10 episodes. Directed by Alvin J. Neitz. Cast: Ben Wilson, Neva Gerber, Lafe McKee, Robert Walker, Charles Brinley, Alfred Hollingsworth, Jack Henderson.

The GREEN ARCHER (1925--Pathé), 10 episodes. Directed by Spencer Bennet. Cast: Allene Ray, Walter Miller, Burr McIntosh, Stephen Gratten, Frank Lackteen, Walter P. Lewis, Jack Tanner, Ray Allan, William Randall, Dorothy King, Wally Oettel.

CASEY OF THE COAST GUARD (1926--Pathé), 10 episodes. Directed by William Nigh. Cast: Helen Ferguson, George O'Hara, John Jarvis, J. Barney Sherry, Coit Albertson.

The BAR-C MYSTERY (1926--Pathé), 10 episodes. Directed by Robert F. Hill. Cast: Dorothy Phillips, Wallace MacDonald, Ethel Clayton, Philo McCullough, Violet Schram, Johnny Fox, Victor Potel, Billy Bletcher, Fred de Silva.

TROOPER 77 (1926--Rayart), 10 episodes. Directed by Duke Worne. Cast: Herbert Rawlinson, Hazel Deane.

VANISHING MILLIONS (1926--Sierra), 15 episodes. Directed by Alvin J. Neitz. Cast: William Fairbanks, Vivian Rich, Alec B. Francis, Sheldon Lewis, Bull Montana, Edward Cecil.

SNOWED IN (1926--Pathé), 10 episodes. Directed by Spencer Bennet. Cast: Allene Ray, Walter Miller, Frank Austin, Tom London, John Webb Dillon, Natalie Warfield, Wally Oettel, Harrison Martell.

SCOTTY OF THE SCOUTS (1926--Rayart), 10 episodes. Directed by Duke Worne. Cast: Ben Alexander, Paddy O'Flynn.

PHANTOM POLICE (1926--Rayart), 10 episodes. Directed by Robert Dillon. Cast: Herbert Rawlinson, Gloria Joy.

OFFICER 444 (1926--Goodwill), 10 episodes. Directed by Ben Wilson. Cast: Ben Wilson, Neva Gerber, Jack Mower, Phil Ford.

MYSTERY PILOT (1926--Rayart), 10 episodes. Directed by Harry Moody. Cast: Rex Lease, Kathryn McGuire.

HOUSE WITHOUT A KEY (1925--Pathé), 10 episodes. Directed by Spencer Bennet. Cast: Allene Ray, Walter Miller, Frank Lackteen, Charles West, John Webb Dillon, Natalie Warfield, William N. Bailey.

LIGHTNING HUTCH (1926--Arrow), 10 episodes. Directed by Charles Hutchison. Cast: Charles Hutchison, Edith Thornton, Virginia Pearson, Sheldon Lewis, Eddie Phillips, Ben Walker, Violet Schram.

The FIGHTING MARINE (1926--Pathé), 10 episodes. Directed by Spencer Bennet. Cast: Gene Tunney, Walter Miller, Marjorie Gay, Virginia Vance, Frank Hagney, Sherman Ross, Mike Donlin, Wally Oettel, Jack Anthony, Anna May Walthall.

ON GUARD (1927--Pathé), 10 episodes. Directed by Arch B. Heath. Cast: Cullen Landis, Muriel Kingston, Louise Du Pre, Walter P. Lewis, Tom Blake, Hal Forde, Edward Burns, Jack Bardette, Gus De Weil, Tom Poland.

FIGHTING FOR FAME (1927--Rayart), 10 episodes. Directed by Duke Worne. Cast: Ben Alexander.

The CRIMSON FLASH (1927--Pathé), 10 episodes. Directed by Arch B. Heath. Cast: Cullen Landis, Eugenia Gilbert, Tom Holding, J. Barney Sherry, Walter P. Lewis, Ivan Linow, Mary Gardner, Tony Hughes, Gus De Weil, Ed Roseman.

HAWK OF THE HILLS (1927--Pathé), 10 episodes. Directed by Spencer Bennet. Cast: Allene Ray, Walter Miller, Frank Lackteen, Paul Panzer, Wally Oettel, Jack Pratt, Jack Ganzhorn, Parks Jones, Fred Dana, Evangeline Russell, George Magrill, Chief White Horse.

KING OF THE JUNGLE (1927--Rayart), 10 episodes. Directed by Webster Cullinson. Cast: Elmo Lincoln, Sally Long, Gordon

Standing, George Kotsonaros, Arthur Morrison, Cliff Bowes, Virginia True Boardman.

MELTING MILLIONS (1927--Pathé), 10 episodes.   Directed by Spencer Bennet.   Cast: Allene Ray, Walter Miller, E. H. Calvert, Frank Lackteen, William N. Bailey, John J. Richardson, Bob Burns, Ernie Adams, John Cossar, William Van Dyke, Richard C. Travers, Ann Gladman, Eugenia Gilbert, Albert Roccardi.

The MASKED MENACE (1927--Pathé), 10 episodes.   Directed by Arch B. Heath.   Cast: Larry Kent, Jean Arthur, Tom Holding, Laura Alberta, John F. Hamilton, Gus De Weil, Agnes Dome.

The MANSION OF MYSTERY (1927--Capitol), 10 episodes.   Directed by Robert J. Horner.   Cast: William Barrymore, Teddy Reavis.

PERILS OF THE JUNGLE (1927--Weiss Brothers), 10 episodes. Directed by Jack Nelson.   Cast: Eugenia Gilbert, Frank Merrill, Bobby Nelson, Milburn Moranti, Albert J. Smith, Will Herman, Walter Maly, Harry Belmore.

The SCARLET BRAND (1927--New-Cal Film Corp.), 10 episodes. Directed by Neal Hart.   Cast: Neal Hart.

The YELLOW CAMEO (1928--Pathé), 10 episodes.   Directed by Spencer Bennet.   Cast: Allene Ray, Ed Hearn , Cyclone, Noble Johnson, Tom London, Maurice Klein, Ed Snyder, Frank Redman.

The MAN WITHOUT A FACE (1928--Pathé), 10 episodes.   Directed by Spencer Bennet.   Cast: Allene Ray, Walter Miller, E. H. Calvert, Sojin, Jeanette Loff.

MARK OF THE FROG (1928--Pathé), 10 episodes.   Directed by Arch B. Heath.   Cast: Donald Reed, Margaret Morris, George Harcourt, Gus De Weil, Frank Lackteen, Tony Hughes, Frank B. Miller, Helen Greene, Ed Roseman, Sidney Paxton, Morgan Jones, William Willis.

The MYSTERIOUS AIRMAN (1928--Weiss Brothers), 10 episodes. Directed by Harry Revier.   Cast: Walter Miller, Eugenia Gilbert.

POLICE REPORTER (1928--Weiss Brothers), 10 episodes.   Directed by Jack Nelson.   Cast: Walter Miller, Eugenia Gilbert.

PIRATES OF THE PINES (1928--Goodart), 10 episodes.   Directed by J. C. Cook.   Cast: George O'Hara.

The CHINATOWN MYSTERY (1928--Syndicate Pictures), 10 episodes.   Directed by J. P. McGowan.   Cast: Joe Bonomo, Ruth Hiatt, Francis Ford, Al Baffet.

EAGLE OF THE NIGHT (1928--Pathé), 10 episodes.   Directed

by Jim Fulton. Cast: Frank Clarke, Shirley Palmer, Josef Swickard, Max Hawley, Earle Metcalfe, Roy Wilson, Jack Richardson, Maurice Costello.

The TIGER'S SHADOW (1928--Pathé), 10 episodes. Directed by Spencer Bennet. Cast: Gladys McConnell, Hugh Allan.

The TERRIBLE PEOPLE (1928--Pathé), 10 episodes. Directed by Spencer Bennet. Cast: Allene Ray, Walter Miller, Wilfred North, Fred Vroom, Tom Holding, Larry Steers, Mary Foy, Alice McCormack, Allen Craven.

The FIRE DETECTIVE (1929--Pathé), 10 episodes. Directed by Spencer Bennet and Thomas L. Storey. Cast: Gladys McConnell, Hugh Allan, Leo Maloney, John Cossar, Frank Lackteen, Larry Steers.

QUEEN OF THE NORTHWOODS (1929--Pathé), 10 episodes. Directed by Spencer Bennet and Thomas L. Storey. Cast: Ethlyne Clair, Walter Miller.

The BLACK BOOK (1929--Pathé), 10 episodes. Directed by Spencer Bennet and Thomas L. Storey. Cast: Allene Ray, Walter Miller, Frank Lackteen, Paul Panzer, Marie Mosquini, Edith London, Willie Fung, Edward Cecil, John Webb Dillon, Evan Pearson, Clay de Roy.

THE INDEPENDENT SERIALS

The RETURN OF CHANDU (Principal Pictures, 1934), 12 episodes. Producer, Sol Lesser. Director, Ray Taylor. Screenplay, Barry Barrington. Camera, John Hickson. Music, Abe Myer.
With Bela Lugosi, Maria Alba, Clara Kimball Young, Lucien Prival, Deane Benton, Phyllis Ludwig, Cyril Armbruster.

Many actors who were later destined for stardom managed to keep busy in their salad days with work in serials. Boris Karloff, who paid his dues early in his career with appearances in several silent and sound cliffhangers, as well as minor roles in features, finally acquired richly deserved fame as the monster in Frankenstein (1931), and never again returned to the lowly chapter play. His rival in horror films, Bela Lugosi, was not so fortunate.

After years on the stage in Europe and America, as well as appearances in an occasional film, Lugosi finally achieved fame in Universal's production of Dracula, released in early 1931. Lugosi had played the vampire Count on stage since 1927, and he was so familiar with the character by the time the picture was filmed that the role had become inseparably him in a unique and startling manner; and even though, incredibly, Universal considered other actors for the part (including Paul Muni!), the studio finally came to realize that Lugosi was the obvious and only choice.

Dracula had been filmed once before, in 1922, as Nosferatu, a classic German silent film directed by F. W. Murnau. In that picture (re-made in 1979 by Werner Herzog), Count Dracula (here referred to as "Baron Orlock" because Murnau hadn't legally purchased the film rights to Bram Stoker's original novel), was played by Max Schreck, whose appearance was one of sallow, totally corrupt evil; his was a desiccated monster spreading pestilence and disease

in his deadly wake.   Nine years later, at Universal, Lugosi's
own interpretation was quite different.   Lugosi portrayed
Dracula as an outwardly cultured, apparently suave Continental charmer, handsome and immaculately clad; but beneath
the civilized veneer and the impeccable evening dress was
the satanic evil of a resurrected dead man who had preyed
on the blood of living human beings for centuries, a perverse
demon who looked normal enough to be accepted in high society by his potential victims.   This aspect of Lugosi's Dracula, more than any other single factor, elevates his conception of the role above all subsequent representations.   His
predecessor, Max Schreck, with his hairless, rat-like coun-
tenance, was so visually horrifying that he could only skulk
about in shadows, and Christopher Lee's later attempt at
the role, in which he wore a pair of canine fangs that he
must have inherited from Rin-Tin-Tin, suffered from the
same problem to a lesser degree.   Of the major interpreters
since (and there have been many deservedly minor ones as
well), only John Carradine in the '40s (adhering more closely
to the novel's description) and Frank Langella (in the dismal
1979 remake of Dracula) approached the role along the same
lines Lugosi had, though neither proved to be anywhere near
as successful.   The 1931 Dracula, though most of the film
was directed in plodding fashion by Tod Browning, was Lugosi's film and Lugosi made it a huge success at the box-
office.   Despite the generally uninspired direction, the opening scenes of the picture are magnificent, and Lugosi's performance, even after decades of spoofs and mimicry by com-
edians, remains one of the greatest ever created in movies.

After Dracula, Lugosi was riding high, a youthful and
virile 48 and considered by many to be the logical successor
to Lon Chaney, Sr.   Then, just when he seemed to have it
all, Lugosi made the single greatest mistake of his career--
he turned down the role of the monster in James Whale's
Frankenstein, feeling the part unworthy of him because it
lacked dialogue.   His decision was a monumental blunder,
for Boris Karloff, hitherto an obscure character actor, was
cast instead and rocketed to overnight stardom with his sen-
sitive and impressive portrayal.   And as if to rub salt in
Lugosi's wounds, Frankenstein was a much better film than
Dracula; Lugosi had, in fact, by refusing to play the monster,
created his own rival.

The effect on his career was almost immediate, and
Lugosi's situation wasn't improved by the ineptitude of his
agent at the time, who proceeded to sign the actor for ap-

pearances in films of minimal prestige and generally inferior quality. Only one year after Dracula, Lugosi accepted a top-billed but minor role in The Death Kiss (1932), a low-budget murder mystery set in a movie studio. White Zombie, released in 1932, a happy exception to Lugosi's run of bad luck, was a poetic, lyrical horror film that was in many respects superior to Dracula, but like Lugosi's other pictures of that period it was a low-budget, independent production, and was ignored by many reviewers despite its artistry. Not long afterwards, Lugosi descended even further down the professional ladder and was appearing in an occasional serial. The Whispering Shadow, a turgid 12-chapter opus released by Mascot in 1933 had been his first, and in 1934 he appeared, with billing above the title, in Principal Pictures' The Return of Chandu.

Deane Benton, Bela Lugosi and Phyllis Ludwig in The Return of Chandu (Principal, 1934).

Produced by Sol Lesser and directed by old serial hand Ray Taylor, The Return of Chandu was based on a popular radio adventure series of the time, and for a variety of reasons remains one of the more interesting of the independently produced serials. As the plot unfolds, Frank Chandler (Chandu), a powerful mystic, is in love with Nadji, an Egyptian princess who is at the center of a diabolical plot hatched by the members of a secret society, the Ubasti. Believing themselves to be descendants of the sunken continent Lemuria's original inhabitants, the Ubasti slavishly worship the dormant body of their goddess, who has lain through the centuries in a hidden temple awaiting the day when a human sacrifice will awaken her. The fanatical cultists intend to sacrifice Nadji to their goddess, and the Princess, who had escaped from the Ubasti once before, is again kidnapped by them and taken to their temple, where she is brought before the high priest Vindyhan and prepared for death. Chandu, after several hectic skirmishes with Vindyhan's followers, arrives at the temple and intervenes, rescuing Nadji just before a mystical thunderbolt descends from the heavens and destroys the Ubasti temple and its inhabitants.

This plot is certainly colorful and dynamic enough to provide enough good material for a feature, and in the right hands it might even have been as good as Flash Gordon, but the main problem with The Return of Chandu is Ray Taylor's flaccid direction and the inevitable padding found in nearly all serials, necessitated by the lengthy amount of footage required. Indeed, The Return of Chandu works considerably better in its feature form, Chandu on the Magic Isle, where a little judicious editorial pruning improves the film's pace substantially. Originally, Sol Lesser offered exhibitors the option of booking The Return of Chandu in a unique format: a 70-minute feature version of the serial's first few chapters (under the same title as the serial), to be followed by eight additional 20-minute episodes. This was an original distribution concept that Lesser had attempted with his earlier 12-chapter production of Tarzan the Fearless starring Buster Crabbe, but the gimmick failed to catch on; serial fans didn't care for it, and audiences preferring full-length pictures were understandably indignant when they discovered at the end of the feature that they were required to return for further chapters in order to see the complete story.

Though cheaply and quickly produced, The Return of Chandu is not lacking in production values. Some of the sets are impressively atmospheric, and one eerie prop, a huge cat idol worshipped by the cultists, is a memorable creation. The film also benefited greatly from the presence of the immense gates seen in the jungle scenes of RKO's King Kong;

the massive set is used repeatedly in The Return of Chandu, with excellent results. Lugosi's performance in this serial is good, but ineffective at times as a result of Taylor's mediocre work in the director's chair. Interestingly enough,

Two years before The Return of Chandu, Lugosi played the evil Roxor in the feature, Chandu the Magician (Fox, 1932). Irene Ware is in his grasp.

The Return of Chandu wasn't Lugosi's first encounter with the character. Two years before, at Fox studios (before their merger with 20th Century), Lugosi had starred in the feature Chandu the Magician, one of his many quickly-forgotten assignments immediately after Dracula. But Chandu the Magician, like White Zombie, hardly deserved to be forgotten. In this film Lugosi had played not Chandu (an ineffective Edmund Lowe was cast in the role), but the evil Roxor, a mad scientist bent on conquering the world with a potent death ray. Stylishly filmed, with artfully designed and strangely beautiful miniatures, Chandu the Magician was well directed

by the great William Cameron Menzies and Marcel Varnel,
with glistening photography by ace cameraman James Wong
Howe. The picture isn't perfect, and its major flaw is the
cloying and excessive "comedy relief" supplied by Herbert
Mundin; but the general design of the film, the casting, and
the all-around sense of wonder are appealing, and the fantasy
"dream sequence," with Roxor gloating as he envisions his
intended destruction of the world's capital cities with the
death ray, is a scene of real scope and power, and an in-
dication of what the later serial could have accomplished,
given more time and resources.

        Lugosi wasn't the only performer in The Return of
Chandu who had seen better days.   Clara Kimball Young,
once a star in the silent era and now a middle-aged character
actress, humbly accepted a matronly supporting role in the
film.   And while the serials were the end of the rope for
many, they offered tangible hope for others.   Lucien Prival,
an obscure character actor often seen in small parts at the
major studios, fared better with small outfits like Principal,
and in The Return of Chandu he was cast in the major role
of Vindyhan, Chandu's evil nemesis.   The serials, like the
"B" pictures, were also a useful training ground for fresh
new talent, and in The Return of Chandu the mystic's nephew
and niece were played, respectively, by 19-year-old Deane
Benton and pretty 17-year-old Phyllis Ludwig.   Sometimes,
as in the case of young Jennifer Jones, who began her career
in Republic's serial Dick Tracy vs. Crime, Inc. under the
name Phyllis Isley, these young hopefuls quickly rose above
their beginnings, but more often, as with Chandu's Benton
and Ludwig, an obvious lack of talent prevented further ad-
vancement.

        Throughout the thirties and forties, Lugosi continued
to appear in inferior horror films and serials, only occa-
sionally landing a decent role in a respectable production.
Those who have suggested that Lugosi was difficult to cast
because of his Hungarian accent either don't remember or
haven't seen his appearance in a small role opposite Greta
Garbo in MGM's Ninotchka (1939), or his poignant vignette
as a tragic gypsy in Universal's The Wolf Man (1941).   He
exuded Continental elegance in the former and ethnic pathos
in the later, proving his versatility; and he displayed so-
phistication and a genuine sense of humor as the sadistic
Ygor in Son of Frankenstein (1939) and the sequel, Ghost of
Frankenstein (1942).   In these two films Lugosi's character,
a sly demented shepherd with a broken neck (the result of

having been unsuccessfully hung for grave robbing!) who be-
friends the Frankenstein monster and uses the creature for
his own evil purposes, could easily have been morbid and
tasteless, but in Lugosi's skilled hands the part became a
ghoulish foray into black comedy, and the role is one of his
very best.   Strangely enough, and most unfortunately, casting
directors didn't seem aware of Lugosi's accomplishment (perhaps because he was so good in the role, and so well disguised by his elaborate makeup).   This performance that
by all rights should have breathed new life into his failing
career passed unnoticed by the industry, and his professional
fortunes continued to decline.   For Lugosi, the rest was
nearly all downhill, and the increasingly poor films he appeared in for poverty row studios like Monogram and PRC
were seen by few and remembered by still fewer.   His last
shot at a major film appearance came when he entertainingly
resurrected Dracula in a comic turn for Universal's Abbott
and Costello Meet Frankenstein in 1948.

In recent years a "cult" has formed around bad movies,
films ostensibly so awful that their very ineptitude supposedly
makes them entertaining.   This is, of course, the "it's so
bad it's good" "camp" notion of the sixties reborn, and while
it has some validity (Who among us hasn't at one time or
another laughed at some unintentionally ludicrous film we've
stumbled across?), it is also unavoidably steeped in ignorance.
A recent popular book on the worst movies ever made was
an appallingly uninformed volume, and clearly, many of the
films discussed were chosen solely for the controversy their
selection would provoke, with admittedly mediocre (but by
no means atrocious) pictures like Abraham Lincoln (1930)
and Parnell (1937) lambasted because it gave the rather irresponsible authors an opportunity to fire snide broadsides
at directors like D. W. Griffith and stars like Clark Gable.

Bela Lugosi, inevitably, received his share of insults,
too.   While some of the better known pictures chosen, like
the abysmal Burt Reynolds-Cybill Shephard musical At Long
Last Love, certainly did deserve the treatment they received,
many of the films so criticized were the lowest of the low,
unbelievably cheap trash like Plan 9 from Outer Space (1959),
produced by fast-buck promoters on the outermost fringes of
the film industry.   It was a tragic Lugosi, whose career began its downward path as far back as The Return of Chandu,
who finally ended his days in obscure films like Plan 9 from
Outer Space and Glen or Glenda?, and with his pronounced
accent and theatrical acting style (misunderstood by so many

modern viewers), Lugosi provides a tempting and easy target
for the chroniclers of bad movies and the attendees at trash
film festivals. Predictably enough, Lugosi's good films,
like Dracula and Son of Frankenstein, are never screened at
these allegedly humorous little retrospectives; only the celluloid dregs from Lugosi's last, sad days, for above all the
bad movie cultists must feel superior to the object of their
scorn. A bloated, artless dud of a picture like Cleopatra
(1963) may well deserve mockery and contempt, but laughing
at Plan 9 from Outer Space is far easier, and safer, even
though the mere discussion of such amateurish junk in the
same breath with professionally made films is patently ab-
surd.

Often, the reasons why a movie is bad, or how an
excellent and underrated actor like Bela Lugosi lost his
prestige and finally his career in "B" pictures and serials
can be fascinating. But among the last things the worshippers
of trash and camp seem to be interested in are film history
and intelligent discussion.

THE LOST CITY (Sherman S. Krellberg, 1935), 12 epi-
sides. Producer, Sherman S. Krellberg. Director, Harry
Revier. Screenplay, Perley Poore Sheehan, Eddie Craneman
and Leon D'Usseau; Original Story by Zelma Carroll, George
M. Merrick and Robert Dillon. Camera, Eddie Linden and
Roland C. Price. Special Effects, Norman Dawn and Kenneth
Strickfadden. Art Director, Ralph Berger. Music, Lee
Zahler.
With William (Stage) Boyd, Kane Richmond, Claudia Dell,
Josef Swickard, George F. Hayes, Ralph Lewis, Eddie Fea-
therstone, William Bletcher and Margot D'Use.

One of the more diverting aberrations to emerge from
Hollywood's "poverty row" during the thirties, The Lost City,
appropriately enough, was shot at the old Mack Sennett studios and released early the following year. This uninten-
tional giggle fest, created by independent producer Sherman
S. Krellberg, is one of those rare films in which grotesque,
overwrought acting, ham-handed direction, and the screenplay's bizarre excesses all combine nearly to justify applica-
tion of the label "camp". Indeed, the awkward gaucheries
of this vulgar little testimonial to bad taste must have seemed
outlandish even to the more unsophisticated audiences of 1935.

The Lost City goes too far at every turn, and keeps right on going far beyond the limits of credibility.

The muddled, lurid plot, such as it is, concerns a mad scientist, Zolok, who plans to conquer the world with death rays and futuristic weapons which he controls from a super-scientific city concealed within an African mountain.

The embarrassed cast of The Lost City (Sherman S. Krellberg, 1935): Eddie Featherstone, Josef Sickard, Claudia Dell and Kane Richmond.

Generating huge atmospheric storms and magnetic disturbances through his machinery, Zolok explodes ocean liners, destroys bridges and floods cities in pursuit of his goal. The artificial cause of these disasters is established by Bruce Gordon, a young electrical engineer, who tracks the source of the catastrophes to Africa and journeys there with his assist-

ant Jerry in an effort to stop the devastation. In the Lost
City, Dr. Manyus, an elderly scientific genius, is being
held captive by Zolok. It is Manyus who, very much against
his will, is actually responsible for creating the technological
wonders of the Lost City, and Zolok keeps Manyus in control
by threatening to harm the scientist's young daughter Natcha,
who is also a prisoner.

      Zolok discovers that Bruce and Jerry are now in the
area and in possession of an electrical detecting machine that
will enable them to discover the location of his city. Using
the reluctant Natcha as bait, Zolok forces her to scream
into a microphone which broadcasts her voice into a hut in
the jungle. Bruce and Jerry, hearing the girl's pleas for
help, are lured into the hut and fall through a concealed trap
door into Zolok's domain. Forming an alliance with Manyus
and Natcha, Bruce and Jerry confront Zolok, who reveals
his intentions of world conquest and eventually decides to
eliminate the intruders; he considers the resourceful Bruce
Gordon in particular threatening to his plans. Bruce and
Jerry manage to escape the Lost City with Manyus and Natcha,
though, and in the surrounding jungle they endure and survive perilous encounters with the exotic Queen Rama, her
murderous natives, and Butterfield, a scurrilous white trader,
before they are recaptured by giant black zombies created
by Zolok and under the command of Gorzo, the mad scientist's hunchbacked slave. Once more in Zolok's power, Manyus and Natcha watch in horror as Bruce is about to be executed by a disintegration ray; suddenly Gorzo, who has
turned against Zolok, helps to rescue him. Bruce, Jerry,
Natcha, Manyus, and Gorzo then flee from the Lost City, and
Zolok, now totally insane, attempts to murder them with a ray
gun. In the process he accidentally destroys himself and his
own laboratory. From a safe vantage point in the jungle,
Bruce and Natcha watch as the Lost City and all the horrors
it contains are annihilated by a colossal explosion.

      While there is the nucleus of a potentially exciting,
if outlandish, adventure film at the heart of this cluttered
mélange, the material would be far better suited to feature
use; it is just too sparse for extended serial treatment.
This is clear in the heavily-padded middle chapters of The
Lost City, which degenerate into standard low-budget jungle
tedium, momentarily relieved (and just barely) only by the
presence of Margot D'Use as the sultry and devious Queen
Rama. The main concept of the Lost City itself, and the
captive father-daughter angle, were hardly fresh even at the

time, although still basically workable; unfortunately the writers saw fit to throw in everything they could think of, and then some, cluttering up the script with preposterous gimmicks, cackling hunchbacks and a virtual army of unnecessary supporting characters.

Nor were matters improved by the acting. William (Stage) Boyd (so named in order to distinguish him from another actor, future Hopalong Cassidy William Boyd) inexplicably plays Zolok in loud-mouthed, oily, big-city gangster fashion, and while this is undoubtedly the most unusual interpretation of a "mad scientist" ever to reach the screen, the approach is hardly suitable, nor are the results effective. The leading lady is a real liability; blonde Claudia Dell emotes in a bug-eyed, hand-fluttering manner (literally bugging her

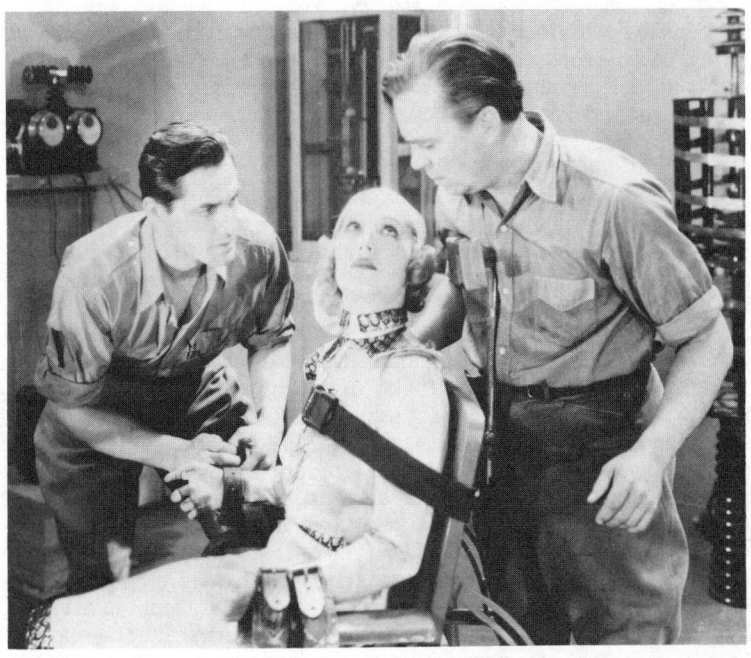

Kane Richmond (l.) and Eddie Featherstone are dumbfounded by Claudia Dell's bad acting in The Lost City (Sherman S. Krellberg, 1935).

eyes and fluttering her hands in the opening credits, her fran-

tic actions underscored by Lee Zahler's primitive, hyper-
active music), and her atrocious performance emerges as
the film's single most laughable aspect. Dell wasn't all that
inept as an actress (she came to a tragic end shortly after
The Lost City when she committed suicide by leaping from
the "H" in the giant "Hollywood" sign overlooking Los Angeles), and she was used to better advantage in small roles
in prestigious features like Cleopatra (1934) and Algiers
(1938). In this serial, however, she is clad in unattractive
costumes and directed in such a ridiculous style that her efforts are comical ("It's no use father ... he's so cru-el!,"
she simpers at one point, commenting on Zolok's activities).
The direction by Harry Revier, a veteran of the silents, is
at the root of nearly all The Lost City's problems; Revier,
who was seemingly incapable of adjusting to the subtler re-
quirements of the sound era, pushes his wild-eyed cast so
far over the edge of believability that audience derision is
inevitable. Revier's culpability is proven by the performance
he extracts from star Kane Richmond; otherwise an acceptable
and convincing actor in serials like Spy Smasher, Richmond
is terrible in The Lost City, and the film is surely the nadir
of his career.

The technical effects in this serial are a mixed bag;
they range from excellent to inept. The opening views of
exploding ships and bridges are badly shot with inadequate,
small-scale models that are made even more unconvincing
by the interpolation of newsreel scenes depicting real disasters. At one point, obvious test footage of Zolok's hidden
city, with separate elements of the matte painting out of
register, was edited into the film (apparently inadvertently),
and the resulting shot is not only hopelessly artificial, but
incongruous and puzzling as well. While these inadequacies
might otherwise have been excusable in a serial (especially
an independent one), there is enough good work in The Lost
City to suggest that the film could have been better technically. The sets were by Ralph Berger, who would later design Flash Gordon, and the superb photography by Eddie Linden contained interesting and at times striking compositions.
Linden managed one fascinating in-the-camera effects shot
in which Zolok enlarges a native to giant proportions in his
laboratory; the scene was executed in a single take through
the simple but convincing use of forced perspective. Exactly what Linden was doing photographing a lowly serial in
the first place is perplexing, for only a couple of years before he had shot Merian C. Cooper's King Kong at RKO!

The Lost City has been out of general circulation for

some years now, available for public viewing mainly in the form of 16mm "dupe" prints of the choppy, re-edited public domain feature version. The serial's blatantly racist attitudes towards its black characters no doubt has much to do with its unofficial suppression; reportedly, when a New York television station attempted to screen the film in the fifties public outcry was volatile, and the picture was immediately withdrawn. But with the current faddish interest in bad movie "cult" films, a widespread revival of The Lost City seems very likely, and Sherman S. Krellberg's exploitive and strangely fascinating 1935 cliffhanger may yet find its appropriate audience.

The NEW ADVENTURES OF TARZAN (Burroughs-Tarzan Pictures, Inc. , 1935), 12 episodes. Producers, Ashton Dearholt, George W. Stout and Ben S. Cohen. Director, Edward Kull. Screenplay, Charles F. Royal; adaptation by Charles F. Royal and Edward F. Blum, from the novels by Edgar Rice Burroughs. Camera, Edward Kull, Ernest F. Smith.
With Herman Brix, Ula Holt, Frank Baker, Dale Walsh, Harry Ernest, Ashton Dearholt and Lewis Sargent.

Like many writers whose material has been adapted to other media, Edgar Rice Burroughs, who created Tarzan for the pulp magazines in 1912, was often dissatisfied with the results of those adaptations. Burroughs, whose talent certainly deserved a better showcase than the lurid and gaudy publications that presented his work, had more reason for complaint than most of his peers. Tarzan, as conceived by Burroughs, was in reality Lord Greystoke, a scion of English royalty orphaned in the wilds of Africa and raised by a tribe of gorillas. As an adult, Greystoke discovers his true identity and returns to civilization, claiming his heritage, but he eventually prefers to return to the jungle he has grown to love. Burroughs, an imaginative and prolific writer, imbued this concept with a deep, poetic respect for nature, and the formula proved an instant and spectacular success. It wasn't long before Hollywood noticed and beckoned; the first Tarzan film was Tarzan of the Apes, a 1918 feature starring Elmo Lincoln in the leading role, but the picture was only superficially faithful to Burroughs' original novel of the same title, eschewing the character's cultured background in order to concentrate on Tarzan's perilous up-

Herman Brix and Ula Holt (both at center) in The New Adventures of Tarzan (Burroughs-Tarzan Pictures, Inc., 1935).

bringing in the jungle and his later courtship of Jane Porter (Enid Markey).

Subsequent Tarzan features and serials released throughout the silent era took their cue from this initial production, and by the time the "definitive" Tarzan in the person of Olympic swimming champion Johnny Weissmuller appeared on the sound screen in 1932, the story and characters bore little resemblance to Burroughs' original creations. Nevertheless, Tarzan the Ape Man, directed by W. S. Van Dyke, was a huge success. Although expensively mounted, it is surprisingly crude even by contemporary standards, relying on an overabundance of stock footage from Trader Horn (a previous MGM jungle epic) as well as extensive and painfully obvious rear-screen projection. The cast, however, managed to counterbalance the production's technical flaws effectively, with Weissmuller scoring well in the title role, and winsome 21-year-old Maureen O'Sullivan especially noteworthy as Jane, whose surname was inexplicably changed from "Porter" to "Parker."

Although Weissmuller's Tarzan was established as un-

educated and inarticulate in this film, and would remain so
throughout the MGM series, the picture still had enough of
the mythic stature inherent in the novels to make the fantasy
acceptable; and many scenes, such as Tarzan's climactic
and near-fatal battle with a monstrous gorilla, provided genuine thrills. Tarzan and His Mate, the follow-up released
in 1934, was also a box-office hit, and unlike most sequels
was a distinct improvement over the original, with a more
generous budget, vastly superior process photography, and
the added attraction of copious eroticism from the diverting
O'Sullivan, whose revealing semi-nude scenes encountered
some censorship problems.

Burroughs, who unlike many writers had shrewdly
retained legal control over his work, licensing the rights for
only two or three films at a time, had meanwhile reached
an agreement with another producer, and in 1933 Tarzan
appeared in a different incarnation as Buster Crabbe (the
future Flash Gordon) interpreted the role in Tarzan the Fearless, a serial distributed by Principal Pictures. If Burroughs
was hoping for a more faithful interpretation of his material,
he was no doubt disappointed, for Tarzan Crabbe was required to communicate in moronic grunts, and was even more
taciturn than Weissmuller. The results were embarrassingly
bad, and damaging to Crabbe's professional reputation. The
film itself was a cheap and crude poverty-row effort, its
only tangible asset being the beauty of blonde leading lady
Jacqueline Wells. Crabbe fared much better the same year
in King of the Jungle, a big-budget Paramount feature in
which he appeared as a Tarzan-inspired wild man envisioned
by Paramount as a potential competitor to MGM's Weissmuller. This incongruous rivalry was amusingly spoofed in
the 1934 MGM musical Hollywood Party, with Jimmy Durante
portraying a comical ape-man character named "Schnarzan,"
but King of the Jungle failed to excite the box office to any
spectacular degree, and the hoped-for sequel never materialized.

Having further reinforced its relationship with Burroughs, MGM continued unabated with the Weissmuller series,
but by the late thirties creative inertia had set in, and the
films were becoming more and more standardized with each
entry, the plots growing more contrived, Weissmuller ma-
turing physically, and O'Sullivan donning progressively more
clothing in deference to the ever-vigilant censors. Eventually,
with the introduction of saccharine "family interest" in the
person of Johnny Sheffield as Boy, Tarzan and Jane's adopted

son, the films degenerated into little more than Andy Hardy
in a tree house.   Losing faith in a stale property that the
studio understandably felt was played out, MGM decided not
to continue its association with Burroughs, and in 1942 the
series was shunted over to RKO.   O'Sullivan wisely chose to
renounce the jungle and remain at Metro.   Weissmuller, to
put it as gently as possible, had considerably fewer options,
and continued to play Tarzan at RKO in tiresome monosyllabic
fashion, with the films steadily decreasing in prestige as
their star's waistline grew wider.

Well into his forties, Weissmuller eventually called it
quits and handed the reins over to Lex Barker, moving on
to Columbia, where he found employment in the low-budget
Jungle Jim series, which one critic succinctly described as
"Tarzan with clothes on."   After its first two excellent films,
MGM had foolishly restricted its creative options by continuing its narrow treatment of the Tarzan character, ignoring
and steadfastly refusing to explore the obvious dramatic possibilities in Tarzan's further education.   Burroughs' jungle
lord finally did learn how to talk (belatedly) with the appearance of Gordon Scott, who played Tarzan in the color films
released in the late fifties and early sixties.   One of these,
Tarzan's Greatest Adventure (1959), almost lives up to its
title; but by this time few people remembered that Tarzan
had once been played, as written by Burroughs, in a forgotten 1936 serial produced by Burroughs himself.

Back in 1934, Burroughs had forged a business partnership with Ashton Dearholt, a friend who had formerly been
a representative for RKO in Guatemala, and together they
created Burroughs-Tarzan Pictures, Incorporated.   Burroughs
had high hopes for the organization as a vehicle for his properties, and conceived Tarzan in Guatemala, which would be
filmed on location in Guatemala as their first project.   Almost immediately, Burroughs encountered resistance from
the Hollywood power structure.   Attempts to borrow Johnny
Weissmuller and Buster Crabbe from their respective studios
proved unsuccessful, and the author ultimately signed Herman
Brix, yet another Olympic athlete turned aspiring actor, at
the magnanimous salary of $75.00 per week.

Arriving in tropical Guatemala late in 1934 with an
entourage totaling 29 cast and crew members, Burroughs and
Dearholt soon discovered, the hard way, the very definite
advantages of big-studio backlot filmmaking.   The neophyte
producers were continuously plagued by illness and rough

weather, with actor Don Castello, cast in the important role
of Tarzan's foe Raglan, rendered inactive by sickness shortly
after filming began. Dearholt himself was forced to assume
the vacated role (even though Castello's name appears in the
credits) and, in addition to the improvised casting, there
were romantic entanglements as well, with Dearholt being
attracted to leading lady Ula Holt, and Burroughs becoming
involved with Mrs. Dearholt, whom he would ultimately marry.
Despite the emotional difficulties and the extremely primitive
conditions inhibiting their work, the expedition somehow managed to shoot all the necessary footage after four months of
arduous toil, with filming finally completed in March of 1935.

The finished picture, expectedly, is a considerable
mess, decidedly ragged and lacking in technical finesse when
compared with other serials released during the same period
(a timorous apology for the inferior quality of the soundtrack
recording is even presented in the opening titles). Released
as The New Adventures of Tarzan (in order to distinguish
the film from the already established MGM pictures), the
serial's plot is a hopeless, convoluted mélange that, through
unlikely contrivance, moves Tarzan from his native Africa
to Guatemala as he attempts to rescue a friend held captive
by savages in a hidden Mayan city. This geographical trans-
fer, however, is less important than the conception of the
leading role, which adheres to that in Burroughs' novels.
As Tarzan, Herman Brix is visually perfect, although an in-
experienced and rather wooden novice actor. An early scene
showing Tarzan abroad a luxury liner en route to Guatemala,
suavely attired in a dinner jacket as he socializes with the
other passengers, offers a hint of the character's previously
unrealized depths, and another related sequence provides the
(intentionally) ludicrous sight of Tarzan, still impeccably attired, swinging on the ship's rigging as he pursues a thief
on the decks below. The humor in this scene grows organ-
ically out of the incongruity of the situation itself, rather
than being artificially injected through the low-brow antics
of chimpanzees and other extraneous "comedy relief," and
could well have served as an example to other interpreters
of such material.

The film's direction, alas, is stodgy and uninspired,
coming to life only sporadically, and Brix does not have the
strong guidance he needed at that early point in his career.
Several years later, after he changed his professional name
to Bruce Bennett in renunciation of his serial origins, he
would build a solid reputation as a dependable featured player

in classy "A" productions like Mildred Pierce and The Treasure of the Sierra Madre.   The rest of the cast of The New
Adventures of Tarzan were hardly as fortunate; their performances range from merely competent to inept, and most
of them faded into oblivion immediately after the movie's
release (the serial was later re-edited with new footage into
a feature, Tarzan and the Green Goddess, in 1938).

Burroughs-Tarzan Pictures, Incorporated was a short-
lived enterprise, producing only one other film of note, a
1937 documentary entitled Tundra.   If The New Adventures
of Tarzan doesn't quite measure up to its own possibilities
or the hopes of Edgar Rice Burroughs, it is still one of the
more noteworthy independent productions of the thirties, and
the important fact is that in this picture Burroughs finally
did present his most famous creation essentially intact to
the movie-going public, audaciously bucking the Hollywood
system and indulging his sensibilities as few writers are
ever able to in the motion-picture industry.   He achieved
all this at a time when independent production was far less
common than it is today.   Seen in this light, The New Adventures of Tarzan is virtually unique.

INDEPENDENT SERIAL INDEX

The VOICE FROM THE SKY (1930--Ben Wilson Productions), 10 episodes. Directed by Ben Wilson. Cast: Wally Wales, Jean Delores.

The MYSTERY TROOPER (1931--Syndicate Pictures), 10 episodes. Directed by Stuart Paton and Harry Webb. Cast: Robert Frazer, Buzz Barton, Blanche Mehaffey, Al Ferguson, Charles King, Red Eagle, White Cloud.

SIGN OF THE WOLF (1931--Metropolitan), 10 episodes. Directed by Harry Webb and Forrest Sheldon. Cast: Virginia Brown Faire, Joe Bonomo, Jack Mower, Josephine Hill, Al Ferguson, Robert Walker, Edmund Cobb, Harry Todd.

The LAST FRONTIER (1932--RKO), 12 episodes. Directed by Spencer Bennet. Cast: Lon Chaney, Jr. (Tom Kirby), Dorothy Gulliver (Betty Halliday), Mary Jo Desmond (Aggie Kirby), Francis X. Bushman, Jr. (Jeff Maillad), Joe Bonomo (Blackie), Slim Cole (Happy), Judith Barrie (Rose Matland), Richard Neil (Tiger Morris), William Desmond (Custer), LeRoy Mason (Butch), Yakima Canutt (Wild Bill Hickok), Pete Morrison (Hank), Claude Payton (Colonel Halliday), Fritzi Femm (Momma Morris), Bill Nesteld (Tex).

TARZAN THE FEARLESS (1933--Principal), 12 episodes. Directed by Robert F. Hill. Cast: Buster Crabbe (Tarzan), Jacqueline Wells (Mary Brooks), E. Alyn Warren (Dr. Brooks), Edward Woods (Bob Hall), Philo McCullough (Jeff Herbert), Matthew Betz (Nick Muran), Frank Lackteen (Abdul), Mischa Auer (Eltar), Carlotta Monti (Priestess), Symona Bonifice (Arab Woman), Darby Jones (Head Bearer).

The RETURN OF CHANDU (1934--Principal), 12 episodes. Feature version: Chandu on the Magic Island. Directed by Ray Taylor. Cast: Bela Lugosi (Chandu), Maria Alba (Princess Nadji), Clara Kimball Young (Dorothy Regent), Lucien Prival (Vindyhan), Deane Benton (Bob Regent), Phyllis Ludwig (Betty Regent), Cyril Armbruster (Sutra), Murdoch MacQuarrie (The Voice), Wilfred Lucas (Capt. Wilson), Josef Swickard (Tyba), Jack Clark (Vitras), Bryant Washburn (Prince Andra), Peggy Montgomery (Judy), Elias Lazaroff (Bara), Dick Botiller (Morta), Frazer Acosta (Nito), Harry Walker (Tagora), Charles Meacham (James), Don Brodie (Reporter).

YOUNG EAGLES (1934--First Division), 12 episodes.   Cast:
Bobby Cox (Bobby Ford), Jim Vance (Jim Adams).

QUEEN OF THE JUNGLE (1935--Screen Attractions), 12 episodes.
Directed by Robert F. Hill.   Cast: Reed Howes (David Worth),
Mary Kornman (Joan Lawrence), Dickie Jones (David as a child),
Marilyn Spinner (Joan as a child), William Walsh (John Lawrence),
Lafe McKee (Kali), George Chesbro (Ken Roberts), Eddie Foster
(Rocco), Robert Borman (Captain Blake), Barney Furey (Abdullah).

The LOST CITY (1935--Sherman S. Krellberg), 12 episodes.
Directed by Harry C. Revier.   Cast: William "Stage" Boyd (Zolok),
Kane Richmond (Bruce Gordon), Claudia Dell (Natcha), Josef Swick-
ard (Dr. Manyus), George F. Hayes (Butterfield), Ralph Lewis
(Reynolds), William Bletcher (Gorzo), Eddie Featherstone (Jerry
Delaney), Milburn Morante (Andrews), Margo D'Use (Queen Rama),
Jerry Frank (Appolyn), Gino Corrado (Ben Ali), Sam Baker (Hugo).

The NEW ADVENTURES OF TARZAN (1935--Burroughs-Tarzan
Pictures), 12 episodes.   Feature version: Tarzan and the Green
Goddess.   Directed by Edward Kull.   Cast: Herman Brix (Tarzan),
Ula Holt (Ula Vale), Frank Baker (Major Martling), Dale Walsh
(Alice Martling), Harry Ernest (Gordon Hamilton), Ashton Dearholt
(Raglan), Lewis Sargent (George), Merrill McCormick (Bouchart),
Jiggs (Nkima), Earle Dwire (Renegade), Mrs. Gentry (Queen Maya).

CUSTER'S LAST STAND (1936--Stage and Screen), 15 episodes.
Directed by Elmer Clifton.   Cast: Rex Lease (Kit Cardigan), Wil-
lian Farnum (Fitzpatrick), Reed Howes (Blade), Jack Mulhall (Lt.
Cook), Josef Swickard (Maj. Trent), Creighton Hale (Hank), Milburn
Moranti (Buckskin), Lona Andre (Belle Meade), Dorothy Gulliver
(Red Fawn).

The CLUTCHING HAND (1936--Stage and Screen), 15 episodes.
Directed by Albert Herman.   Cast: Jack Mulhall (Craig Kennedy),
Ruth Mix (Shirley McMillan), Marion Shilling (Verna Gironda), Wil-
liam Farnum (Gordon Gaunt), Yakima Canutt (Number 8), Rex Lease
(Walter Jameson), Reed Howes (Sullivan), Mae Busch (Mrs. Gir-
onda), Bryant Washburn (Denton), Robert Frazer (Dr. Gironda),
Gaston Glass (Louis Bouchard), Mahlon Hamilton (Montgomery),
Robert Walker (Mitchell), Joseph W. Girard (Cromwell), Frank Leigh
(Wickham), Charles Locher (Hobart), Franklyn Farnum (Nicky),
Richard Alexander (Olaf).

The BLACK COIN (1936--Stage and Screen), 15 episodes.   Directed by Albert Herman.   Cast: Ralph Graves (Prescott), Ruth
Mix (Dorothy Dale), Dave O'Brien (Terry Navarro), Constance Ber-
gen (Virginia Caswell), Matthew Betz (Jensen), Robert Frazer (Hackett), Snub Pollard (Vic Moran), Robert Walker (Shark Malone), Bryant Washburn (Caswell), Clara Kimball Young (Donna Luise), Josef
Swickard (Don Pedro), Blackie Whiteford (McGuire), Yakima Canutt
(Ed McMahan), Jackie Miller (Bobby), Lane Chandler (Sir Philip).

SHADOW OF CHINATOWN (1936--Victory), 15 episodes.   Directed by Robert F. Hill.   Cast: Bela Lugosi (Victor Poten), Herman Brix (Martin Andrews), Luana Walters (Sonya), Joan Barclay (Joan Whiting), Maurice Liu (Willy Fu), Charles King (Grogan), William Buchanan (Healy), Forrest Taylor (Capt. Walters), James B. Leong (Wong), Henry F. Tung (Dr. Wu), Paul Fung (Tom Chu), George Chan (Old Luee), John Elliot (Captain), Moy Fing (Wong's Brother), Jack Cowell (White Chink), with Lester Dorr, Henry Wall, Roger Williams.

BLAKE OF SCOTLAND YARD (1937--Victory), 15 episodes.   Directed by Robert F. Hill.   Cast: Ralph Byrd (Blake), Joan Barclay (Hope Mason), Dickie Jones (Bobby), with Herbert Rawlinson, Lloyd Hughes, Nick Stuart.

THE SERIALS OF MASCOT

The PHANTOM EMPIRE (Mascot Pictures, 1935), 12 episodes. Producer, Nat Levine. Directors, Otto Brower and B. Reeves Eason. Screenplay, Wallace MacDonald, Gerald Geraghty and Harry Friedman; continuity by John Rathmell and Armand Schaefer. Camera, Ernest Miller and William Nobles. Art Direction, Mack D'Agostino, Jack Coyle and Ralph DeLacy. Special Effects, Ellis "Bud" Thackery, Howard Lydecker and Theodore Lydecker.
With Gene Autry, Frankie Darro, Betsy King Ross, Dorothy Christy, Wheeler Oakman, Frank Glendon, Smiley Burnette and William Moore.

The Phantom Empire is the screen's only musical science-fiction western, a distinction of dubious worth but, if nothing else, it earns the film a unique position in the tarnished annals of serial history. Comparisons with Flash Gordon, released less than a year later by Universal, are, of course, inevitable. Although containing futuristic elements in their design, both films actually take place in the present, with their unwilling protagonists thrown into a fantastic setting by circumstances beyond their control. But while Flash Gordon is almost always classified as science-fiction, it is actually more of a romantic fantasy, a space-opera with whatever "science" the scriptwriters injected into the film having more in common with the magic and alchemy of the sword and sorcery pulps than anything else. The Phantom Empire, although lacking the rocket ships and space travel of Flash Gordon, contains many of the same plot elements (ray guns, tele-screens, etc.), but is nonetheless much more solidly based in science-fiction.

This represents producer Nat Levine's recognition of the popularity by SF pulp fiction in the thirties; for while Flash Gordon was the composite result of Alex Raymond's

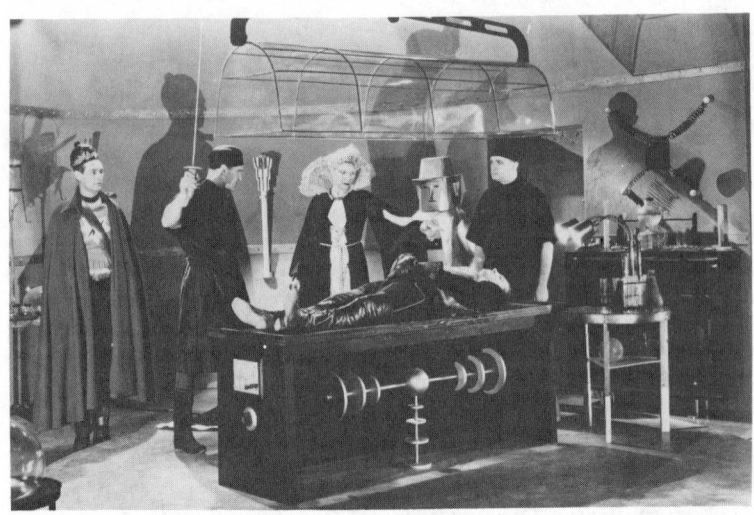

Dorothy Christie (center) attempts to revive a comatose Gene
Aubry by scientific means in The Phantom Empire (Mascot,
1935).

visual designs coupled with the Germanic fantasy prevalent
at Universal Pictures during this period, Levine's scriptwriters were drawing their main inspiration from the pulp
magazines, although with more than a little element of cau-
tion.   Apparently concerned that pure SF might not appeal
to a mass audience, Levine carefully hedged his bets by combining his outrageous science-fiction plot with the tried-and-
true western genre (publicity "hype" at the time of release
claimed that Phantom Empire writer Wallace MacDonald had
originated the basic story idea while under anesthesia in a
dentist's chair!).   This combining of two seemingly disparate
genres actually represented a shrewd move on Levine's part,
for if The Phantom Empire failed to excite or alienated audiences with its science-fiction elements, then it could certainly be counted on to succeed as a western!

    The script wasn't the only area where Levine was
playing it safe; popular western star Ken Maynard was originally announced as the star of The Phantom Empire, but
after having experienced difficulties with the financially de-
manding and temperamental Maynard on a couple of earlier

productions, Levine decided instead to risk casting an unknown in the lead, singing Texas cowboy Gene Autry. Autry was already under contract to Levine at the time, drawing all of $100 dollars a week, and he had appeared in bit parts for the producer in other films. Levine's decision was fortunate as far as Autry was concerned, for The Phantom Empire not only helped to popularize the musical western film, but started Autry on a successful climb towards a quarter of a century of western super-stardom, firmly establishing him as a top star in his field and leading to his incredibly profitable career as a broadcasting executive. As a performer, Autry may have been bland and his talent questionable, but his huge success and popularity in films cannot be denied.

After casting Autry, Levine also signed up bit-player Smiley Burnette at the rate of $75 per week, along with Betsy King Ross, billed as "The World's Champion Trick Rider." Dorothy Christie, who had played Stan Laurel's wife in the Laurel and Hardy feature Sons of the Desert was cast as Queen Tika, the ultimately sympathetic ruler of the underground city of Murania; and the remainder of the cast was fleshed out with familiar character actors as well as old serial stand-bys like Wheeler Oakman. Levine, by ruthlessly cutting corners wherever possible, managed to bring in The Phantom Empire at a final negative cost of only $70,000--quite a feat considering that the serial's 12 chapters have a combined running time of nearly four hours!

Exteriors for the film were shot on the Mack Sennett lot in San Fernando Valley and also in Bronson Canyon, an area of bizarre rock formations that was also used as a backdrop in Flash Gordon, Buck Rogers, One Million B.C. and countless other serials and "B" films. In a further economy move, Queen Tika's massive throne room set was not a constructed artifice at all, but the actual interior of an unfinished solar observatory that was still under construction, this "set" being extended and enhanced by glass paintings. A fascinating aspect of The Phantom Empire is the relatively high quality of the special effects; the film made excellent use of glass shots and models which were used both alone and in tandem with process and rear projection photography. This effects work is a vast improvement over that seen in earlier serials produced by Mascot and other studios. It is, for the most part, far superior to the effects in Flash Gordon, even though Flash Gordon was budgeted at several times the cost of The Phantom Empire. The Mascot

serial does have its share of shoddy production values, however, as can be seen in the design of the Muranian robots,
the most ludicrous and unconvincing mechanical men ever
put on screen, complete with wide brimmed hats!   These
very same robot costumes were put to use again 16 years
later in Columbia Pictures' 1951 serial, Captain Video, in
which they were even more unconvincing.   On the average
though, The Phantom Empire's special effects work was
quite impressive, and one effect in particular is memorable
for the ingenuity with which it was achieved.

      In the serial's spectacular conclusion, the entire city
of Murania is disintegrated by one of Queen Tika's own machines; the buildings slowly lose their structural form and
are reduced to pools of liquid metal.   This sequence was
realized by producing several large "still" photos of the miniature city, and then dissolving the emulsion of the photos
until it simply oozed downward, destroying the image.   This
is a perfect example of the creativity that filmmakers are
forced to resort to when they are saddled with a low budget,
and although the scene was cheaply done, it is undeniably
striking.   The Phantom Empire's special effects were the
work of Ellis "Bud" Thackery and the Lydecker brothers,
Howard and Theodore, who would later distinguish themselves
with their technical contributions to well-made serials such
as The Adventures of Captain Marvel and Spy Smasher at
Republic Pictures.

      The Phantom Empire opens with Gene Autry and his
musical Radio Riders performing in a show broadcast from
Radio Ranch, a popular tourist resort owned by Gene and
his partner, Tom Baxter.   Later, Tom's teenage children,
Frankie and Betsy, see a band of strangely-garbed horsemen
(whom they call "Thunder Riders"), and learning of this,
Gene decides to investigate.   Meanwhile, the dastardly Professor Beetson and his henchmen have arrived at Radio Ranch
by plane.   They are searching for radium deposits they know
are on Autry's property, and their nefarious intention, of
course, is to steal the valuable mineral.   Staging an ambush,
Beetson and his accomplices shoot Gene and leave him for
dead, and then attack a lone Thunder Rider, seriously wound-
ing him.   From hiding, Beetson and his gang watch as more
Thunder Riders appear to carry off their dying friend and,
following, they enter a hidden cave.   By means of a high-
speed elevator, they travel down a long shaft into the futuristic underground city of Murania, ruled by Queen Tika, and
through deception seek her cooperation in their plot against
Autry.

On the surface, Frankie and Betsy find Gene still alive, and they are pursued by another group of Thunder Riders. Running away, the three of them accidently plummet over the edge of a cliff, but manage to save themselves by clinging desperately to a bush growing from the face of it and they are then rescued by several friends of the children. Returning to the ranch, Gene is wrongly accused of murdering his partner Tom Baxter, who has actually been killed by the treacherous Beetson. Attempting to prove his innocence, Autry escapes, and even though he is pursued by the sheriff in Beetson's plane, he manages to elude both the law and yet another group of the mysterious Thunder Riders. Gene tries to outdistance his pursuers in a car, but the brakes fail and the vehicle hurtles off the road, immediately bursting into flames. Witnessing this, both the sheriff and the Thunder Riders believe that Autry has died in the accident, but he has survived and manages to return to Radio Ranch in time to stage the show he is legally obligated to broadcast at regular intervals if he is not to lose his property.

After another struggle with Beetson's stooges, Gene is captured by the Muranian Thunder Riders and taken to their city, where he is promptly sentenced to death. Argo, Queen Tika's devious Prime Minister, is plotting to overthrow the Queen, however, and sensing that he may be able to use the surface-dweller towards this purpose, saves Autry from death in the disintegration chamber. Autry immediately finds himself entangled in a seemingly endless series of confrontations with mechanical men and rebel soldiers, and during an intense battle he is killed in a searing radium blast. Unfortunately for the movie-going public, Gene is restored to life by the advanced super-science of Murania, and he returns to the surface after releasing Frankie and Betsy from the clutches of the Muranians. The trio then escapes in Beetson's plane, but they are forced to crash-land when Queen Tika's ray gun, fired from Murania, disables the craft. Surviving the crash, Autry is once more defeated by Beetson's gang and the children are again captured by the Muranians and taken to a dungeon in the subterranean city.

Pete and Oscar, Gene's irritatingly comical sidekicks, rescue him from Beetson, and at the same time Frankie and Betsy escape from Queen Tika; but Gene, unaware of this, is taken prisoner once more when he re-enters Murania in an effort to save the children. Meanwhile, Pete and Oscar, in a rare exhibition of intelligence, infiltrate Murania disguised as robots, and when Argo's long-anticipated rebellion

against the Queen finally begins, Gene and his friends ally
themselves with Queen Tika, whom Argo then captures.   In
the ensuing struggle, Argo and his friends gain control
of the Queen's laboratory and the powerful disintegrating ray,
but there is a power feedback and the ray goes wild, destroying the city.   Gene and his friends plead with Queen Tika
to leave Murania and come with them to the surface, but she
refuses, preferring to stay behind.   She perishes tragically
with Murania and all its secrets.   Escaping this apocalypse,
Gene Autry (seemingly oblivious that he has been indirectly
responsible for the destruction of an entire city and its popu-
lation) and his companions return to Radio Ranch, where they
finally capture Beetson and force the murderer to confess
his guilt.

       As should be obvious from this synopsis, The Phantom
Empire, like many other serials, had its share of idiocies
in the script department.   Particularly ridiculous was the
cliff-hanging device through which Autry, bound by a contract
to broadcast his radio show regularly or else lose the deed
to his ranch, was forced to return to the surface at the most
inopportune moments in order to perform.   Even if he was
in the middle of a battle for his life against his Muranian
foes, Gene always managed somehow to hold off his attackers,
escape, and make his way back to the surface just in time
to sing the required song before returning to Murania and
continuing the fight!

       The songs themselves, bland little ditties such as In
My Vine-Covered Cottage and Just Come On In, could have
easily been dispensed with entirely, but Autry was, after all,
a singing cowboy.   In order to avoid paying any royalties for
music, however, the dollar-conscious Nat Levine saw to it
that Autry and Smiley Burnette only sang songs that they
themselves had composed.   In fact, Levine, seemingly able
to squeeze blood from the proverbial turnip, reaped even
further profits from The Phantom Empire when he re-edited
the serial into the feature films, Radio Ranch and Men With
Steel Faces, both of which were released in the early forties
for exhibition in theaters that did not normally play serials.

       It would be natural to assume that The Phantom Em-
pire, hardly a particularly well-known film, would have simply
faded into the past and been forgotten by everyone but the
most devoted of film buffs.   Such is not the case, however.
Early in 1979, NBC Television premiered a mid-season re-
placement series called Cliffhangers, a weekly show com-

prised of three continuing dramatic segments.   This show,
according to its producers, sought to recapture the fun and
escapism of the old chapter plays, albeit with tongue firmly
planted in cheek.   Whatever the intentions of the show (and
they were unfortunately hazy), one of the weekly segments
demands brief examination here.   Entitled The Secret Empire, this segment related the misadventures of a frontier
marshal and his young companion who discover a sprawling
futuristic city hidden underground.   If this sounds familiar,
a lot of other people thought so, too, but when the office of
Cliffhangers producer Kenneth Johnson was contacted by Star-
log magazine concerning the matter, he denied knowledge of
The Phantom Empire or any "inspiration" derived from it.

Of course, no illegalities or copyright infringements
were involved, since The Phantom Empire had long since
passed into the public domain.   The copyright on the film
was never renewed after it lapsed, and anyone wishing to
use material connected with the film, even to the extent of
selling copies or video-tapes of the film itself, would be
perfectly free to do so.   What the since-cancelled Cliffhangers
series amply demonstrates, though, is the appalling lack of
creativity in modern entertainment, and no matter how unintentionally ludicrous certain elements of The Phantom Empire may be, Nat Levine's 1935 serial was, at least, a unique
and original concept.

MASCOT SERIAL INDEX--SILENT FILMS

The GOLDEN STALLION (1927), 10 episodes. Directed by Harry Webb. Cast: Maurice "Lefty" Flynn, Joe Bonomo, White Fury, Molly Malone, Josef Swickard, Burr McIntosh.

ISLE OF SUNKEN GOLD (1927), 10 episodes. Directed by Harry Webb. Cast: Anita Stewart, Duke Kahanamoku.

HEROES OF THE WILD (1927), 10 episodes. Directed by Harry Webb. Cast: Jack Hoxie, Joe Bonomo, Tornado, White Fury.

VULTURES OF THE SEA (1928), 10 episodes. Directed by Richard Thorpe. Cast: Johnnie Walker, Shirley Mason, Tom Santschi, Boris Karloff, Frank Hagney, John Carpenter, George Magrill, Joe Bennet.

The VANISHING WEST (1928), 10 episodes. Directed by Richard Thorpe. Cast: Jack Daugherty, Leo Maloney, Yakima Canutt, Jack Perrin, William Fairbanks, Eileen Sedgwick, Fred Church, Mickey Bennett, Helen Gibson.

The FATAL WARNING (1929), 10 episodes. Directed by Richard Thorpe. Cast: Helen Costello, Ralph Graves, George Periolat, Phillip Smalley, Lloyd Whitlock, Boris Karloff, Sid Crossley, Thomas Lingham, Symona Bonifice.

SOUND FILMS

KING OF THE KONGO (1929), 10 episodes. Directed by Richard Thorpe. Cast: Jacqueline Logan (Diana Martin), Walter Miller (Larry Trent), Richard Tucker (Chief of the Secret Service), Boris Karloff (Scareface Macklin), Larry Steers (Jack Drake), Harry Todd (Commodore), Richard Neil (Prisoner), Lafe McKee (Trader John), J. P. Leckray (Priest), William Burt (Mooney), J. Gordon Russell (Derelict), Robert Frazer (Native Chief), Ruth Davis (Poppy), Joe Bonomo (Gorilla).

The LONE DEFENDER (1930), 12 episodes. Directed by Richard Thorpe. Cast: Rin-Tin-Tin (himself), Walter Miller (Ramson), June Marlowe (Dolores), Buzz Barton (Buzz), Josef Swickard (Juan

Valdez), Lee Schumway (Halkey), Frank Lanning (Burke), Bob Kortman (Jenkins), Arthur Morrison (Limpy), Lafe McKee (Sheriff), Bob
Irwin (Deputy), Arthur Metzeff (Dutch), Bill McGowan (Henchman).

The PHANTOM OF THE WEST (1930), 10 episodes. Directed by
Ross Lederman. Cast: Tom Tyler (Jim Lester), Dorothy Gulliver
(Mona Cortez), William Desmond (Martin Blain), Tom Santschi (Bud
Landers), Tom Dugan (Oscar), Philo McCullough (Royce Macklin),
Joe Bonomo (Keno), Kermit Maynard (Peter Drake), Frank Lanning
(Francisco Cortez), Frank S. Hagney (Sheriff Ryan), Dick Dickinson
(Stewart), Halee Sullivan (Ruby Blain), Al Taylor (Deputy).

KING OF THE WILD (1930), 12 episodes. Directed by Richard
Thorpe. Cast: Walter Miller (Robert Grant), Nora Lane (Muriel
Armitage), Dorothy Christie (Mrs. LaSalle), Tom Santschi (Harris),
Boris Karloff (Mustapha), Cyril MacLaglen (Bimi), Carroll Nye (Tom
Armitage), Victor Potel (Peterson), Martha LaLande (Mrs. Colby),
Mischa Auer (Dakka), Lafe McKee (Officer), with Otto Hoffman,
Fletcher Norton, Albert DeWarton, Merrill McCormick, Earle Doug-
las, Larry Steers, Eileen Schofield, Walter Ferdna, Norman Feu-
sier.

The VANISHING LEGION (1930), 12 episodes. Directed by B.
Reeves Eason. Cast: Harry Carey (Cardigan), Edwina Booth (Caro-
line Hall), Rex (himself), Frankie Darro (Jimmie Williams), Philo
McCullough (Stevens), William Desmond (Sheriff), Joe Bonomo (Stuffy),
Edward Hearn (Jed Williams), Alex Taylor (Sheriff), Lafe McKee
(Hornback), Dick Hatton (Dodger), Peter Morrison (Dopey).

The GALLOPING GHOST (1931), 12 episodes. Directed by B.
Reeves Eason. Cast: Harold "Red" Grange (himself), Dorothy
Gulliver (Barbara), Walter Miller (Elton), Gwen Lee (Irene), Fran-
cis X. Bushman (Buddy), Tom Dugan (Jerry), Theodore Lorch (the
Mystery Man), Tom London (Mullins), Eddie Hearn (Harlow), Ernie
Adams (Brady), Frank Brownlee (Tom), Stepin Fetchit (Snowball).

The LIGHTNING WARRIOR (1931), 12 episodes. Directed by Ar-
mand Schaefer and Ben Kline. Cast: Rin-Tin-Tin (himself), Frankie
Darro (Jimmy Carter), Hayden Stevenson (Mr. Carter), George Brent
(Alan Scott), Pat O'Malley (Sheriff), Georgia Hale (Dianne), Theodore
Lorch (Pierre LaFarge), Lafe McKee (John Hayden), Frank Brownlee
(Angus MacDonald), Bob Kortman (Wells), George McGrill (Adams),
Yakima Canutt (Ken Davis), Frank Lanning (Indian George), with
Helen Gibson, Kermit Maynard.

The SHADOW OF THE EAGLE (1932), 12 episodes. Directed by
Ford Beebe. Cast: John Wayne (Craig McCoy), Dorothy Gulliver
(Jean Gregory), Walter Miller (Danby), Kenneth Harlan (Ward),
Richard Tucker (Evans), Pat O'Malley (Ames), Yakima Canutt (Boyle),
Edmund Burns (Clark), Roy D'Arcy (Gardner), Billy West (Clown),
Edward Hearn (Nathan Gregory), Lloyd Whitlock (Green), Little Billy
(Midget), Ivan Linlow (Strong Man), James Bradbury, Jr. (Ventrilo-
quist), Ernie S. Adams (Kelly), Bud Osborne (Moore), Monte Monta-
gue (Policeman).

LAST OF THE MOHICANS (1932), 12 episodes. Cast: Harry Carey.

The HURRICANE EXPRESS (1932), 12 episodes. Directed by Armand Schaefer and J. P. McGowan. Cast: John Wayne (Larry Baker), Shirley Grey (Gloria Martin), Tully Marshall (Edwards), Conway Tearle (Stevens), J. Farrell McDonald (Jim Baker), Matthew Betz (Jordan), James Burte (Hemingway), Lloyd Whitlock (Walter Gray), Joseph Girard (Matthews), Edmund Breese (Stratton), Glenn Strange (Jim), Al Ferguson (Sandy), Fred Toomes (Porter), Eddie Parker (Co-Pilot).

The DEVIL HORSE (1932), 12 episodes. Directed by Otto Brower. Cast: Harry Carey (Norton Roberts), Noah Beery (Canfield), Frankie Darro (Wild Boy), Apache (the Devil Horse), Carli Russell (Wild Boy at age 5).

The WHISPERING SHADOW (1933), 12 episodes. Directed by Albert Herman and Colbert Clark. Cast: Bela Lugosi (Professor Strang), Viva Tattersall (Vera Strang), Malcolm McGregor (Jack Foster), Henry B. Walthall (President Bradley), Robert Warwick (Detective Raymond), Ethel Clayton (Countess), Roy D'Arcy (Steinbeck), Karl Dane (Sparks), Lloyd Whitlock (Young), Bob Kortman (Slade), Lafe McKee (Jerome), George J. Lewis (Bud Foster), Jack Perrin (Williams), Max Wagner (Kruger), Kernan Crippe (Foreman), Eddie Parker (Driver), Gordon DeMain (Detective), George Magrill (Mitchell), Tom London (Dupont), Lionel Backus (Jarvis), Norman Feusier (Deane).

The THREE MUSKETEERS (1933), 12 episodes. Feature version: Desert Command. Directed by Armand Schaefer and Colbert Clark. Cast: Jack Mulhall (Clancy), Raymond Hatton (Renard), Francis X. Bushman (Schmidt), John Wayne (Tom Wayne), Ruth Hall (Elaine Corday), Lon Chaney, Jr. (Armand Corday), Hooper Atchley (El Kadur), Gordon DeMain (Colonel Duval), Robert Frazer (Major Booth), Noah Berry, Jr. (Stubbs), Al Ferguson (Ali), Edward Piel (Ratkin), William Desmond (Capt. Boncour), George Magrill (El Maghreb), Robert Warwick (Col. Brent), Wilfred Lucas (El Shaitan), Merill McCormick (Henchman), Ken Cooper (Arab), Yakima Canutt (Arab).

FIGHTING WITH KIT CARSON (1933), 12 episodes. Directed by Armand Schaefer and Colbert Clark. Cast: Johnny Mack Brown (Kit Carson), Betsy King Ross (Joan Fargo), Noah Beery (Kraft), Noah Beery, Jr. (Nakomas).

The WOLF DOG (1933), 12 episodes. Directed by Harry Fraser and Colbert Clark. Cast: Rin-Tin-Tin, Jr. (Pal), Frankie Darro (Frank), George J. Lewis (Bob), Boots Mallory (Irene), Henry B. Walthall (Jim Courtney), Hale Hamilton (Bryan), Fred Kohler (Stevens), with Niles Welch, Stanley Blystone, Tom London, Sarah Padden, Max Wagner, Carroll Nye, Cornelius Keefe, Harry Northrup, Lane Chandler, Dickie Moore, Donald Reed, Gordon DeMain, George Magrill, Lionel Backus, Lew Meehan, Yakima Canutt, Leon Holmes, Jack Kenney, Wes Wagner.

The MYSTERY SQUADRON (1933), 12 episodes. Directed by Colbert Clark and David Howard. Cast: Bob Steele (Fred (Cromwell), Guinn "Big Boy" William (Bill Cook), Lucille Brown (Dorothy Gray), Jack Mulhall (Davis), Purnell Pratt (Johnson), Lafe McKee (Gray).

The LOST JUNGLE (1934), 12 episodes. Directed by Armand Schaefer and David Howard. Cast: Clyde Beatty (himself), Cecilia Parker (Ruth Robinson), Syd Saylor (Larry Henderson), Warner Richmond (Sharkey), Wheeler Oakman (Kirby), Maston Williams (Thompson), J. Crauford Kent (Explorer), Lloyd Whitlock (Howard), Lloyd Ingraham (Bannister), Edward J. LeSaint (Capt. Robinson), Lew Meehan (Flynn), Max Wagner (Slade), Wes Warner (Jackman), Jack Carlyle (Cook), Jim Corey (Steve), Wally Wales (Sandy), Ernie S. Adams (Pete), Charles Wittaker (Slim), Harry Holman (Maitland), Mickey Rooney (Mickey).

BURN 'EM UP BARNES (1934), 12 episodes. Directed by Colbert Clark and Armand Schaefer. Cast: Frankie Darro (Bobby), Jack Mulhall (Burn 'Em Up Barnes), Lola Lane (Marjorie Temple), Julian Rivero (Tony), Edwin Maxwell (Warren), Jason Robards (Drummond), Francis McDonald (Ray Ridpath), James Bush (George), Stanley Blystone (Joe Stevens), Al Bridge (Tucker), Bob Kortman (Frazer), Tom London (Parsons), Eddie Hearn (Parker), John Davidson (Chase), Lloyd Whitlock (District Attorney), Bruce Mitchell (Lambert).

The LAW OF THE WILD (1934), 12 episodes. Directed by Armand Schaefer and B. Reeves Eason. Cast: Rex (himself), Rin-Tin-Tin, Jr. (himself), Bob Custer (Sheldon), Ben Turpin (Henry), Lucille Brown (Alice), Richard Cramer (Nolan), Ernie Adams (Raymond), Edmund Cobb (Jim Lugar), Charles Whitaker (Mack), Dick Alexander (Salter), Jack Rockwell (Sheriff), George Chesebro (Parks).

MYSTERY MOUNTAIN (1934), 12 episodes. Directed by Otto Brower and B. Reeves Eason. Cast: Ken Maynard (Ken Williams), Tarzan (himself), Verna Hillie (Jane Corwin), Edward Earle (Blayden), Edmund Cobb (The Rattler), Lynton Brent (Matthews), Syd Saylor (Breezy), Carmencita Johnson (Little Jane), Lake McKee (Corwin), Al Bridge (Henderson), Ed Hearne (Lake), Bob Kortman (Hank), with Wally Wales, George Chesbro, Hooper Atchley, Gene Autry, Smiley Burnette, Jack Kirk, Lew Meehan, Jack Rockwell, William Gould, Tom London, Philo McCullough, Frank Ellis, James Mason, Steve Clark, Cliff Lyons, Art Mix, Curley Dresden.

The PHANTOM EMPIRE (1935), 12 episodes. Feature versions: Radio Ranch and Men With Steel Faces. Directed by Otto Brower and B. Reeves Eason. Cast: Gene Autry (himself), Frankie Darro (Frankie), Betsy King Ross (Betsy), Dorothy Christy (Queen Tika), Wheeler Oakman (Argo), Charles K. French (Mal), Warner Richmond (Rab), Frank Glendon (Beetson), Smiley Burnette (Oscar), William Moore (Pete), Edward Piel, Sr. (Dr. Cooper), Frankie Marvin (Frankie), Jack Carlyle (Saunders), with Wally Wales, Fred Burns, Jay Wilsey, Stanley Blystone, Richard Talmadge, Frank Ellis, Henry Hall, Jim Corey.

The MIRACLE RIDER (1935), 15 episodes.   Directed by Armand Schaefer and B. Reeves Eason.   Cast: Tom Mix (Tom Morgan), Jean Gale (Ruth), Charles Middleton (Zaroff), Jason Robards (Carlton), Edward Hearn (Janes), Pat O'Malley (Sam Morgan), Robert Frazer (Chief Black Wing), Ernie Adams (Stelter), Wally Wales (Burnett), Bob Kortman (Longboat), Blackhawk (Chief Two Hawks), Chief Standing Bear (Chief Long Elk).

The ADVENTURES OF REX AND RINTY (1935), 12 episodes.   Directed by Ford Beebe and B. Reeves Eason.   Cast: Rex (himself), Rin-Tin-Tin, Jr. (himself), Kane Richmond (Frank Bradley), Norma Taylor (Dorothy Bruce), Mischa Auer (Tanaga), Smiley Burnette (Jensen), Harry Woods (Crawford).

FIGHTING MARINES (1935), 12 episodes.   Directed by B. Reeves Eason and Joseph Kane.   Cast: Grant Withers (Lawrence), Adrian Morris (McGowan), Ann Rutherford (Frances), Robert Warwick (Col. Bennet), George J. Lewis (Schiller), Jason Robards (Kota), Pat O'Malley (Grayson), Warner Richmond (Metcalf), Frank Reicher (Steinbeck), Robert Frazer (Douglas), Frank Glendon (Buchanan), Richard Alexander (Ivan), Donald Reed (Pedro), Tom London (Miller), Stanly Blystone (Gibson), Milburn Stone (Red), with Franklin Adreon, Billy Arnold, Lee Shumway, Grace Durkin.

THE SERIALS OF REPUBLIC

DICK TRACY (Republic, 1937), 15 episodes. Producer, Nat Levine. Associate Producer, J. Laurence Wickland. Directors, Ray Taylor and Alan James. Screenplay, Barry Shipman and Winston Miller; original story by Morgan Cox and George Morgan. Camera, William Nobles and Edgar Lyons.
With Ralph Byrd, Kay Hughes, Smiley Burnette, Lee Van Atta, John Piccori, Carleton Young, Fred Hamilton, Francis X. Bushman and John Dilson.

In 1935, Herbert J. Yates, a tobacco executive and owner of Consolidated Film Industries (a lab which processed footage and produced optical effects for movies), merged with Mascot studios and created Republic Pictures. Having thus established himself in the production end of the industry, Yates, with no illusions about his intended product, immediately set about creating a steady and dependable supply of "B" westerns and, of course, serials. The last serial to carry the Mascot logo had been Fighting Marines in 1935, completed during the corporate transition and distributed through Republic's exchanges. The first Republic serial proper to boast the studio's "shield" logo (later changed to a depiction of an imposing eagle defiantly perched atop the company name chiseled in solid granite) was Darkest Africa (1936). Released in 15 chapters, Darkest Africa was a considerable improvement over Mascot's productions. Starring real-life wild animal trainer Clyde Beatty as himself in a fantastic and improbable tale concerning a hidden jungle city populated by flying "batmen," Darkest Africa was a top-notch effort as serials went, offering vigorous pacing, interesting set design, and fascinating miniature work. With one or two memorable exceptions, Mascot serials like The Whispering Shadow (1933) had been numbing endurance tests, about par for the course for chapter plays in the thirities, but

Darkest Africa set a new standard in cliffhangers for the industry; it was Republic's first, and one of its best.

The following year, Republic adapted the first of its many comic strip inspirations with Dick Tracy, the detective strip created by Chester Gould for the Chicago Tribune in 1931. The bizarre Gould milieu, with villains named Pruneface, The Mole, and Flat Top, and drawn to match, was largely rejected by Republic; even Tracy's girl friend Tess Trueheart underwent a name change and became "Gwen Andrews." Republic no doubt was only attempting to make the subject more realistic, but this meddling disappointed fans of Gould's strip. The resulting serials, which pitted the stalwart Tracy against a master criminal known as "The Spider," was lethargic, over-plotted, and surprisingly dull considering Republic's promising debut the year before with Darkest Africa. Far better were the three sequels, Dick Tracy Returns (1938), Dick Tracy's G-Men (1939), and Dick Tracy vs. Crime, Inc. (1941). These serials benefited from tighter screenplays as well as improved acting from Byrd, who had been a trifle stiff in the original; and Dick Tracy Returns had a superior villain in the person of Charles Middleton as the sinister "Pa Stark," leader of a cut-throat gang comprised of his five murderous sons.

While Republic deserves credit for being the first studio to adapt the character, the best Dick Tracy films were produced as features by RKO. Beginning in 1946 with Dick Tracy (retitled Dick Tracy, Detective for its TV showings), Morgan Conway, a suitably tough but stolid and ultimately inadequate choice for the lead, took over from Byrd. Fortunately, though, RKO's writers were faithful to Gould's original concept, and the cast performed in a subdued tongue-in-cheek manner with entertaining results. Conway returned in 1947 with a sequel, Dick Tracy vs. Cueball; then, happily, Ralph Byrd was on hand once more for the last two installments in this mini-series, Dick Tracy's Dilemma (1947) and Dick Tracy Meets Gruesome (1947). This final entry, with guest star Boris Karloff in fine serio-comic form as the title fiend, was a delight, and is perhaps the best illustration of the vast differences between Republic's and RKO's treatment of the same material; for while Republic's traditional serial adaptations provided a few genuine thrills, the RKO features remain the more sophisticated interpretation.

Opposite: Ralph Byrd reaches for a convenient knife in Dick Tracy (Republic, 1937).

A publicity portrait of Tom Tyler as he appeared in <u>Adventures of Captain Marvel</u> (Republic, 1941).

ADVENTURES OF CAPTAIN MARVEL (Republic, 1941),
12 episodes. Associate Producer, Hiram S. Brown, Jr.
Directors, William Witney and John English. Screenplay,
Sol Short, Ronald Davidson, Norman S. Hall, Joseph Poland
and Arch B. Heath. Camera, William Nobles. Special
Effects, Howard Lydecker. Music, Cy Feuer.
With Tom Tyler, Frank Coghlan, Jr., William Benedict,
Louise Currie, Robert Strange, Harry Worth, Bryant Wash-
burn and John Davidson.

Adventures of Captain Marvel, although highly overrated by many, remains one of the better serials to emerge
from Republic Pictures. Based on the then-popular comic
book character, the title figure in Adventures of Captain Marvel somehow broke all the rules and survived virtually intact
in its transition from the pulp page to the screen; the sorry
fate of Republic's other releases like Captain America, which
were almost unrecognizable perversions of their source material, was avoided.

In the comic books, Captain Marvel was, for its time,
a brilliant creation. Superman and Batman were adult characters with whom the children who read comics identified
and secretly dreamed of emulating. Perhaps sensing what
they perceived to be a flaw in this situation, the publishers
soon created juvenile sidekicks for heroes like Batman (e.g.,
Robin, the boy wonder) in the obvious hope of providing more
accessible role models for their juvenile audience. The
movies, in "B" westerns and serials, had been following this
approach for years by casting young actors like Frankie
Darro in support of adult stars such as Gene Autry. This
concept was based on an unnecessary and erroneous assump-
tion made by adults who had forgotten what it was like to be
a child; for the young fans of comic books and serials saw
themselves not as the child sidekick, but as the adult hero.
The creators of the Captain Marvel comic books understood
this, and shrewdly developed the character along those lines.

The resulting creation was Billy Batson, a young boy
awarded superhuman powers by an emissary of the ancient
gods. Speaking one magic word, "Shazam," Billy was transformed into the adult Captain Marvel, and back again, whenever he desired. Drawn in appropriately simplistic and
juvenile style, the Captain Marvel comic books were soon
selling more than one million copies a month, out-distancing
Superman at the newsstands, and with that kind of huge

success creating a ready-made audience it was only natural
that the producers of serials would purchase screen rights
to the property.

In Republic's Adventures of Captain Marvel the only
changes made in the original concept were relatively minor
in nature.   Billy Batson was matured somewhat from a juvenile to a whining adolescent (as played by Frank Coghlan,
Jr.), and the whimsical supporting characters and fanciful
milieu of the comics were replaced by a standard Republic
"masked villain" serial plot concerning a golden scorpion
idol with the ability to transform ordinary stone into gold,
and the efforts of a mysterious antagonist, "The Scorpion,"
to gain posession of the device.

As Captain Marvel the studio cast Tom Tyler, a hard-
riding "B" western cowboy who frequently essayed bit roles
in major Hollywood productions like Gone with the Wind, and
whose most unusual role to date had been as an immortal
resurrected Egyptian mummy in Universal's The Mummy's

Tom Tyler and friends in Adventures of Captain Marvel (Republic, 1941).

Hand (1940). With very few notable exceptions, most of the
leading men in serials, and Republic's leading men in particular, resembled nothing more than ambling sequoia trees
giving very unconvincing impersonations of human beings.
Tom Tyler was typical, but fortunately his shortcomings inadvertently worked to his advantage in Adventures of Captain
Marvel. Well aware of Tyler's dramatic ineptitude and almost insurmountable problems with delivering his lines, Republic's writers compensated by reducing Captain Marvel's
dialogue to the barest possible minimum. Tyler only speaks
a few short sentences in each episode, which has the un-
intentional but welcome effect of making the character seem
more mysterious--and atmosphere was an element sorely
lacking in Republic serials. Visually, though, Tyler was a
perfect choice, and the only time the actor's performance
degenerates into total inadequacy occurs in the serial's con-
cluding episode, when he is required to deliver a few con-
tinuous sentences of dialogue, and stammers out his lines in
a halting, nasal voice that is entirely inappropriate. The
remainder of the cast for Adventures of Captain Marvel was
filled with familiar Republic character actors, and blonde
Louise Currie occupied the studio's usual thankless heroine
position in bland fashion.

      As was usually the case with Republic, Adventures of
Captain Marvel excelled in the area of special effects. Brothers Howard and Theodore Lydecker were the heads of the
studio's miniature department, and their meticulous and convincing work often proved to be the only worthwhile quality
in many of Republic's serials. Thrilling scenes of exploding
buildings, crashing planes and burning cars were executed
using large-scale models shot outdoors in natural sunlight,
and it was the realistic lighting more than anything else that
enabled these sequences to mesh so smoothly with the normal
live-action shots. Most "B" pictures and serials, with their
necessarily rushed schedules, routinely intercut studio-shot
miniatures with real exteriors, and it was the obvious difference in lighting styles that often revealed the trickery for
what it was. As Republic moved into the late forties and
early fifties, gradually reducing the budgets of their serials,
many of their more exciting special effects from the earlier
productions were used again as stock footage, with the scripts
of these later serials actually conceived and written around
the studio's extensive library of effects sequences.

      While Columbia's successful but undeniably cheap
Superman serial of 1948 would use crude and unconvincing

animation to enable its hero to fly, the Lydeckers filmed the flying shots for Adventures of Captain Marvel in ingenious fashion and the results were often stunning. A hollow dummy of Tom Tyler was constructed, slightly larger than life-size for visual impact, with pulleys mounted inside the outstretched arms and legs. Rigged in this manner, the effigy was towed along invisible wires strung across mountainous terrain or from a street to the upper floors of a building, producing a convincing image from a distance. These shots were intercut with facial close-ups and full-length body shots of Tyler himself suspended before footage of passing clouds and scenery projected onto a standard process screen. With an occasional daredevil leap from a stuntman in Tyler's costume edited into the action, the illusion was complete, spoiled only intermittently by the variable quality of the rear-projection in the process shots.

Adventures of Captain Marvel is about evenly composed of flaws and virtues, the movie's only partially realized effectiveness being inevitably curtailed by many of the drawbacks common to Republic serials. Unlike Universal and Columbia, which scored their serials with stock musical tracks culled from their backlog of features (often in tandem with classical compositions), Republic always produced original scores for its cliffhangers. While this was admirable in principle, and the music was often quite good, just as often the scores were bland, uninspired, and ultimately detrimental rather than beneficial to the films they accompanied. Despite a few successfully energetic flourishes the compositions for Adventures of Captain Marvel (by Cy Feuer) are droning and repetitious, and the music is a definite hindrance to the picture.

Not entirely triumphant, Adventures of Captain Marvel, like all serials, must be measured against others of its type, and on that admittedly paltry scale the film manages to succeed, if only through the merits of its glistening photography and technical slickness.

SPY SMASHER (Republic, 1942), 12 episodes. Associate Producer, William J. O'Sullivan. Director, William Witney. Screenplay, Ronald Davidson, Norman S. Hall, Joseph Poland, William Lively and Joseph O'Donnel. Camera, Reggie Lanning. Special Effects, Howard Lydecker. Music, Mort Glickman.

Marguerite Chapman and Kane Richmond in Spy Smasher (Republic, 1942).

With Kane Richmond, Sam Flint, Marguerite Chapman, Hans Schumm, Tristram Coffin and Frank Corsaro.

Well-aware that it was catering to a mostly juvenile, unsophisticated audience, Republic, like other serial producers, frequently turned to comic books and newspaper strips for inspiration. Having previously negotiated with Fawcett Publications for the rights to Captain Marvel, the studio also obtained permission to film Fawcett's other big seller, Spy Smasher. Republic's resulting production, released in 12 compact chapters at the height of the Second World War in 1942, was its serial magnum opus, and with Universal's Flash Gordon achieved the highest peak of quality the cliffhangers would ever reach.

Spy Smasher, a masked free-lance American agent
working in occupied France, is discovered and captured by
the Nazis while attempting to learn the location of a powerful German agent called "The Mask," the ringleader and
mastermind of an Axis spy ring based in the United States.
Spy Smasher is sentenced to the firing squad by his captors,
but at the last minute is rescued by Pierre Durand, a member of the French underground who arranges for Spy Smasher's
clandestine return to America.   Upon his arrival in the United
States, he joins forces with his twin brother Jack, and discovers that The Mask intends to attack Admiral Corby, chief
of the U. S. Foreign Service and father of Jack's fiancée,
Eve.   They successfully thwart The Mask's plans, and subsequently learn that the enemy spy has formed a counterfeit
money ring in an attempt to disrupt Allied financial stability.
Spy Smasher again averts The Mask's efforts and, learning
that his friend Durand has been captured and sentenced to
death by hanging, rescues the heroic Frenchman from the
noose.   Nevertheless, Durand perishes tragically when he
and Spy Smasher are then trapped aboard a flooding submarine, but with his dying partner's help Spy Smasher manages
to escape through one of the sub's torpedo tubes.   Informed
that Nazi agents are now in posession of a futuristic "bat
plane" capable of taking off and landing vertically, Spy Smasher
plans to seize the vehicle, and nearly achieves his goal when
the plane crashes and bursts into flames.   Spy Smasher,
miraculously thrown clear of the wreckage and rescued by
his brother, discovers that The Mask now intends to sabotage
a squadron of American bombers which is about to conduct
a test flight by destroying the planes with a powerful ray
gun, but Spy Smasher once again intervenes and disposes of
the ominous weapon.   Notified by the government that ex-
plosive mines are about to be smuggled out to sea by The
Mask's henchmen, Spy Smasher triumphantly prevents the
disaster, destroying the marine bombs before they can be
used against Allied vessels.   Eve Corby is then captured by
The Mask's agents, who are aware of her connection with
Spy Smasher.   Jack, masquerading as his costumed brother,
forfeits his life in a noble attempt to rescue her, and Spy
Smasher, grimly vowing retribution, finally defeats The Mask
and destroys his spy ring.

Slick and technically proficient, Spy Smasher was directed by William Witney, who in partnership with fellow
craftsman John English helmed many of Republic's more successful chapter plays during the studio's peak years.   Although Witney directed Spy Smasher alone (which no doubt

Kane Richmond (l.) and Franco Corsaro take aim in Spy Smasher (Republic, 1942).

accounts for the picture's cohesive design), it was common practice in serial production to assign two directors to each film, one handling action sequences and the other supervising dialogue scenes, thereby effectively condensing the shooting schedule. Although this technique resulted in unavoidable choppiness in the cliffhangers made by other studios, Republic always seemed to pull it off better than anyone else. The seams don't show in Spy Smasher; even the tricky scenes with Kane Richmond performing opposite his non-existent "twin brother," for which cinematographer Reggie Lanning employed split-screen methods as well as well-disguised doubles, could have easily been ruined or shot in a cruder and more obvious manner, but Lanning pulled it off without a hitch.

Like Buster Crabbe, Spy Smasher's leading man Kane Richmond was a capable, greatly underrated actor who spent most of his career toiling in cheap features and serials, and

he was finally unable to advance from those lower echelons
of fame.   In Spy Smasher, Richmond is convincing and sin-
cere, even exhibiting a sense of humor at times and effectively
breathing some three-dimensional life and characterization
into a shallow comic book figure that could have easily appeared laughable.   In support, shovel-jawed Hans Schumm
as The Mask was essentially just another stock Republic villain, but Marguerite Chapman as Eve Corby was beautiful
and a definite asset to the serial despite her predictably
minor role.   Shortly afterwards, Chapman went on to achieve
mild success in several features.

     Far better than the previous year's Adventures of Cap-
tain Marvel, Spy Smasher was a winner on every level and
alone almost justifies the serial genre.   While many "patriotic" films of the World War Two era lost their impetus and
their believability as soon as that era was over, and while
other war movies that were much more highly respected at
the time (e.g., The Purple Heart) now seem dated, repul-
sive, and even comical in their volatile racial jingoism, Spy
Smasher, a lowly cliffhanger based on a comic book and
originally intended to carry a prologue appearance by J. Edgar Hoover himself (!), survives rather well as a much more
agreeable and inoffensive document of those years.

     PERILS OF NYOKA (Republic, 1942), 15 episodes.   As-
sociate Producer, William J. O'Sullivan.   Director, William
Witney.   Screenplay, Ronald Davidson, William Lively, Joseph
O'Donnel and Joseph Poland.   Camera, Reggie Lanning.
Special Effects, Howard Lydecker.   Music, Mort Glickman.
With Kay Aldridge, Clayton Moore, William Benedict, Lorna
Gray, Charles Middleton, Tristram Coffin.

     Republic Pictures, more so than the other producers
of serials, seemed to maintain a rigid, inflexible notion of
the type of paying customer who formed the target audience
for cliffhangers; in the studio's corporate mind those cus-
tomers were apparently male, unsophisticated, and juvenile.
There was, of course, a great deal of truth in this, as Republic's profitable 20-year operation through the mid-fifties
proved; still, designing a film to fit pre-existing exhibition
patterns does not mean that all spontaneity and creativity
must be drained from the finished product; at Republic however, this was unfortunately a common result.   Republic's

Frances Gifford in the title role of <u>Jungle Girl</u> (Republic, 1941).

serials, although visually the slickest, glossiest chapter plays
produced by the industry, were more often than not mechan-
ically plotted, uninspired, and lacking the vitality sometimes
present in the releases from Universal and Columbia.   Worse
yet, Republic's productions were almost totally sexless.   The
stolid characters portrayed by Republic's leading men were
apparently eunuchs; they were never permitted a screen kiss,
and always seemed more interested in firing their guns and
engaging in fist fights than in even momentary pursuit of the
opposite sex.   Universal (perhaps unconsciously, but effectively
nevertheless), had broken this rule in Flash Gordon, with
Buster Crabbe and Jean Rogers accorded a few chaste kisses
and the sultry Priscilla Lawson on hand to provoke further
interest.   With Flash Gordon Universal had proven the adapt-
ability of the serial to a potentially more adult audience,
but Republic, although it certainly noticed the resulting profits,
apparently failed to understand the reasons for Universal's
success, and continued down the same path with its own
bland formula.

Happily, there are welcome exceptions to every rule,
and the first of these at Republic arrived in the form of a
mediocre novel by Edgar Rice Burroughs, Jungle Girl.   Burroughs had dashed off this uninspired and quickly forgotten
tale in an obvious attempt to create a female equivalent of
Tarzan, and Republic, cognizant of the profits reaped by
MGM with its popular Tarzan series, purchased the screen
rights.

Released in 1941, Jungle Girl related the juvenile tale
of Nyoka, a girl who grows to maturity in the wild after her
father, driven from society by the criminal activities of his
twin brother, takes refuge in the jungle with his daughter.
Needless to say, the evil twin brother eventually puts in an
appearance, along with the inevitable scheming witch doctors
and wild animals.   Jungle Girl, like most serials, didn't
offer much depth or opportunity for thought; what it did offer
was beautiful Frances Gifford in the title role, enticingly
clad in her jungle mini-skirt.   Jungle Girl, largely as a
result of Gifford's performance, was an immediate success,
and the following year Republic released The Perils of Nyoka,
a sequel with a much more colorful plot.   Professor Campbell, an archaeologist, and his assistant Larry Grayson have
discovered a moldering papyrus indicating the location of the
"Tablets of Hippocrates," containing the lost medical knowledge of the ancient Greeks.   Embarking on an expedition to
the Arabian desert in search of Nyoka, the only person able

Kay Aldridge aids a wounded Clayton Moore in Perils of
Nyoka (Republic, 1942).

to decipher the obscure map, they find her living with a tribe
of Bedouin nomads and endeavoring to find her missing father,
who was lost during a previous expedition. Vultura, the
exotic and ruthless leader of a band of Arab thieves, learns
of Campbell's expedition and its purpose. She plots to seize
the Tablets for herself, and steals the map before Nyoka can
examine it. Nyoka and Larry track Vultura to her hidden
temple, and are attacked by Satan, Vultura's pet gorilla.
Nyoka is captured by the ape and Vultura imprisons her, but
Larry returns with help; leading an attack on the temple, he
frees Nyoka, who has reclaimed the map. Translating the
papyrus, Nyoka follows the instructions and leads the Campbell expedition to a distant valley, where they find an in-
scription containing further directions. They then discover
Nyoka's long-lost father, who is afflicted with amnesia, but
eventually regains his memory and leads them to the tomb
of The Moon God, where the Tablets of Hippocrates are concealed. They find to their dismay that Vultura has arrived
before them and taken the Tablets back to her temple, and
Nyoka returns to Vultura's outpost with Larry to attempt to
recover the Tablets. They are discovered, however, and
Vultura's trained gorilla, enraged, hurls a spear at Nyoka.
It misses and accidentally kills Vultura instead. Larry shoots
the crazed ape, and the other members of the Campbell expedition arrive, overpowering Vultura's remaining guards.
Afterwards the Campbell expedition, recovering the treasure,
decide to use its wealth for the construction of a hospital
where the information contained on the Tablets can be used
for the benefit of humanity.

The Perils of Nyoka, with its wild story and outlandish
incidents, is one of Republic's more enjoyable concoctions.
Leading lady Kay Aldridge was a worthy successor to Frances
Gifford, but was somewhat overshadowed by the performance
of Lorna Gray as the perverse Vultura--reportedly Gray was
paid a higher fee for her supporting role than Aldridge was
for the lead! Also present were Flash Gordon's Emperor
Ming, Charles Middleton (in the uncommonly swarthy guise
of an Arab henchman), and a pre-Lone Ranger Clayton Moore.
Obviously, feminine pulchritude combined with jungle thrills
was a very popular formula, for Republic mimicked The
Perils of Nyoka with a follow-up in the same mold, The Tiger
Woman, released in 1944.

Allen Saunders, a trouble-shooter for the Inter-Ocean
Oil Company, is dispatched to the South American jungle
town of Alta Vista to investigate delays in the development

An uncommonly swarthy Charles Middleton (c.) and villainous Lorna Gray (r.) interrogate an effectively bound Kay Aldridge and Robert Strange (l.) in <u>Perils of Nyoka</u> (Republic, 1942).

of a new oil field. In the jungles surrounding Alta Vista, the Tiger Woman, a mysterious white queen, rules over a lost tribe from her temple. The Inter-Ocean Company has reached an agreement with this tribe which allows them to transport men and equipment through the jungle unharmed, but saboteurs have obstructed progress on their well and the Tiger Woman is wrongfully suspected. Dagget, the shady owner of a general store in Alta Vista and secretly an agent for a rival oil firm, tries to murder Saunders, but the plot fails, succeeding only in convincing Saunders that the Tiger Woman is innocent of all wrongdoing. Dagget and a crooked attorney, Walton, believe that the Tiger Woman is actually Rita Arnold, a missing heiress who was lost in a plane crash over the jungle as a child. Together, they plan to destroy the Inter-Ocean oil project, establish proof of the Tiger Woman's true identity, then murder her and collect her fortune

More jungle cheesecake: Beautiful Linda Stirling in The Tiger Woman (Republic, 1944).

by substituting an imposter in her place. Meanwhile, Saunders and his men have joined forces with the Tiger Woman and her natives; together they work feverishly to complete the oil well before Inter-Ocean's government franchise on the land expires. Dagget and Walton have learned that documents proving the Tiger Woman's identity as Rita Arnold are guarded by her high priest in the queen's jungle temple; but they fail in a subsequent attempt to steal them and are eventually defeated by Allen Saunders, who manages to open the Inter-Ocean oil well on time and persuades the Tiger Woman to leave the jungle and return to America with him.

For a while, it actually looked as though Republic had decided to resurrect the Golden Age of the serial queen; lovely Linda Stirling, a former fashion model, was the star of The Tiger Woman, and with her likable personality and competent performance (she was Republic's female counterpart to Kane Richmond) she went on, as did Kay Aldridge, to roles in several more cliffhangers. This renaissance of more entertaining chapter plays did not last long at Republic, but the allure and genuine talent of Gifford, Aldridge, and Stirling provided a badly-needed if temporary respite from the studio's usual barren product.

CAPTAIN AMERICA (Republic, 1944), 15 episodes. Associate Producer, William J. O'Sullivan. Directors, John English and Elmer Clifton. Screenplay, Royal Cole, Ronald Davidson, Basil Dickey, Jesse Duffy, Harry Fraser, Grant Nelson and Joseph Poland. Camera, Johm McBurnie. Special Effects, Theodore Lydecker, Music, Mort Glickman. With Dick Purcell, Lorna Gray, Lionel Atwill, Charles Trowbridge, Russell Hicks, John Davidson and George Lewis.

Although the serials regularly turned to comic books and adventure pulps for source material, the attitudes of the producers, directors, and writers who adapted that material were often surprisingly cavalier considering the expectations an audience already familiar with these characters must have had. Some properties, like Superman and Spy Smasher, benefited from relatively faithful interpretations, but what finally reached the screen in some other cases was so vastly different from its inspiration that one wonders why the studio even bothered to purchase the rights at all; such a case was Republic's production of Captain America.

The plot is standard cliffhanger tripe. Dr. Cyrus Maldor, curator of the Drummond Museum, believes that the members of an archaeological expedition he once led have cheated him of the wealth and fame that should rightly be his. Swearing vengeance, Maldor disguises himself as the sinister "Scarab" and begins murdering his enemies one by one with a lethal poison called "The Purple Death." Maldor then attempts to steal an experimental machine from a research laboratory, intending to use the device as a weapon, but the theft is interrupted by the masked figure of District Attorney Grant Gardner in his colorful secret identity as Captain America. Although he prevents the crime, Captain America fails to apprehend the disguised Maldor. Maldor then learns that Hillman, who had been a member of the expedition, has discovered an incomplete map that reveals the location of a hidden Mayan treasure; Maldor owns the other part of the map, and plans to steal Hillman's portion in order to claim the treasure for himself. Captain America hears of Maldor's plot, and places Hillman under protective custody, but the resourceful Maldor still manages to acquire Hillman's partial map and now in possession of the complete document, captures Hillman and ruthlessly tortures him in an attempt to read the ancient symbols, which only Hillman can decipher. Captain America intervenes, rescuing Hillman, and Maldor, still at large, is desperate because Hillman has learned his identity and can identify him as the Scarab. Maldor boldly kidnaps Captain America's assistant Gail Richards as insurance, but the clever Gail has discovered the madman's true identity and manages to inform Captain America, who tracks down Maldor, saves Gail, and sends the psychopathic killer to prison and the electric chair.

Captain America was one of the most popular and widely read comic book characters of the forties, but his screen incarnation bears almost no resemblance to the original concept. As created at the height of World War II by the prolific writer-artist team of Joe Simon and Jack Kirby, Captain America in the comics was in reality Steve Rogers, an anemic 4-F draft board reject who, yearning to serve his country, volunteered as a guinea pig for a secret government experiment, the results of which transformed him into a being of superhuman strength and endurance. Before others could be similarly treated, thus producing an army of super-soldiers to aid the war effort, the scientist in charge of the project was murdered by a Nazi agent, his secret formulae dying with him. The assassin was subsequently captured by Rogers, who then adopted the guise of Captain America and

Dick Purcell (or his stunt double) prepares for a thrilling leap in Captain America (Republic, 1944).

went on to fight the Axis while masquerading as a lowly Army private stationed in Europe. With his patriotic red, white, and blue costume and circular shield modeled after the American flag, Captain America was one of the most appropriate (and inevitable) popular fiction creations of the World War II era; fittingly enough, he delivers a shattering knock-out blow to Hitler's jaw on the cover of an early issue.

In Republic's serial production of Captain America, though, gone were the character's shield and several other details of his costume, gone was his secret identity as Steve Rogers and, perhaps most puzzling considering the film's release date, gone was the World War II milieu. Republic's official explanation for the changes in the costume was that if adapted as drawn in the comics, the outfit would hinder stunt men in filming, but this excuse doesn't hold water in light of the even more outlandish garb worn by Captain Marvel and other characters in the studio's previous serials, and it certainly doesn't justify the more serious discrepancies of the adaptation (the comics had also given Captain America the inevitable juvenile cohort, Bucky, but his elimination by Republic was more than welcome). Most likely, Republic simply wanted to reap the almost guaranteed profits it were sure to earn from a pre-sold property with a minimal amount of effort on its part, for while Captain America is every bit as slick as the studio's other chapter plays, it appears to have been designed, even more so than most serials, to facilitate quick and easy production.

But by rejecting Captain America's fantastic origin and transforming the character into a crusading District Attorney, Republic's writers only succeeded in constructing a screenplay that was even more outlandish and unbelievable than a comic book, besides raising the issue of Grant Gardner's highly questionable law enforcement methods. Those methods resulted in almost preposterous levels of violence, for Captain America surely claimed more victims in this film than any other serial hero. The sheer number of deaths he is responsible for is incredible, and if the picture had ever been re-edited into feature form (it never was), the almost non-stop carnage wrought in the pursuit of justice would have been appalling. Republic had a pronounced and decidedly unhealthy obsession with guns (no doubt a result of its ceaseless "B" western production schedule), and the studio put a revolver in the hand of nearly every one of its serial stars (and starlets). In Captain America, though, the bullets fly at an unprecedented rate, with the frantic action scaling

new heights of absurdity when Captain America, trapped inside a large crate, escapes by using his gun to shoot out
the wooden joints in the corners!

The cast of Captain America is mostly uninspired,
with pudgy Dick Purcell sadly deficient in the title role, and
Lorna Gray, who was so memorable in The Perils of Nyoka,
given almost nothing to do as Gail Richards.   The real star
of Captain America is Lionel Atwill as Maldor; in the previous decade, this incisive British character actor had brought
genuine class and polish to the villainous roles he essayed
in major horror films like Mystery of the Wax Museum and
Son of Frankenstein.   By the time he appeared in Captain
America, Atwill's effectiveness was somewhat impaired by
ill health (he passed away only two years later), but even
so he towers over his co-stars and steals every scene he
appears in.   This is admittedly petty theft, but Atwill's performance in Captain America and the serial's unintentionally
comic profusion of cartoon mayhem combine to make it one
of Republic's more entertaining cliffhangers, almost compen-
sating for the studio's disdainful and unfortunate adaptation
of the original comic book character.

KING OF THE ROCKETMEN (Republic, 1949), 12 episodes.
Associate Producer, Franklin Adreon.   Director, Fred Bran-
non.   Screenplay, Royale Cole, William Lively, Sol Shor.
Camera, Ellis W. Carter.   Special Effects, Howard and
Theodore Lydecker.
With Tristram Coffin, Mae Clarke, Don Haggerty, House
Peters, Jr., James Craven and I. Stanford Jolley.

The World War II era, with its obvious dramatic possibilities and opportunities for broad characterizations of
"the enemy," had given Hollywood in general and the morally
simplistic serials in particular a patriotic shot in the arm
at the box office, but the serial market and its profits declined sharply in the post-war years.   After Columbia's
wildly popular Superman (1948), there would be no more huge
successes, and Republic, recalling a few of the sizable li-
cencing fees they had been obligated to pay for the screen
rights to characters like Captain America and Spy Smasher,
now attempted to create their own characters, thus elimin-
ating costly negotiations and increasing the dwindling profits.

Bad casting: Mae Clarke and Tristram Coffin in King of the Rocketmen (Republic, 1949).

What the studio came up with, in 1949, was King of the Rocketmen. Although hardly an inspired concoction, it was Republic's last serial of real merit. The threadbare narrative involves the efforts of Dr. Vulcan, a familiar "mad scientist" type, to gain control of several futuristic weapons invented by the technicians of "Science Associates," a top-secret research institute located in the desert. In the "wrong hands," of course, these devices could prove threatening to society, and Dr. Vulcan is opposed by Science Associates member Jeff King, who flies through the air by means of a rocket suit, and Glenda Thomas, a reporter for "Miracle Science" magazine. Needless to say, they ultimately triumph, despite minor annoyances such as the near-total destruction of New York by a massive tidal wave created with Vulcan's super-scientific gadgetry.

Stuntman Dave Sharpe doubles for Tristram Coffin in King of the Rocketmen (Republic, 1949).

King of the Rocketmen was paltry enough conceptually, but the unbelievably poor casting by Republic was far more damaging. In the lead role as Rocketman was middle-aged, shifty-eyed Tristram Coffin. Otherwise nearly always cast as a greasy felon, Coffin looked and acted more like a Times Square pimp than a hero. His presence was detrimental enough, but the studio reached new lows in its cavalier attitude towards its serial actresses by casting Mae Clarke as Coffin's leading lady. In 1931, a banner year for the actress, Mae Clarke had been a lovely and quite talented 24-year-old blonde, appearing in top-notch films like Waterloo Bridge and Frankenstein, and in Public Enemy she received a grapefruit in the face from James Cagney in a scene that has become a part of American movie folklore. By the time King of the Rocketmen was produced in 1949, Clarke's career and prestige had declined sharply, and at 42 she was hardly ingénue material. It was a sad come-down for an actress who had once been directed by James Whale and William Wellman; perhaps inevitably, her meager wardrobe for King of the Rocketmen consisted almost entirely of lumpy mechanic's coveralls. Glamour was not Republic's strong point.

Saddled with an inadequate star and a fading leading lady, King of the Rocketmen goes downhill quickly, and the only genuine interest lies in the costume and abilities of Rocketman himself. With his black leather flying jacket, silver bullet-shaped helmet, and twin rocket engines on his back, Rocketman is one of the serials' more inspired and memorable creations despite the character's scientific implausibility ("up-down-fast-slow" reads a simplistic and not very convincing control panel mounted on his jacket). The impressive flying scenes, using wired dummies, were filmed in exactly the same manner as those done for The Adventures of Captain Marvel several years earlier, and the final scenes of New York's apocalyptic destruction beneath an immense tidal wave had been seen before, too. This footage was, in fact, taken from the 1933 RKO film, Deluge, and the impressively detailed miniature buildings annihilated in the cataclysm were the work of a technical crew headed by Ned Mann, who was responsible for the special effects in Things to Come. These scenes (which are all that survive of Deluge, a "lost" film), were convincing when they were used in Republic's earlier serials in the thirties, but by 1949 the clothing worn by the crowds fleeing the disaster was obviously out of date, revealing the anachronistic nature of the earlier shots.

Cunningly, Republic's wardrobe department designed Rocketman's costume so that the face of the actor wearing the garb was totally obscured; this simplified the inevitable substitution of doubles and stunt men, and also economically cleared the way for the use of stock footage should a need arise to resurrect the character in future productions. This proved to be a felicitous decision, for three years later in 1952 Radar Men from the Moon was released by Republic. Even though the same Rocketman costume and stock footage flying scenes from King of the Rocketmen were incorporated into the new serial, Rader Men from the Moon was not a sequel and the character was now called "Commando Cody, Sky Marshall of the Universe," a somewhat unwieldy nom de plume to say the least. As Commando Cody, George Wallace was almost as visually inadequate as Tristram Coffin had been (like his predecessor, he looked better with the helmet on), and he was even more wooden dramatically.   Youthful

Opposite: At top, a stolid George Wallace has apparently bored one of his co-stars to death in Radar Men from the Moon (Republic, 1952). Below, Judd Holdren (he's the one on the right) defends himself in Zombies of the Stratosphere (Republic, 1952).

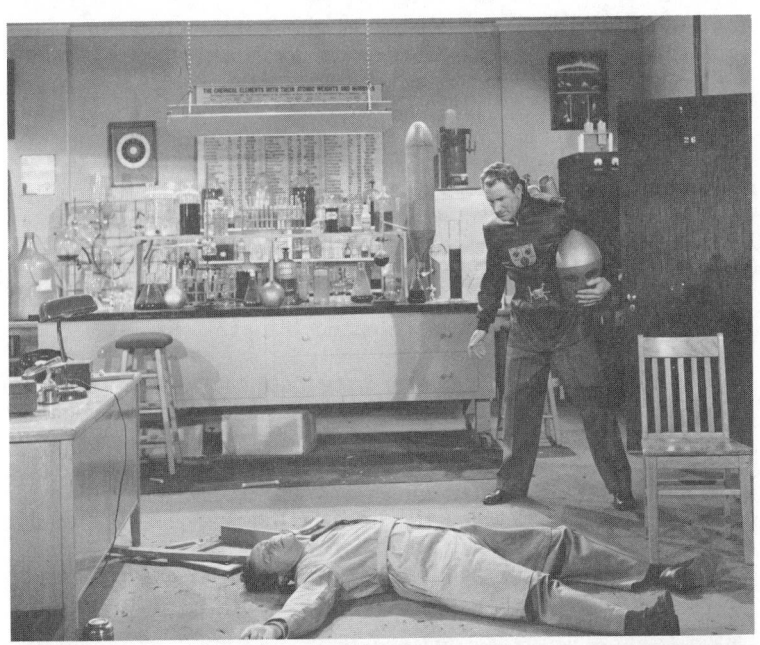

and attractive Aline Towne was a considerable improvement over Mae Clarke, but she had little to do except hand Cody his rocket suit and gun. Radar Men's plot, which concerned an invasion of Earth by aliens from the moon, rejected fantasy and a sense of wonder for more of Republic's stale shoot-'em-up tedium as the soldiers in the lunar vanguard ally themselves with stock gangsters on Earth. This pathetic lack of imagination (a plot thread echoing Republic's earlier The Purple Monster Strikes) was especially appalling considering that two features which have since become classics, Howard Hawks' The Thing and Robert Wise's The Day the Earth Stood Still, had been released the previous year.

Republic didn't seem to have noticed, though, for later in 1952 the studio churned out the improbably titled Zombies of the Stratosphere, which served up more of the same. This time the man in the rocket suit was played by Judd Holdren, whose character was now known as "Larry Martin." Once again Aline Towne handed the hero his rocket suit and gun, and once again the flying scenes from King of the Rocketmen were excavated from the Republic vaults to no great effect, and the serial's only claim to fame lies in the latter-day trivia interest derived from the presence of a young Leonard Nimoy in the cast, contributing the minor supporting role of a Martian invader. Today, riding high on his overrated portrayal of the alien Mr. Spock in the Star Trek films derived from the television series of the sixties, Nimoy doesn't like to be reminded of his youthful transgression at Republic in Zombies of the Stratosphere.

Eventually, Republic used the Rocketman character once more (again under the name Commando Cody) in several low-budget short subjects produced in the early fifties. These films, although they received theatrical distribution, were not serial chapters and were complete stories with resolved endings; and their simultaneous release to television was evidence of the inevitable to the producers of serials. Despite the uninspired use of the character, though, Rocketman remains one of the more interesting creations from the last days of a dying genre.

REPUBLIC SERIAL INDEX

DARKEST AFRICA (1936), 15 episodes. Re-issued as King of Jungleland, feature version: Batmen of Africa. Directed by B. Reeves Eason and Joseph Kane. Cast: Clyde Beatty (himself), Manuel King (Baru), Elaine Shepard (Valerie), Lucien Prival (Dagna), Ray "Crash" Corrigan (Bonga, Samabi), Wheeler Oakman (Durkin), Edward McWade (Gorn), Edmund Cobb (Craddock), Ray Turner (Hambone), Donald Reed (Negus), Harrison Greene (Driscoll), Henry Sylvester (Tomlin), Joseph Boyd (Nagga).

UNDERSEA KINGDOM (1936), 12 episodes. Feature version: Sharad of Atlantis. Directed by B. Reeves Eason and Joseph Kane. Cast: Ray "Crash" Corrigan (himself), Lois Wilde (Diana), Monte Blue (Khan), William Farnum (Sharad), Boothe Howard (Ditmar), C. Montague Shaw (Professor Norton), Lee Van Atta (Billy Norton), Smiley Burnette (Briny), Frankie Marvin (Salty), Lon Chaney, Jr. (Hakur), Lane Chandler (Darius), Jack Mulhall (Lt. Andrews), John Bradford (Joe), Malcolm McGregor (Zogg), Ralph Holmes (Martos), John Meryon (Moloch), Ernie Smith (Gourck), Lloyd Whitlock (Captain Clinton), David Horsley (Naval Sentry), Kenneth Lawton (Naval Doctor).

The VIGILANTES ARE COMING (1936), 12 episodes. Directed by Mack V. Wright and Ray Taylor. Cast: Robert Livingston (Don Loring), Kay Hughes (Doris), Guinn "Big Boy" Williams (Salvation), Raymond Hatton (Whipsaw), Fred Kohler (Burr), Robert Warwick (Raspinoff), William Farnum (Father Jose), Bob Kortman (Petroff), John Merton (Talbot), Ray "Crash" Corrigan (Captain Fremont), Lloyd Ingraham (Colton), William Desmond (Anderson), Yakima Canutt (Barsom), Tracy Lane (Peters), Bud Pope (Ivan), Steve Clemente (Pedro), Bud Osborne (Harris), John O'Brien (Robert Loring), Henry Hall (Señor Loring), Philip Armetta (Dark Feather).

ROBINSON CRUSOE OF CLIPPER ISLAND (1936), 14 episodes. Feature version: Robinson Crusoe of Mystery Island. Directed by Mack V. Wright and Ray Taylor. Cast: Mala (himself), Rex (himself), Buck (himself), Mamo Clark (Melani), Herbert Rawlinson (Jackson), William Newell (Hank), John Ward (Tupper), Selmer Jackson (Canfield), John Dilson (Ellsworth), John Picorri (Porotu), George Chesebro (Draker), Bob Kortman (Wilson), George Cleveland (Goebel), Lloyd Whitlock (Lamar), Tiny Roebuck (Eppa), Tracy Layne (Larkin).

DICK TRACY (1937), 15 episodes.   Directed by Ray Taylor and
Alan James.   Cast: Ralph Byrd (Dick Tracy), Kay Hughes (Gwen
Andrews), Smiley Burnette (Mike McGurk), Lee Van Atta (Junior),
John Piccori (Moloch), Carleton Young, Richard Beach (Gordon
Tracy, before and after), Fred Hamilton (Steve Lockwood), Francis
X. Bushman (Clive Anderson), John Dilson (Ellery Brewster), Wedge-
wood Nowell (H. T. Clayton), Theodore Lorch (Patorno), Edwin
Stanley (Walter Odette), Harrison Greene (Cloggerstein), Herbert
Weber (Tony Martino), Buddy Roosevelt (Burke), George DeNormand
(Claude Destino), Byron K. Foulger (Korvitch), Oscar (himself),
Elmer (himself).

The PAINTED STALLION (1937), 12 episodes.   Directed by Ray
Taylor and Alan James.   Cast: Ray "Crash" Corrigan (Clark Stew-
art), Hoot Gibson (Walter Jamison), Leroy Mason (Dupre), Duncan
Renaldo (Zamoro), Sammy McKim (Kit Carson), Hal Taliaferro (Jim
Bowie), Jack Perrin (Davy Crockett).

S. O. S. COAST GUARD (1937), 12 episodes.   Directed by William
Witney and Alan James.   Cast: Ralph Byrd (Terry), Bela Lugosi
(Boroff), Maxine Doyle (Jean Norman), Herbert Rawlinson (Commander
Boyle), Richard Alexander (Thorg), Lee Ford (Snapper McGee), John
Piccori (Rackerby), Lawrence Grant (Rabinisi), Thomas Carr (Jim
Kent), Carleton Young (Dodds), Allen Connor (Dick Norman), George
Chesebro (Degado), Ranny Weeks (Wies).

ZORRO RIDES AGAIN (1937), 12 episodes.   Directed by William
Witney and John English.   Cast: John Carroll (James Vega, Zorro),
Helen Christian (Joyce), Reed Howes (Philip), Duncan Renaldo (Re-
naldo), Noah Beery (Marsden), Richard Alexander (El Lobo), Bob
Kortman (Trelliger), Paul Lopez (Captain Rurales), Jack Ingram
(Carter), Roger Williams (Manning), Mona Rico (Singer), Jerry
Frank (Duncan).

The LONE RANGER (1938), 15 episodes.   Directed by William
Witney and John English.   Cast: Lee Powell (The Lone Ranger,
Allen King), Silver King (Silver), Chief Thunder Cloud (Tonto), Her-
man Brix (Bert Rogers), Lynn Roberts (Joan Blanchard), Stanley
Andrews (Jeffries), William Farnum (Father McKim), George Cleve-
land (Blanchard), Hal Taliaferro (Bob Stewart), Lane Chandler (Dick
Forrest), George Letz (Jim Clark), John Merton (Kester), Sammy
McKim (Felton), Ralph Bennet (Taggart).

FIGHTING DEVIL DOGS (1938), 12 episodes.   Feature version:
The Torpedo of Doom.   Directed by William Witney and John Eng-
lish.   Cast: Lee Powell (Lt. Tom Grayson), Herman Brix (Frank
Corby), Eleanor Stewart (Janet), Montagu Love (General White),
Hugh Sothern (Warfield), Sam Flint (Colonel Grayson), Perry Ivans
(Crenshaw), Forrest Taylor (Benson), John Piccori (Gould), Carleton
Young (Johnson), John Davidson (Lin Wing), Henry Otho (Sam Hedges),
Reed Howes (Parker), Tom London (Wilson), Edmund Cobb (Ellis).

DICK TRACY RETURNS (1938), 15 episodes.   Directed by William

Witney and John English. Cast: Ralph Byrd (Dick Tracy), Lynn
Roberts (Gwen), Charles Middleton (Pa Stark), Jerry Tucker (Junior),
Dave Sharpe (Ron Merton), Lee Ford (Mike McGurk), Michael Kent
(Steve), John Merton (Champ), Ralph Bennett (Trigger), Jack Roberts
(Dude), Ned Glass (The Kid), Edward Foster (Joe Hanner), Alan
Gregg (Snub), Reed Howes (Rance), Robert Terry (Reynolds), Tom
Seidel (Hunt).

HAWK OF THE WILDERNESS (1938), 12 episodes. Feature ver-
sion: Lost Island of Kioga. Directed by William Witney and John
English. Cast: Herman Brix (Kioga), Mala (Kias), Monte Blue
(Yellow Weasel), Jill Martin (Beth), Noble Johnson (Mokuyi), William
Royle (Solerno), Tom Chatterton (Dr. Munro), George Eldredge
(Allen Kendall), Patrick J. Kelly (Bill), Dick Wessel (Dirk), Snow-
flake (George), Tuffy (Tawnee).

The LONE RANGER RIDES AGAIN (1939), 15 episodes. Directed
by William Witney and John English. Cast: Robert Livingston (The
Lone Ranger, Bill Andrews), Chief Thunder Cloud (Tonto), Silver
Chief (Silver), Duncan Renaldo (Juan Vasquez), Jinx Falken (Sue),
Ralph Dunn (Bart Dolan), J. Farrell MacDonald (Craig Dolan), Wil-
liam Gould (Jed Scott), Rex Lease (Evans), Ted Mapes (Merritt),
Henry Otho (Pa Daniels), John Beach (Hardin), Glenn Strange (Thorne),
Stanley Blystone (Murdock), Edwin Parker (Hank), Al Taylor (Colt),
Carlton Young (Logan), Ernie Adams (Doc Grover).

DAREDEVILS OF THE RED CIRCLE (1939), 12 episodes. Di-
rected by William Witney and John English. Cast: Charles Quigley
(Gene Townley), Herman Brix (Tiny Dawson), Dave Sharpe (Burt
Knowles), Carole Landis (Blanche Granville), Miles Mander (Horace
Granville), Charles Middleton (Harry Crowell).

DICK TRACY'S G-MEN (1939), 15 episodes. Directed by William
Witney and John English. Cast: Ralph Byrd (Dick Tracy), Irving
Pichel (Zarnoff), Ted Pearson (Steve), Phylis Isley (Gwen), Walter
Miller (Robal), George Douglas (Sandoval), Robert Carson (Scott),
Julian Madison (Foster), Ted Mapes (G-Man #1), William Stahl (G-
Man #2), Robert Wayne (G-Man #3), Joe McGuinn (Tommy), Kenneth
Terrell (Ed), Harry Humphrey (Warden Stover), Harrison Greene
(Baron).

ZORRO'S FIGHTING LEGION (1939), 12 episodes. Directed by
William Witney and John English. Cast: Reed Hadley (Zorro),
Sheila Darcy (Volita), William Corson (Ramon), Leander De Cor-
dova (Felipe), Edmund Cobb (Gonzales), C. Montague Shaw (Pablo),
John Merton (Manuel), Budd Buster (Juan), Carleton Young (Juarez),
Guy D'Ennery (Francisco), Paul Marian (Kala), Joe Molina (Tarmac),
Jim Pierce (Moreno), Helen Mitchell (Donna Maria), Curley Dresden
(Tomas), Charles King (Valdez).

DRUMS OF FU MANCHU (1940), 15 episodes. Directed by William Witney and John English. Cast: Henry Brandon (Fu Manchu),
William Royle (Nayland Smith), Robert Kellard (Allen Parker), Gloria

Henry Brandon (r.), in the title role, unmasks a hitherto disguised Robert Kellard in <u>Drums of Fu Manchu</u> (Republic, 1940).

Franklin (Fah Lo Suee), Olaf Hytten (Dr. Petrie), Tom Chatterton (Professor Randolph), Luana Walters (Mary Randolph), Lal Chend Mehra (Sirdar Prahin), George Cleveland (Professor Parker), John Dilson (Howard), John Merton (Loki), Dwight Frye (Anderson), Wheaton Chambers (Dr. Humphrey).

ADVENTURES OF RED RYDER (1940), 12 episodes. Directed by William Witney and John English. Cast: Don "Red" Barry (Red Ryder), Noah Beery (Ace Hanlon), Tommy Cook (Little Beaver), Maude Pierce (The Duchess), Vivian Coe (Beth Andrews), Harry Worth (Calvin Drake), Hal Taliaferro (Cherokee Sims), William Farnum (Colonel Tom Ryder), Bob Kortmann (One-Eye Chapin), Carleton Young (Sheriff Dade), Ray Teal (Shark), Gene Alsace (Deputy Lawson), Gayne Whitman (Harrison), Hooper Atchley (Treadway), John Dilson (Hale), Lloyd Ingraham (Sheriff Luke Andrews), Charles Hutchinson (Brown), Gardner James (H. S. Barnett), Wheaton Chambers (Boswell), Lynton Brent (Len Clark).

KING OF THE ROYAL MOUNTED (1940), 12 episodes. Directed by William Witney and John English. Cast: Allan Lane (Sgt. King), Robert Strange (Kettler), Robert Kellard (Corporal Tom Merrit, Jr.), Lita Conway (Linda Merrit), Herbert Rawlinson (Inspector King), Harry Cording (Wade Garson), Bryant Washburn (Crandall), Budd Buster (Vinegar Smith), Stanley Andrews (Merrit, Sr.), John Davidson (Dr. Shelton), John Dilson (Dr. Wall), Paul McVey (Excellency Zarnoff), Lucien Prival (Admiral Johnson).

MYSTERIOUS DOCTOR SATAN (1940), 15 episodes. Feature version: Doctor Satan's Robot. Directed by William Witney and John English. Cast: Eduardo Cianelli (Doctor Satan), Robert Wilcox (Bob Wayne), William Newell (Speed Martin), C. Montague Shaw (Mr. Scott), Ella Neal (Lois Scott), Dorothy Herbert (Alice Brent), Charles Trowbridge (Governor Bronson), Jack Mulhall (Rand), Edwin Stanley (Colonel Bevans), Walter McGrail (Stoner), Joe McGuinn (Gort), Bud Geary (Hallett), Paul Marion (The Stranger), Archie Twitchell (Airport Radio Announcer), Lynton Brent (Scarlett), Kenneth Terrell (Corwin), Al Taylor (Joe).

ADVENTURES OF CAPTAIN MARVEL (1941), 12 episodes. Reissued as Return of Captain Marvel. Directed by William Witney and John English. Cast: Tom Tyler (Captain Marvel), Frank Coghlan, Jr. (Billy Batson), William Benedict (Murphy), Louise Currie (Betty Wallace), Robert Strange (John Malcolm), Harry Worth (Professor Bentley), Bryant Washburn (Henry Carlyle), John Davidson (Tal Chotali), George Pembroke (Dr. Stephen Lang), Peter George Lynn (Dwight Fisher), Reed Hadley (Rahman Bar), Jack Mulhall (Howell), Kenneth Ducan (Barnett), Nigel De Brulier (Shazam), John Bagni (Cowan), Carleton Young (Martin), Leland Hodgson (Major Rawley), Stanley Price (Owens), Ernest Sarracino (Akbar), Tetsu Komai (Chan Lai).

JUNGLE GIRL (1941), 15 episodes. Directed by William Witney and John English. Cast: Frances Gifford (Nyoka), Tom Neal (Jack Stanton), Trevor Bardette (Meredith-Bradley), Gerald Mohr (Slick Latimer), Eddie Acuff (Curly Rogers), Frank Lackteen (Shamba), Tommy Cook (Wakimbu), Robert Barron (Bombo), Al Kikume (Lutembi), Bud Geary (Brock), Al Taylor (Claggett), Joe McGuinn (Bone), Jerry Frank (the Lion Chief), Kenneth Terrell (Mananga).

KING OF THE TEXAS RANGERS (1941), 12 episodes. Directed by William Witney and John English. Cast: "Slingin' Sammy" Baugh (Sergeant King), Neil Hamilton (Barton), Pauline Moore (Sally Crane), Duncan Renaldo (Pedro Garcia), Charles Trowbridge (Crawford), Herbert Rawlinson (Col. Avery), Frank Darien (Evans), Robert O. Davis (His Excellency), Monte Blue (Captain King), Stanley Blystone (Lynch), Kermit Maynard (Wichita), Roy Barcroft (Ross), Kenneth Duncan (Nick), Jack Ingram (Shorty), Robert Barron (Blake), Frank Bruno (Cole), Monte Montague (Dade).

DICK TRACY vs. CRIME, INC. (1941), 15 episodes. Re-issued as Dick Tracy vs. Phantom Empire. Directed by William Witney

and John English. Cast: Ralph Byrd (Dick Tracy), Michael Owen
(Billy Car), Jan Wiley (June Chandler), John Davidson (Lucifer),
Ralph Morgan (Morton), Kenneth Harlan (Lieut. Cosgrave), John
Dilson (Weldon), Howard Hickman (Chandler), Robert Frazer (Brew-
ster), Robert Fiske (Cabot), Jack Mulhall (Wilson), Hooper Atchley
(Trent), Anthony Warde (Corey), Chuck Morrison (Trask).

SPY SMASHER (1942), 12 episodes. Feature version: Spy Smasher
Returns. Directed by William Witney. Cast: Kane Richmond (Spy
Smasher), Sam Flint (Admiral Corby), Marguerite Chapman (Eve
Corby), Hans Schumm (The Mask), Tristram Coffin (Drake), Franco
Corsaro (Pierre Durand), Hans Von Morhart (Capt. Gerhardt), George
Renavent (the Governor), Robert O. Davis (Col. Von Kohr), Henry
Zynda (Lazar), Paul Bryar (Lawlor), Tom London (Crane), Richard
Bond (Hayes), Crane Whitley (Dr. Hauser), John James (Steve).

PERILS OF NYOKA (1942), 15 episodes.   Re-issued as Nyoka
and the Tigermen, feature version: Nyoka and the Lost Secrets of
Hippocrates. Directed by William Witney. Cast: Kay Aldridge
(Nyoka), Clayton Moore (Larry), William Benedict (Red), Lorna
Gray (Vultura), Charles Middleton (Cassib), Tristram Coffin (Tor-
rini), Forbes Murray (Professor Campbell), Robert Strange (Professor Gordon), George Pembroke (John Spencer), George Renavent
(Maghreb), John Davidson (Lhoba), George Lewis (Batan), Ken Terrell (Ahmed), John Bagni (Ben Ali), Kenneth Duncan (Abou).

KING OF THE MOUNTIES (1942), 12 episodes.   Directed by Wil-
liam Witney. Cast: Allan Lane (Sergeant King), Gilbert Emery
(Commissioner), Russell Hicks (Marshal Carleton), Peggy Drake
(Carol Brent), George Irving (Professor Brent), Abner Biberman
(Admiral Yamata), William Vaughn (Marshall Von Horst), Nestor
Paiva (Count Broni), Brasley Page (Blake), Douglas Dumbrille (Har-
per), William Blakewell (Ross), Duncan Renaldo (Pierre), Francis
Ford (Collins), Jay Novello (Lewis).

G-MEN vs. THE BLACK DRAGON (1943), 15 episodes.   Feature
version: Black Dragon of Manzanar. Directed by William Witney.
Cast: Rod Cameron (Rex), Roland Got (Chang), Constance Worth
(Vivian), Nino Pipitone (Harachi), Noel Cravat (Ranga), George Lewis
(Lugo), Maxine Doyle (Marie), Donald Kirke (Muller), Ivan Miller
(Inspector), Walter Fenner (Williams), C. Montague Shaw (Nichol-
son), Harry Burns (Tony), Forbes Murray (Kennedy), Hooper Atch-
ley (Caldwell).

DAREDEVILS OF THE WEST (1943), 12 episodes.   Directed by
John English. Cast: Allan Lane (Duke Cameron), Kay Aldridge
(June Foster), Eddie Acuff (Red Kelly), William Hade (Barton Ward),
Robert Frazer (Martin Dexter), Ted Adams (Silas Higby), George
Lewis (Turner, Stanley Andrews (Colonel Andrews), Jack Rockwell
(Sheriff Watson).

SECRET SERVICE IN DARKEST AFRICA (1943), 15 episodes.
Re-issued as Manhunt in the African Jungle, feature version: The

Baron's African War. Directed by Spencer Bennet. Cast: Rod
Cameron (Rex Bennett), Joan Marsh (Janet Blake), Duncan Renaldo
(Pierre LaSalle), Lionel Royce (Sultan Abou Ben Ali, Baron Von
Rommler), Kurt Kreuger (Ernest Muller), Frederic Brunn (Wolfe),
Sigurd Tor (Luger), George Renavent (Armand), Kurt Katch (Haupt-
mann), Ralf Harolde (Riverboat Captain), William Vaughn (Captain
Boschert), William Yetter (Commandant), Hans Von Morhart (First
Officer), Erwin Goldi (Colonel Von Raeder).

The MASKED MARVEL (1943), 12 episodes. Feature version:
Sakima and the Masked Marvel. Directed by Spencer Bennet. Cast:
William Forrest (Crane), Louise Currie (Alice Hamilton), Johnny
Arthur (Sakima), Rod Bacon (Jim Arnold), Richard Clarke (Frank
Jeffers), Anthony Warde (Mace), David Bacon (Bob Barton), Bill
Healy (Terry Morton), Howard Hickman (Warren Hamilton), Kenneth
Harlan (Officer), Thomas Louden (Matthews), Edwin Parker (Meggs),
Duke Green (Spike), Dale Van Sickel (Kline), Wendell Niles (News-
caster), Lester Dorr (Reporter).

CAPTAIN AMERICA (1944), 15 episodes. Re-issued as Return
of Captain America. Directed by John English and Elmer Clifton.
Cast: Dick Purcell (Captain America), Lorna Gray (Gail Richards),
Lionel Atwill (Dr. Cyrus Maldor), Charles Trowbridge (Commisioner
Dryden), Russell Hicks (Mayor Randolph), John Davidson (Gruber),
George Lewis (Bart Matson), Tom Chatterton (J. C. Henley), Crane
Whitley (Dirk).

The TIGER WOMAN (1944), 12 episodes. Re-issued as Perils of
the Darkest Jungle, feature version: Jungle Gold. Directed by
Spencer Bennet and Wallace Grissell. Cast: Allan Lane (Allan
Saunders), Linda Stirling (the Tiger Woman), Duncan Renaldo (Jose),
George J. Lewis (Morgan), LeRoy Mason (Walton), Crane Whitley
(Dagget), Robert Frazer (High Priest), Rico De Montez (Tegula),
Stanley Price (Slim), Nolan Leary (Captain Scott), Kenne Duncan
(Gentry), Tom Steele (Tunnel Heavy), Duke Greene (Flint), Eddie
Parker (Travis), Ken Terrell (Depot Heavy), Cliff Lyons (Rand).

HAUNTED HARBOR (1944), 15 episodes. Re-issued as Pirate's
Harbor. Directed by Spencer Bennet and Wallace Grissell. Cast:
Kane Richmond (Jim Marsden), Kay Aldridge (Patricia Harding),
Roy Barcroft (Kane), Clancy Cooper (Yank), Marshall J. Reed
(Tommy), Oscar O'Shea (Galbraith), Forrest Taylor (Dr. Harding),
Hal Taliaferro (Lawson), Edward Keane (Vorhees), George J. Lewis
(Dranga), Kenne Duncan (Gregg), Bud Geary (Snell), Robert Homans
(Port Captain), Duke Green (Neville), Dale Van Sickel (Duff), Tom
Steele (Mead).

ZORRO'S BLACK WHIP (1944), 12 episodes. Directed by Spencer
Bennet and Wallace Grissell. Cast: George J. Lewis (Vic Gordon),
Linda Stirling (Barbara Meredith), Lucien Littlefield (Tenpoint),
Francis McDonald (Hammond), Hal Taliaferro (Baxter), John Merton
(Harris), John Hamilton (the Banker), Tom Chatterton (the Merchant),
Tom London (the Commissioner), Jack Kirk (the Marshall), Jay Kirby

(Randolph Meredith), Si Jenks (Zeke Heydon), Stanley Price (Hedges), Tom Steele (Hull), Duke Greene (Evans), Dale Van Sickel (Danley).

MANHUNT OF MYSTERY ISLAND (1945), 15 episodes. Feature version: Captain Mephisto and the Transformation Machine. Directed by Spencer Bennet, Wallace Grissell and Yakima Canutt. Cast: Richard Bailey (Lance), Linda Stirling (Claire), Roy Barcroft (Mephisto), Kenne Duncan (Brand), Forrest Taylor (Professor Forrest), Forbes Murray (Hargraves), Jack Ingram (Armstrong), Harry Strang (Braley), Edward Cassidy (Melton), Frank Alton (Raymond), Lane Chandler (Reed), Russ Vincent (Ruga), Dale Van Sickel (Barker), Tom Steele (Lyons), Duke Green (Harvey).

FEDERAL OPERATOR 99 (1945), 12 episodes. Feature version: FBI 99. Directed by Spencer Bennet and Wallace Grissell. Cast: Marten Lamont (Jerry Blake), Helen Talbot (Joyce Kingston), George J. Lewis (Jim Belmont), Lorna Gray (Rita Parker), Hal Taliaferro (Matt Farrell), Bill Stevens (Morton), Maurice Cass (Morello), Kernan Cripps (Jeffries), Elaine Lange (The Countess), Frank Jaquet (Hunter), Forrest Taylor (Wolfe), Jay Novello (Heinrick), Tom London (Crawford), Jack Ingram (Riggs).

The PURPLE MONSTER STRIKES (1945), 15 episodes. Feature version: D-Day On Mars. Directed by Spencer Bennet and Fred Brannon. Cast: Dennis Moore (Craig Foster), Linda Stirling (Sheila Layton), Roy Barcroft (the Purple Monster), James Craven (Dr. Cyrus Layton), Bud Geary (Garrett), Mary Moore (Macia the Martian), John Davidson (Emperor of Mars), Joe Whitehead (Stewart), Emmett Vogan (Saunders), George Carleton (Meredith), Kenne Duncan (Mitchell), Rosemonde James (Helen), Monte Hale (Harvey), Wheaton Chambers (Benjamin), Frederick Howard (Crandall), Anthony Warde (Tony), Ken Terrell (Andy).

The PHANTOM RIDER (1946), 12 episodes. Re-issued as Ghost Riders of the West. Directed by Spencer Bennet and Fred Brannon. Cast: Robert Kent (Dr. Jim Sterling), Peggy Stewart (Doris Hammond), Leroy Mason (Fred Carson), George J. Lewis (Blue Feather), Kenne Duncan (Ben Brady), Hal Taliaferro (Nugget), Chief Thunder Cloud (Yellow Wolf), Monte Hale (Cass), Tom Lomdon (Ceta), Roy Barcroft (Marshal), John Hamilton (Senator Williams), Hugh Prosser (Keeler), Jack Kirk (Deputy Sheriff), Rex Lease (Randall), Tommy Coats (Tim), Joe Yrigoyen (Logan).

KING OF THE FOREST RANGERS (1946), 12 episodes. Directed by Spencer Bennet and Fred Brannon. Cast: Larry Thompson (Steve King), Helen Talbot (Marian Brennan), Stuart Hamblen (Professor Carver), Anthony Warde (Burt Spear), LeRoy Mason (Haliday), Scott Elliott (Andrews), Tom London (Judson), Walter Soderling (Miner), Bud Geary (Rance), Harry Strang (Harmon), Ernie Adams (Bailey), Eddie Parker (Stover), Jack Kirk (Holmes), Tom Steele (Martin), Dale Van Sickel (Blaine), Stanley Blystone (Lynch).

DAUGHTER OF DON Q (1946), 12 episodes. Directed by Spencer

Bennet and Fred Brannon. Cast: Adrian Booth (Dolores Quantaro), Kirk Alyn (Cliff Roberts), LeRoy Mason (Carlos Manning), Roy Barcroft (Mel Donovan), Claire Meade (Maria Montenez), Kernan Cripps (Grogan), Jimmy Ames (Romero), Eddie Parker (Tompkins), Tom Steele (Norton), Dale Van Sickel (Murphy), Fred Graham (Rollins), Tom Quinn (Riggs), Johnny Daheim (Kelso), Ted Mapes (Gray), Stanford Jolley (Lippy), Buddy Roosevelt (Moody).

The CRIMSON GHOST (1946), 12 episodes. Feature version: Cyclotrode X. Directed by William Witney and Fred Brannon.

The ghoulish title villain plots his crimes in The Crimson Ghost (Republic, 1946).

Cast: Charles Quigley (Duncan Richards), Linda Stirling (Diana Farnsworth), Clayton Moore (Ashe), I. Stanford Jolley (Blackton), Kenne Duncan (Chambers), Forrest Taylor (Van Wyck), Emmett Vogan (Anderson), Sam Flint (Maxwell), Joe Forte (Parker), Stanley Price (Fator), Wheaton Chambers (Wilson), Tom Steele (Stricker), Dale Van Sickel (Harte), Rex Lease (Bain), Fred Graham (Zane).

SON OF ZORRO (1947), 13 episodes. Directed by Spencer Bennet and Fred Brannon. Cast: George Turner (Jeff Stewart), Peggy Stewart (Kate Wells), Roy Barcroft (Boyd), Edward Cassidy (Sheriff Moody), Ernie Adams (Judge Hyde), Stanley Price (Pancho), Edmund

Cobb (Stockton), Ken Terrell (Thomas), Wheaton Chambers (Baldwin), Fred Graham (Quirt), Eddie Parker (Melton), Si Jenks (Fred), Jack O'Shea (Hood), Jack Kirk (Charlie), Tom Steele (Leach), Dale Van Sickle (Murray).

JESSE JAMES RIDES AGAIN (1947), 13 episodes. Directed by Fred Brannon and Thomas Carr. Cast: Clayton Moore (Jesse James), Linda Stirling (Ann), Roy Barcroft (Lawton), John Compton (Steve), Tristram Coffin (Clark), Tom London (Bolton), Holly Bane (Tim), Edmund Cobb (Wilkie), Gene Stutenroth (the Sheriff), Fred Graham (Hawks), LeRoy Mason (Finlay), Edward Cassidy (Grant), Dave Anderson (Sam), Eddie Parker (Captain Flint), Tom Steele (Goff), Dale Van Sickel (Brock).

The BLACK WIDOW (1947), 13 episodes. Feature version: Sombra the Spider Woman. Directed by Spencer Bennet and Fred Brannon. Cast: Bruce Edwards (Steve), Virginia Lindley (Joyce), Carol Forman (Sombra), Anthony Warde (Ward), Ramsay Ames (Ruth Dayton), I. Stanford Jolley (Jaffa), Theodore Gottlieb (Hitomu), Virginia Carroll (Dr. Curry), Gene Stutenroth (Walker), Sam Flint (Weston), Tom Steele (Bard), Dale Van Sickel (Bill), LeRoy Mason (Dr. Godfrey), Forrest Taylor (Bradley), Ernie Adams (Blinkey), Keith Richards (Burns).

G-MEN NEVER FORGET (1948), 12 episodes. Feature version: Code 645. Directed by Fred Brannon and Yakima Canutt. Cast: Clayton Moore (Ted O'Hara), Roy Barcroft (Murkland, Cameron), Ramsay Ames (Frances Blake), Drew Allen (Duke), Tom Steele (Parker), Dale Van Sickel (Brent), Edmund Cobb (Cook), Stanley Price (Benson), Jack O'Shea (Slater), Barry Brooks (George), Doug Aylesworth (Hayden), Frank O'Connor (District Attorney), Dian Fauntelle (Miss Stewart), Eddie Acuff (Fiddler).

DANGERS OF THE CANADIAN MOUNTED (1948), 12 episodes. Feature version: R. C. M. P. and the Treasure of Genghis Khan. Directed by Fred Brannon and Yakima Canutt. Cast: Jim Bannon (Christopher Royal), Virginia Belmont (Bobbie Page), Anthony Warde (Mort), Dorothy Granger (Skagway Kate), Bill Van Sickel (Dan Page), Tom Steele (Fagin), Dale Van Sickel (Boyd), I. Stanford Jolley (Pelance), Phil Warren (George), Lee Morgan (Dale), James Dale (Andy), Ted Adams (Oldtimer), John Crawford (Danton), Jack Clifford (Marshal), Eddie Parker (Lowry).

ADVENTURES OF FRANK AND JESSE JAMES (1948), 13 episodes. Directed by Fred Brannon and Yakima Canutt. Cast: Clayton Moore (Jesse James), Steve Darrell (Frank James), Noel Neill (Judy Powell), George J. Lewis (Rafe Henley), Stanley Andrews (Powell), John Crawford (Amos Ramsey), Sam Flint (Thatcher), House Peters, Jr. (Sheriff Towey), Dale Van Sickel (Dale), Tom Steele (Steele), James Dale (Nichols), I. Stanford Jolley (Ward), Gene Stutenroth (Marshal), Lane Bradford (Bill), George Chesebro (Station Agent), Jack Kirk (Stage Driver).

FEDERAL AGENTS vs. UNDERWORLD, INC. (1949), 12 episodes. Feature version: Golden Hands of Kurigal. Directed by Fred Brannon. Cast: Kirk Alyn (Dave Worth), Rosemary La Planche (Laura), Roy Barcroft (Gordon), Carol Forman (Nila), James Dale (Steve Evans), Bruce Edwards (Professor Williams), James Craven (Professor Clayton), Tristram Coffin (Chambers), Tom Steele (Mort), Dale Van Sickle (Professor Graves), Jack O'Shea (Ali), Marshall Reed (O'Hara), Bob Wilke (Zod), Robert St. Angelo (Native), George Douglas (Courier), Dave Anderson (Porter).

GHOST OF ZORRO (1949), 12 episodes. Directed by Fred Brannon. Cast: Clayton Moore (Zorro, Ken Mason), Pamela Blake (Rita), Roy Barcroft (Kilgore), George J. Lewis (Moccasin), Eugene Roth (Crane), John Crawford (Mulvaney), I. Stanford Jolley (Green), Steve Clark (White), Steve Darrell (Marshal Simpson), Dale Van Sickel (Hodge), Tom Steele (Brace), Alex Montoya (Yellow Hawk), Marshall Reed (Fowler), Frank O'Connor (Doctor), Jack O'Shea (Freight Agent), Holly Bane (Larkin).

KING OF THE ROCKET MEN (1949), 12 episodes. Feature version: Lost Planet Airmen. Directed by Fred Brannon. Cast: Tristram Coffin (Jeff King), Mae Clarke (Glenda Thomas), Don Haggerty (Tony Dirken), House Peters, Jr. (Burt Winslow), James Craven (Professor Millard), I. Stanford Jolley (Professor Bryant), Douglas Evans (Chairman), Ted Adams (Martin Conway), Stanley Price (Gunther Von Strum), Dale Van Sickel (Martin), Tom Steele (Knox), David Sharpe (Blears), Eddie Parker (Rowan), Michael Ferro (Turk), Frank O'Connor (Guard), Buddy Roosevelt (Phillips).

The JAMES BROTHERS OF MISSOURI (1950), 12 episodes. Directed by Fred Brannon. Cast: Keith Richards (Jesse James), Robert Bice (Frank James), Noel Neill (Peggy Sawyer), Roy Barcroft (Ace), Patricia Knox (Belle), Lane Bradford (Monk), Eugene Roth (Marshal Rand), John Hamilton (Lon), Edmund Cobb (Sheriff), Hank Patterson (Duffy), Dale Van Sickel (Simpson), Tom Steele (Slim), Lee Roberts (Brandy), Frank O'Connor (Citizen), Marshall Reed (Dutch), Wade Ray (Deputy Sheriff), Nolan Leary (Pop Keever).

RADAR PATROL vs. SPY KING (1950) 12 episodes. Directed by Fred Brannon. Cast: Kirk Alyn (Chris Calvert), Jean Dean (Joan Hughes), Anthony Warde (Ricco), George J. Lewis (Manuel), Eve Whitney (Nitra), John Merton (Baroda), Tristram Coffin (Lord), John Crawford (Sands), Harold Goodwin (Miller), Dale Van Sickel (Ames), Tom Steele (Gorman), Eddie Parker (Dutch), Forbes Murray (Chairman), Stephen Gregory (Hugo).

The INVISIBLE MONSTER (1950), 12 episodes. Feature version: Slaves of the Invisible Monster. Directed by Fred Brannon. Cast: Richard Webb (Lane Carson), Aline Towne (Carol Richards), Lane Bradford (Burton), Stanley Price (the Phantom Ruler), John Crawford (Harris), George Meeker (Long), Keith Richards (Doctor), Dale Van Sickel (Martin), Tom Steele (Haines), Marshall Reed (Police

Officer), Forrest Burns (Guard), Eddie Parker (Stoner), Frank
O'Connor (Hogan), Charles Sullivan (Grogarty).

DESPERADOES OF THE WEST (1950), 12 episodes.   Directed by
Fred Brannon.   Cast: Richard Powers (Ward), Judy Clark (Sally),
Roy Barcroft (Hacker), I. Stanford Jolley (Dawson), Lee Phelps
(Rusty), Lee Roberts (Larson), Cliff Clark (Colonel Arnold), Ed-
mund Cobb (Bowers), Hank Patterson (Hard Rock), Dale Van Sickel
(Reed), Tom Steele (Gregg), Sandy Sanders (Karn), John Cason
(Casey), Guy Teague (Jack), Bud Osborne (Joe), Stanley Blystone
(Storekeeper).

FLYING DISC MAN FROM MARS (1951), 12 episodes.   Directed
by Fred Brannon.   Cast: Walter Reed (Kent Fowler), Lois Collier
(Helen), Gregory Gay (Mota), James Craven (Dr. Bryant), Harry
Lauter (Drake), Richard Irving (Ryan), Sandy Sanders (Steve), Michael
Carr (Trent), Dale Van Sickel (Watchman), Tom Steele (Taylor),
George Sherwood (Gateman), Jim O'Gatty (Gradey), John DeSimone
(Curtis), Jester Dorr (Crane), Dick Cogan (Kirk).

DON DAREDEVIL RIDES AGAIN (1951), 12 episodes.   Directed
by Fred Brannon.   Cast: Ken Curtis (Lee Hadley), Aline Towne
(Patricia Doyle), Roy Barcroft (Stratton), Lane Bradford (Weber),
Robert Einer (Gary), John Cason (Hagen), L. Standord Jolley (Sher-
iff), Hank Patterson (Buck), Lee Phelps (Uncle Michael), Sandy
Sanders (Dirk), Guy Teague (Deputy Sheriff), Tom Steele (Black),
Michael Ragan (Miller).

GOVERNMENT AGENTS vs. PHANTOM LEGION (1951), 12 epi-
sides.   Directed by Fred Brannon.   Cast: Walter Reed (Hal Dun-
can), Mary Ellen Kay (Kay Roberts), Dick Curtis (Regan), John
Pickard (Sam Bradley), Fred Coby (Cady), Pierce Lyden (Armstrong),
George Meeker (Willard), John Phillips (Patterson), Mauritz Hugo
(Thompson), Edmund Cobb (Turner), Eddie Dew (Barnett), George
Lloyd (Coroner), Dale Van Sickel (Brice), Tom Steele (Brandt),
Arthur Space (Crandall), Norval Mitchell (District Attorney), Frank
Meredith (Motorcycle Officer).

RADAR MEN FROM THE MOON (1952), 12 episodes.   Feature
version: Retik, the Moon Menace.   Directed by Fred Brannon.
Cast: George Wallace (Commando Cody), Aline Towne (Joan Gilbert), Roy Barcroft (Retik), William Bakewell (Ted Richards), Clayton Moore (Graber), Bob Stevenson (Krog), Don Walters (Henderson), Tom Steele (Zerg), Dale Van Sickel (Alon), Wilson Wood (Hank),
Noel Cravat (Robal), Baynes Barron (Nasor), Paul McGuire (Bream),
Ted Thrope (Bartender), Dick Cogan (Jones).

ZOMBIES OF THE STRATOSPHERE (1952), 12 episodes.   Di-
rected by Fred Brannon.   Cast: Judd Holdren (Larry Martin), Aline
Towne (Sue Davis), Wilson Wood (Bob Wilson), Lane Bradford (Marex),
Stanley Waxman (Dr. Harding), John Crawford (Roth), Craig Kelly
(Mr. Steele), Ray Boyle (Shane), Leonard Nimoy (Narab), Tom Steele
(Truck Driver), Dale Van Sickel (Telegraph Operator), Roy Engel

(Lawson), Jack Harden (Kerr), Paul Stader (Fisherman), Gaye Kellogg (Dick), Jack Shea (Policeman).

JUNGLE DRUMS OF AFRICA (1953), 12 episodes. Feature version: U-238 and the Witch Doctor. Directed by Fred Brannon. Cast: Clayton Moore (Alan King), Phyllis Coates (Carol Bryant), Johnny Spencer (Bert Hadley), Roy Glenn (Naganto), John Cason (Regas), Henry Rowland (Kurgan), Steve Mitchell (Gauss), Bill Walker (Chief Douranga), Don Blackman (Ebola), Felix Nelson (Nodala), Joe Fluellen (Matambo), Bill Washington (Tembo), Tom Steele (Second Constable), Robert Davis (1st Native), Bob Johnson (2nd Native).

CANADIAN MOUNTIES vs. ATOMIC INVADERS (1953), 12 episodes. Feature version: Missile Base at Taniak. Directed by Franklin Adreon. Cast: Bill Henry (Sgt. Don Roberts), Susan Morrow (Kay Conway), Arthur Space (Marlof), Dale Van Sickel (Beck), Pierre Watkin (Comm. Morrison), Mike Ragan (Reed), Stanley Andrews (Anderson), Harry Lauter (Clark), Hank Peterson (Larson), Edmund Cobb (Warner), Gayle Kellogg (Corp. Guy Sanders), Tim Steele (Mack), Jean Wright (Mrs. Warner).

TRADER TOM OF THE CHINA SEAS (1954), 12 episodes. Feature version: Target: Sea of China. Directed by Franklin Adreon. Cast: Harry Lauter (Tom Rogers), Aline Towne (Vivian Wells), Lyle Talbot (Barent), Robert Shayne (Major Conroy), Fred Graham (Kurt Daley), Richard Reeves (Rebel Chief), Tom Steele (Gursan), John Crawford (Bill Gaines), Dale Van Sickel (Native), Victor Sen Yung (Wang), Jan Arvan (Khan), Ramsey Hill (British Colonel), George Selk (Ole).

MAN WITH THE STEEL WHIP (1954), 12 episodes. Directed by Franklin Adreon. Cast: Richard Simmons (Jerry Randall), Barbara Bestar (Nancy Cooper), Dale Van Sickel (Crane), Mauritz Hugo (Barnet), Lane Bradford (Tosco), Pat Hogan (Chief), Roy Barcroft (Sheriff), Stuart Randall (Harris), Edmund Cobb (Lee), Il Stanford Jolley (Sloane), Guy Teague (Price), Alan Wells (Quivar), Tom Steele (Gage).

PANTHER GIRL OF THE KONGO (1955), 12 episodes. Feature version: The Claw Monsters. Directed by Franklin Adreon. Cast: Phyllis Coates (Jean Evans), Myron Healey (Larry Sanders), Arthur Space (Doctor Morgan), John Day (Cass), Mike Regan (Rand), Morris Buchanan (Tembu), Roy Glenn, Jr. (Chief Danka), Archie Savage (Ituri), Ramsay Hill (Commissioner Stanton), Naaman Brown (Orto), Dan Ferniel (Ebu), James Logan (Harris).

KING OF THE CARNIVAL (1955), 12 episodes. Directed by Franklin Adreon. Cast: Harry Lauter (Bert King), Fran Bennett (June Edwards), Keith Richards (Daley), Robert Shayne (Carter), Gregory Gay (Zorn), Rick Vallin (Art), Robert Clarke (Jim), Terry Frost (Travis), Mauritz Hugo (Sam), Lee Roberts (Hank), Chris Mitchell (Bill), Stuart Whitman (Mac), Tom Steele (Matt), George DeNormand (Garth).

THE SERIALS OF COLUMBIA

BATMAN (Columbia, 1943), 15 episodes. Producer, Rudolph C. Flothow. Director, Lambert Hillyer. Screenplay, Victor McLeod, Leslie Swabacker and Harry Fraser. Camera, James S. Brown, Jr. Music, Lee Zahler.
With Lewis Wilson, Douglas Croft, J. Carrol Naish, Shirley Patterson, William Austin, Charles C. Wilson and Charles Middleton.

More than any other chapter play released by the studio, Batman provides a classic example of Columbia Pictures' approach to serial production. Highly underrated and even misunderstood by many film historians and movie buffs, Columbia's serial formula involved light-hearted, gentle spoofing of the subject matter, and Batman, adapted from the successful comic book character created by Bob Kane and published by National Comics, provided adequate grist for the Columbia serial mill. In the original comic books, Batman was a grim, ruthless vigilante, a costumed denizen of the night who had sworn to battle the underworld of Gotham City in revenge for the murder of his parents, years before, at the hands of a criminal. In reality millionaire Bruce Wayne, Batman (with his young ward Dick Grayson, who masquerades as Robin, the Boy Wonder) masterminds his proficient crime-fighting activities from a hidden cave located beneath his mansion on the outskirts of Gotham City.

This melodramatic concept establishes Batman as an obsessed, costumed avenger, and at the same time "justifies" and glosses over crime-fighting techniques of dubious legality with a patina of morality via the "revenge" motif. The idea might have provided the impetus for a great, shadowy mystery film at RKO or Warners in the forties. But major Hollywood studios weren't taking comic books very seriously at that time (they wouldn't until decades later, in the seventies, when the age of the average filmgoer, and

Douglas Croft (l.) and Lewis Wilson, ready for action in Batman (Columbia, 1943).

presumably his intelligence as well, fell sharply), and judging from the results seen in Batman, the serial department at Columbia wasn't taking them seriously either. The screenplay for Batman by-passed most of the character's background and motivation, substituting instead a wild, barnstorming plot detailing the nefarious activities of Dr. Daka, an insane Oriental master spy who plans to steal Gotham City's radium supply in order to aid the Axis war effort. Operating from headquarters concealed behind a "tunnel of horrors" exhibit at a carnival, Daka dispatches a seemingly endless army of hoods and mindless zombies in pursuit of his goal, but they are defeated at every turn by Batman. Daka, suspecting that Batman and Bruce Wayne are one and the same, kidnaps Wayne's girlfriend Linda, and Batman eventually traces Daka to his lair, where the madman meets his inevitable doom in an alligator pit.

This genial insanity was directed by Lambert Hillyer, an experienced hand at "B" westerns who also made two minor fantasy classics, The Invisible Ray, a Boris Karloff and Bela Lugosi vehicle, and Dracula's Daughter, both released in 1936. While The Invisible Ray was a solid, competent thriller, Dracula's Daughter stands as the better of the two films, and is rich in stylish atmosphere. Hillyer injected much of that atmosphere into Batman, with many sequences contributing a grim quality that effectively counterbalances the lighter passages of the film. The scenes in which Batman interrogates criminals in his gloomy Batcave while the bats cast their shadows on the hapless prisoner provided badly-needed relief from the wooden performances of Lewis Wilson in the title role and Douglas Croft as Robin. Lovely Shirley Patterson, an obscure prisoner of the Columbia contract roster, was a definite asset to the film as Linda, but the biggest delight in Batman is J. Carrol Naish as Daka. Interpreting his role with tongue firmly in cheek, Naish leers and mugs his way through the fifteen chapters in such an entertaining manner that he more than compensates for the deficiencies of Wilson and Croft. An incisive and highly-regarded character actor who often appeared in far more highly-regarded films (e. g. , Beau Geste and Blood and Sand), Naish clearly realizes that he is "slumming" here, and cuts loose with a vengeance, serving the audience a few thick slices of prime ham without ever making the mistake of being totally contemptuous of his material.

That mistake wouldn't be made until 1966, when the television series Batman premiered on the ABC network. An immediate, wildfire success due to a clever advertising campaign and a massive wave of publicity, the Batman television series reveled in its trendy "Pop Art" presentation, garish photography, and big name "guest villians." Realized in vulgar, self-conscious "camp" fashion by producer William Dozier and head writer Lorenzo Semple, Jr. , the characters and plotlines were ridiculed to the nth degree, not with the saving grace of style or wit, but in the broadest manner possible in order to make the "humor" accessible to a mass audience of would-be sophisticates. But the public (which never seems to be as lacking in intelligence as some of the people in control of politics and the media seem to think), quickly tired of the antics of stars Adam West and Burt Ward and the show's facile stupidities. The series burned itself out after its third season, stranding manufacturers with warehouses stuffed full of unsold Batman tie-in merchandise. One would think that writer Lorenzo Semple, Jr. would have learned his lesson from this short-lived travesty, but a decade

Batman unmasked.   Shirley Patterson and Lewis Wilson as they appeared in <u>Batman</u> (Columbia, 1943).

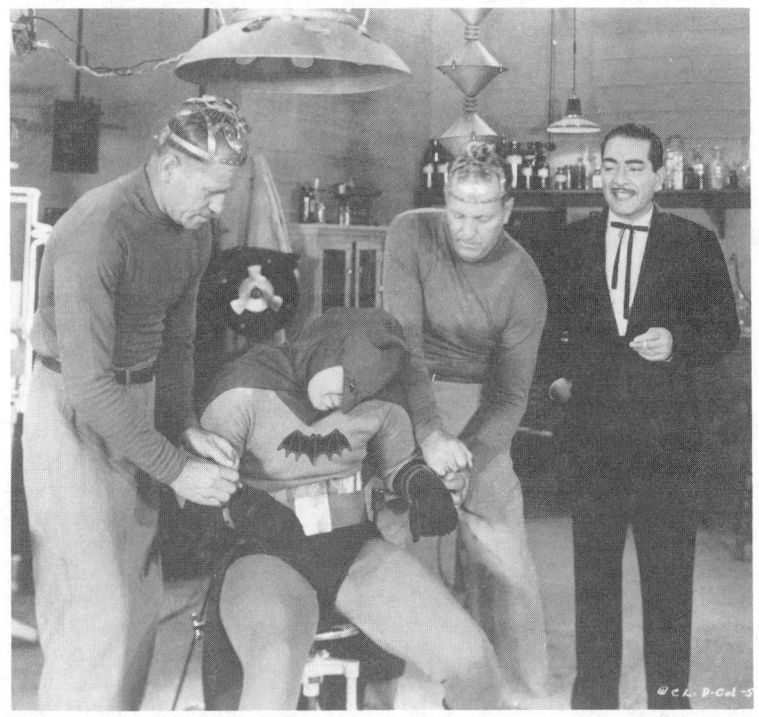

A leering J. Carrol Naish (r.) instructs his zombie minions to confine an unconscious Lewis Wilson in <u>Batman</u> (Columbia, 1943).

later he was still at it, scripting the adominable "spoof" remakes of <u>King Kong</u> (1976) and <u>Flash Gordon</u> (1980). In 1966 <u>Batman</u> was reissued by Columbia as <u>An Evening with Batman and Robin</u>, with all fifteen chapters of the serial strung together into a presentation of marathon length. This revival threw the shortcomings and conceits of the TV series into even sharper contrast, but the film wasn't received very well by younger viewers, who were understandably impressed by the television show's James Bond-inspired gagetry. The old serial was also criticized for its World War II jingoism and blatant racism, with fruity dialogue containing such epithets as "dirty slant-eyed Jap rats" eliciting hoots of derision

from mid-sixties audiences. Batman had spawned a sequel
serial entitled Batman and Robin, also released by Columbia,
but this 1949 rehash starring Robert Lowery and John Duncan in the title roles was abysmally cheap even by serial
standards and, after the rather indifferent reception of the
first film, plans to reissue Batman and Robin as well didn't
get very far.

    Lambert Hillyer never directed another serial, but
his technique on Batman was continued by fellow director
James W. Horne, who was also under contract to Columbia.
Horne, who had directed Laurel and Hardy (he did their best
feature, Way Out West), had his serial actors emote with
flamboyant, exaggerated gestures, a technique that made both
the heroes and the villains look ridiculous and placed the
material in an atmosphere of unreality that somehow made
the proceedings all the more entertaining. One of Horne's
best serials, The Green Archer (1940), starred excellent
character actor Victor Jory as ace detective Spike Holland,
who is investigating theft and treachery at a mysterious castle
estate. With Horne's usual touches, in addition to such sub-
limely ridiculous devices as fast-motion photography (in one
scene several characters are awaiting Jory's arrival at the
castle, and there is an immediate cut to a riotous speeded-
up shot of Jory running across the front lawn towards the
estate), The Green Archer is a delight. Incredibly, though,
no one seemed to realize or appreciate what Horne was doing;
serial fans who took their fare seriously were disappointed,
and exhibitors followed suit by complaining about the "unbelievable" stories and characters in Horne's "inept" serials!
Executives at Columbia either failed to notice or (more likely)
really didn't care about Horne's approach, and he continued
willingly on the same demented course, with actors like James
Craven (who provided the oily menace in The Green Archer),
supplying screamingly funny performances in serial after
serial.

    Although their efforts weren't appreciated by most
film-goers at the time, James W. Horne in his serials and
Lambert Hillyer in Batman both made effective use of a formula that was far superior to the obvious "camp" of the tiresome and ultimately forgettable Batman television series,
and their unpretentious, genuine sense of humor and playful
attitude towards their genre provided infinitely superior entertainment.

SUPERMAN (Columbia, 1948), 15 episodes. Producer, Sam Katzman. Directors, Spencer Bennet and Tommy Carr. Screenplay, Arthur Hoerl, Lewis Clay and Royal Cole, adaptation by George H. Plympton and Joseph F. Poland. Camera, Ira H. Morgan. Art Direction, Paul Palmentola. Music, Mischa Bakaleinikoff.
With Kirk Alyn, Noel Neill, Carol Forman, Tommy Bond, Pierre Watkin and George Meeker.

Because of its wide popularity as a comic strip, and considering its visual possibilities, Superman would appear to have been a natural choice for live-action serial treatment, and it is somewhat surprising to note that it wasn't until 1948, in the waning days of the serials, that the first Superman chapter play was produced. The difficulties of filming the required special effects depicting this character's fantastic abilities, such as flying, X-ray vision and enormous strength, must have been among the reasons for the delay, for this factor alone would have strained the most generous of serial budgets. The main drawback preventing an earlier production of Superman, though, was simply the enormous amount of money and the restrictive licensing demands made by National Comics Publications, Inc. (now known as DC Comics), the copyright holders and publishers of the Superman comic books.

Republic Pictures had sought the rights to produce a Superman serial in the late thirties, but negotiations quickly broke down when National Comics stipulated that the proposed serial could only be released once, after which all control of the film would revert to them. Republic, a studio that reissued its films on a regular basis, balked at this demand and abandoned the project. Unfortunately, Republic's writers had already concocted a Superman screenplay by this time, and in order to make use of the effort already expended, they were told simply to retool their existing material and cobble together a new script that would ultimately evolve into The Mysterious Doctor Satan (1940). The protagonist was clumsily transformed from Superman into a masked hero named "The Copperhead," who was now forced into performing some incredibly athletic feats, such as scaling the outside walls of buildings in scenes where the scriptwriters had previously indicated that Superman should simply fly to the upper floors of a skyscraper. At any rate, it is a tragedy that Republic never produced Superman as a serial, for while the film would undoubtedly have suffered from the usual flaws that plagued

Kirk Alyn, about to leap into the air and change into a cartoon in <u>Superman</u> (Columbia, 1948).

their output, at least it would have been slick and good to look at, and would certainly have benefited from the studio's expertise with miniatures and special effects.

Aside from an early radio series featuring the voice of Bud Collier as Superman, an excellent group of 17 animated cartoons had been released by Paramount Pictures in the early forties, using Collier's voice. Beautifully animated by the Max Fleischer studios in a rich and florid style that perfectly complements the heroic subject matter, these little technicolor epics are among the best cartoons ever made, with intricate draftsmanship and subtlety of movement and detail that the modern animation industry could never duplicate. Ultimately, because of rising production costs (it has been reported that the first cartoon in the series, lasting only ten minutes, was budgeted at $100,000!), the series was taken out of Fleischer's hands after the ninth film, and the remaining eight cartoons were produced more cheaply at Famous Studios, where the quality of the animation, though still good, declined noticeably.

By 1948 National Comics had finally been approached by someone who was willing to meet their terms; Sam Katzman was interested in producing a Superman serial for Columbia Pictures. Katzman was a producer of prodigious output and minuscule budgets, whose cheap "B" pictures were among the sleaziest and most profitable ever made. Like nearly every other tight-fisted producer, Katzman mercilessly exploited unknown young performers on the way up and, sadly, once-successful stars whose careers were on the downslide. As an example, when Bela Lugosi's fortunes fell on hard times in the late thirties and he was virtually unemployed because of the dearth of horror films being produced at the time, he had the misfortune to stumble into Sam Katzman's awaiting arms and was forced to degrade his already tarnished professional reputation at impoverished Monogram Pictures, where he appeared in a series of abysmal horror pictures (The Ape Man) and wretched haunted house "comedies" (Spooks Run Wild) with Leo Gorcey and The East Side Kids. Association with Katzman may have provided gainful employment, but wallowing in the Katzman mire did little for the actor's prestige. These awful films, with their wandering, sloppily constructed plots, their uninspired direction, and their embarrassed actors (who often seem to be trying to hide their faces from the camera in shame), are tacky monuments to crass commercialism--entertainment of the lowest common denominator produced as cheaply as possible for the

sole purpose of reaping the greatest possible profit. Artistry
never entered into the equation, and for a clue to the nature
of Katzman's aesthetics one need look no farther than the exhibitor's pressbook for his 1948 serial Congo Bill and Katzman's opinion of his leading lady, fifties "B" movie floozy
Cleo Moore: "No less an authority than Sam Katzman, recognized as Hollywood's serial king, is confident that Cleo,
a blonde with a classy chassis, will become a star judging
by her performance in Congo Bill." She didn't, of course,
but Katzman was a natural for serials.

When Katzman finally began production on Superman,
the aforementioned special effects problems manifested themselves immediately. After early attempts at depicting Superman's flying ability by suspending star Kirk Alyn from wires
in front of a rear projection screen proved a failure (the resulting test shots reportedly looked so bad, with the wires
supporting Alyn painfully obvious, that even the none-too dis-
criminating Katzman refused to use the footage), Katzman
arrived at the solution to his technical problems with char-
acteristic economy: whenever Superman would be required
to fly, or for that matter perform any feat that would demand extensive special effects work, Kirk Alyn would simply
be replaced onscreen by an animated cartoon figure super-
imposed over the live-action scenery. This technique was so
brazen, so audacious, that it almost worked. Superman was,
after all, derived from a comic strip, and the animation might
have unintentionally provided a link, however tenuous, with
the character's gaudy pulp-paper origins. Animation combined with live-action is a valid technique (as the animated
monster in Forbidden Planet proves), and if the animation
used by Katzman had been of the same detailed quality as
the work in the early Fleischer cartoons, this procedure
would have worked. Unfortunately, though, Katzman opted
for jerky animation work that was crudely and inexpensively
rendered, and the ploy just doesn't come off. It is also used
far too often, in chapter after chapter, with the filmmakers
using what is, at best, a stop-gap measure, like a crutch.
Even the most mundane action (Superman crashing through
the wall of a cave, for instance) was represented by cut-rate
animation, and one is hard put to decide which Superman
shows more life, Kirk Alyn or his cartoon doppelganger.

The first chapter of Superman, depicting the character's
origin, opens as the planet Krypton, populated by a race of
super-humans, is annihilated by a series of massive earth-
quakes. A scientist, Jor-El, manages to save his infant son

by sending him to Earth in a small rocket ship just before
Krypton explodes in a flurry of grainy stock-footage. Via
cartoon animation that would shame The Flintstones, the rocket
ship speeds to Earth and crashes near a country road where
a passing couple, the Kents, discover the surviving infant
and adopt him as their own. As the years pass and he grows
to maturity, the last inhabitant of Krypton astounds his foster
parents with his strange powers and abilities. As Clark Kent,
the adult Superman travels to the city of Metropolis, where
he secures employment as a reporter with The Daily Planet,
the city's largest newspaper. Keeping his true identity a
secret, Superman vows to use his great powers in the service of mankind, and he uses his position with The Daily
Planet to keep abreast of world events that may require his
attention.

His services are needed soon enough; the sinister
Spider Lady, a criminal mastermind, has gained control of
a powerful machine, the Reducer Ray, and threatens to destroy Metropolis unless the authorities yield to her demands.
Superman, meanwhile, has discovered to his consternation
that his powers are vulnerable to the weakening effects of
Kryptonite, a radioactive fragment of his native world, and
the Spider Lady's henchmen, learning this, obtain the Kryptonite and use it to thwart Superman's efforts at capturing
them. Despite this setback, Superman ultimately tracks down
the Spider Lady to her hidden lair, using a special lead lining beneath his costume to protect himself from the Kryptonite rays. In the ensuing struggle, the Spider Lady, attempting to escape, is destroyed when the Reducer Ray accidentally explodes.

Like Flash Gordon, released twelve years earlier,
Superman was enormously popular, playing evening performances at first-run theaters, and it gave the dying serials,
facing stiff competition from the newly-established medium
of television, a badly-needed shot in the arm. Unfortunately,
as was also the case with Flash Gordon, these beneficial effects were short-lived. Superman, although it was above
par in its field, was still no masterpiece even within those
restrictive boundaries, and the serial's popularity was probably more attributable to its flamboyant subject matter than
to any other quality. As Superman, Kirk Alyn is rather
stolid, but he has the right physique for the costume and
does manage to show some perspective about his role and a
sense of humor in approaching it, a factor which places him
a definite cut above the average leading man in serials; and

as Clark Kent, Alyn supplies some tolerable if rather obvious comedy relief.   Noel Neill, interpreting Lois Lane, is younger, fresher, and far more charming than she ever was in the same role in the later Adventures of Superman television series, and Pierre Watkin is appropriately bombastic as Daily Planet editor Perry White.   Former child star Tommy Bond, an Our Gang alumnus, rounded out the cast in the minor supporting role of cub reporter Jimmy Olsen, which he plays in a surprisingly abrasive manner.   The only real casting flaw in Superman is unfortunately a major one: Carol Forman as the Spider Lady.   Decked out in a blonde wig and tight black gown, Forman's performance is atrocious; she flubs her lines in several scenes and appears unable to place more than three words together into a coherent sentence. Forman was attractive, and if it hadn't been for the static emotional quality of her acting she would have been endearingly inept as a serial villainess; but her performances weren't much better in her other serial appearances, with Republic's 1947 potboiler, The Black Widow, demonstrating how one inadequate performer (Forman, in the title role) can damage a film that would have otherwise been moderately acceptable.

Two years after Superman, in 1950, Sam Katzman had a sequel to the first serial completed and in the theaters. Atom Man vs. Superman featured the same principal cast as the previous film, but the services of Carol Forman were wisely dispensed with, and the villainy was placed in the hands of Lyle Talbot, who was cast in the pivotal role of Lex Luthor, Superman's arch-nemesis from the comic books.   This bound the sequel even more closely than its predecessor to its source material, but once again the picture suffered from Katzman's restrictive economies, and the paltry special effects budget was again padded with cheap animation.

In 1951, a new Superman, in the person of George Reeves, appeared in the film Superman and the Mole Men, released by Lippert Pictures.   Significantly, this picture was not produced as a serial, but as a feature-length film intended to be exhibited as a test-run for the later television series.   Superman and the Mole Men, produced by Robert Maxwell and efficiently directed by Lee Sholem from a screenplay by Maxwell (writing under the pen name of Richard Fielding), relates the story of three alien creatures who emerge from their underground civilization through the shaft of an oil well under construction near the small town of Silsby. Clark Kent and Lois Lane, on hand to cover the opening of the well (the deepest ever drilled) for the Metropolis Daily

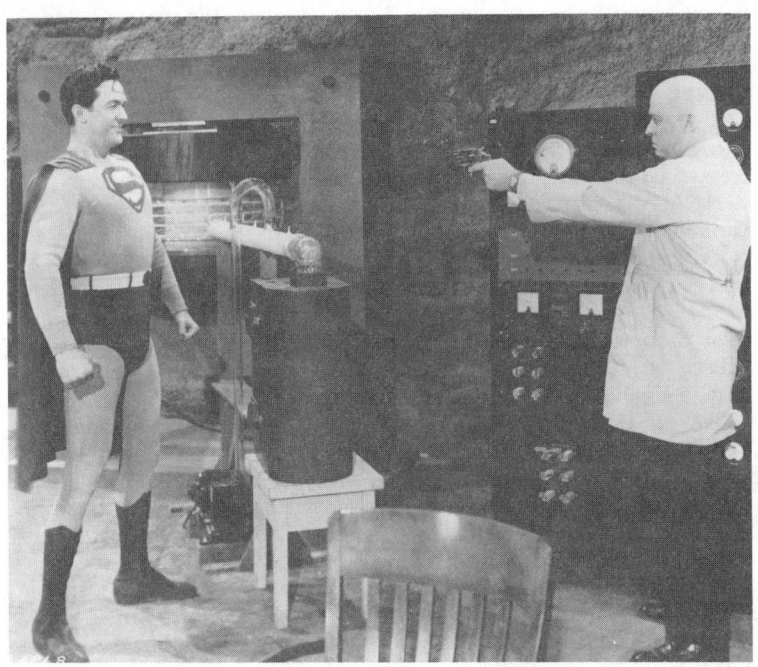

Kirk Alyn laughs off a few slugs in Atom Man vs. Superman (Columbia, 1950). That's Lyle Talbot taking aim.

Planet, soon find themselves covering an even bigger story: the three harmless creatures, who are merely curious about the world they have entered, are seen by the townspeople, who react in typical redneck fashion and promptly form a bloodthirsty lynch mob. Instigated by their ignorant ring-leader, Luke Benson, the mob has hunted the creatures down and is about to destroy them when Kent, as Superman, intervenes and rescues the aliens, eventually returning them to their subterranean domain.

Surprisingly mature and thoughtful in theme and plot, Superman and the Mole Men, a bizarre mixture of The Ox-Bow Incident and The Day the Earth Stood Still, was a low-budget but carefully realized and produced film. The flaws are minor ones of pacing and technique: a couple of chase

scenes go on for longer than they should, and Katzman-like
animation is used for one dreadfully tacky shot of Superman
flying, but these are merely lapses among the considerable
virtues of the film.   George Reeves, as Superman, although
obviously padded with artificial shoulders, is outstanding.
Reeves succeeds in bringing real depth to what could easily
have been a one-dimensional role, and his excellent diction
and expressive theatrical "body language" (e. g. , the familiar
fists-on-hips stance of defiance) are light years ahead of
Kirk Alyn's portrayal in effectiveness.   Reeves interpreted
Superman as aloof and all-powerful, yet moralistic and com-
passionate, and at age 37 Reeves was both young enough to
function as a romantic figure and mature enough to lend the
proper air of authority to the role.   He was so good as Superman that he never really escaped identification with the character, as a result of this film and the subsequent television
series, and some have suggested that his untimely death in
1959, an alleged suicide, stemmed directly from his despair
over being type-cast in the role.   As Lois Lane, Phyllis
Coates, too, is superb in an even more thankless role, bringing to the part a classy, sophisticated sarcasm and insolence
which is worthy of Katharine Hepburn.   Coates followed up
her appearance here by playing Lois Lane in the first 26
episodes of the television series, after which Noel Neill,
Kirk Alyn's leading lady, returned to the role.   Jeff Corey,
always an underrated character actor, is also impressive as
Luke Benson, a totally unsympathetic character whose evil
stems not from greed or ambition, but from his own ignorance and banality.

Many images from Superman and the Mole Men are
memorable: Superman, defying the lynch mob ("You obviously
can't be trusted with guns, so I'm just going to have to take
them away from you!"); Superman making his first appearance
in the town, confiscating Benson's rifle, bending it like rubber,
and then sternly lifting Benson into the air like a child as
he reprimands him ("It's men like you who make it difficult
for people to understand one another"); and Superman saving
Benson from the retribution of the creatures, who finally
turn on their persecutor and attempt to destroy him with a
ray gun (Benson, sheepishly, to Superman: "You saved my
life ... " and Superman, in reply, "That's more than you
deserve!").

In particular, one scene in Superman and the Mole
Men demonstrates what screen fantasy is (or should be) all
about; after his suspicious debut in Silsby, Superman learns

A superior interpretation: George Reeves and Phyllis Coates in the feature film, Superman and the Mole Men (Lippert, 1951).

that Benson's mob has just left town to hunt the creatures. Reeves crouches low, gazes skyward, and miraculously lifts off the ground and into the air as he flies in pursuit. This scene is simply shot, from one stationary angle, without the benefit of animation, optical work, or miniatures of any kind, with Reeves merely wearing a leather harness beneath his costume from which wires are attached to an off-camera pulley system; and yet the shot is so expertly played and photographed that these few fleeting frames of films contain more magic and excitement than the entire footage of the over-produced, over-designed, and grossly over-budgeted multi-million dollar Superman feature released by Warner Brothers in 1978. This updated "epic," with its meandering, disjointed screenplay, blatant commercial plugs, mannered, self-conscious acting, shockingly cheap special effects, grainy photography, big-name performers waltzing smugly through their roles, and an eternal ten-minute credit crawl at the end, amply demonstrates all that is wrong with the "New Hollywood."

Superman and the Mole Men, with its excellent cast and impressive technical credits (the film was shot at RKO studios, producers of King Kong and Citizen Kane), was more than anything else a painful reminder of just how far the serials had declined, and the long-running television series that the film launched was undoubtedly a major factor in their demise (Superman and the Mole Men, reduced by ten minutes from its original 58 and retitled Unknown People, was later presented as a two-part episode of the television series).

Due to the original contractual agreement between Columbia Pictures and National Comics, the two Kirk Alyn serials, Superman and Atom Man vs. Superman have not been seen by the public since their initial release more than thirty years ago, and the official explanation now given by DC Comics is that the films were so cheaply produced that modern audiences would never accept them. Despite their many faults, though, these two films represent some of the most faithful adapting of a comic strip character to the live-action screen ever done in Hollywood; for while Superman and the Mole Men trancended its subject matter, the Kirk Alyn serials wholeheartedly embraced it, and they are in their own way nearly as successful. Their cheapness is undeniable, but since that cheapness was in large part necessitated by National Comics' licensing restrictions in the first place, there is really no valid reason why the serials shouldn't once again be made available for public viewing, along with the George Reeves television series, the 1978 Warner Brothers feature, and its sequels.

COLUMBIA SERIAL INDEX

JUNGLE MENACE (1937), 15 episodes. Directed by George Melford and Harry Fraser. Cast: Frank Buck (Frank Henry), John St. Polis (Edward Elliott), Charlotte Henry (Dorothy Elliott), William Bokewell (Tom Banning), Richard Tucker (Robert Banning), LeRoy Mason (Murphy), Sasha Siemel (the Tiger Man), Willie Fung (Chiang), Duncan Renaldo (Rogers), Robert Warwick (MacLeod).

The MYSTERIOUS PILOT (1937), 15 episodes. Directed by Spencer Bennet. Cast: Frank Hawks (Jim Dorn), Dorothy Sebastian (Jean McNain), Rex Lease (Kansas), Guy Bates Post (Bergelot), Kenneth Harlan (Snowden), Yakima Canutt (Luke), Frank Lackteen (Yoroslaf), Robert Terry (Casper), George Rosener (Fritz), Clara Kimball Young (Martha), Harry Harvey (Soft Shoe), Tom London (Kilgour), Ted Adams (Carlson), Earl Douglas (Jerry), Robert Walker (Boyer), Roger Williams (McCarthy), Esther Ralston (Vivian McNain).

The SECRET OF TREASURE ISLAND (1938), 15 episodes. Directed by Elmer Clifton. Cast: Don Terry (Larry Kent), Gwen Gaze (Toni Morrel), Grant Withers (Grindley), Hobart Bosworth (Dr. X), William Farnum (Westmore), Walter Miller (Collins), George Rosener (Captain Cuttle), Dave O'Brien (Jameson), Yakima Canutt (Dreer), Warner Richmond (Captain Faxton), Bill Boyle (Thorndyke), Sandra Karina (Zanya), Joe Caits (Jerry), Colin Campbell (Hawkins), Patrick J. Kelly (Professor).

The GREAT ADVENTURES OF WILD BILL HICKOK (1938), 15 episodes. Directed by Mack V. Wright and Sam Nelson. Cast: Gordon Elliott (Wild Bill Hickok), Carol Wayne (Ruth Cameron), Frankie Darro (Jerry), Dickie Jones (Bud), Sammy McKim (Boots), Kermit Maynard (Kit Lawson), Roscoe Ates (Snake Eyes), Monte Collins (Danny), Reed Hadley (Blakely), Chief Thunder Cloud (Gray Eagle), Mala (Little Elk), Walter Wills (Bruce), J. P. McGowan (Scudder), Eddie Waller (Stone), George Chesebro (Metaxa), Alan Bridge (Blackie).

The SPIDER'S WEB (1938), 15 episodes. Directed by Ray Taylor and James W. Horne. Cast: Warren Hull (Richard Wentworth), Iris Meredith (Nita Van Sloan), Richard Fiske (Jackson), Kenneth Duncan (Ram Singh), Forbes Murray (Commissioner Kirk), Marc Lawrence (Steve), Charles Wilson (Chase), Donald Douglas (Jenkins).

Warren Hull (r.) in The Spider's Web (Columbia, 1938).

FLYING G-MEN (1939), 15 episodes. Directed by Ray Taylor and James W. Horne. Cast: Robert Paige (Hal Andrews), Robert Fiske (Bart Davis), James Craig (John Cummings), Lorna Gray (Babs McKay), Sammy McKim (Billy McKay), Don Beddoe (Hamilton), Forbes Murray (Brewster), Dick Curtis (Korman), Ann Doran (Secretary), Nestor Paiva (Everett), George Chesebro (Red), Bud Geary (Radio Man), Tom Steele (Williams), George Turner (Crawford), Hugh Prosser (Stokes).

MANDRAKE THE MAGICIAN (1939), 12 episodes. Directed by Sam Nelson and Norman Deming. Cast: Warren Hull (Mandrake), Doris Weston (Betty), Al Kikume (Lothar), Rex Downing (Tommy), Edward Earle (Andre), Forbes Murray (Houston), Kenneth MacDonald (Webster), Don Beddoe (Raymond), Dick Curtis (Dorgan), John Tyrell (Dirk), Ernie Adams (Brown), George Chesebro (Baker), George Turner (Hall).

OVERLAND WITH KIT CARSON (1939), 15 episodes. Directed by Sam Nelson and Norman Deming. Cast: Bill Elliott (Kit Car-

son), Iris Meredith (Carmelita), Richard Fiske (David Brent), Bobby
Clark (Andy), Trevor Bardette (Arthur Mitchell), LeRoy Mason (John
Baxter), Olin Francis (Pierre), James Craig (Tennessee), Francis
Sayles (Dr. Parker), Kenneth MacDonald (Winchester), Dick Curtis
(Drake), Richard Botiller (Natchez).

The SHADOW (1940), 15 episodes. Directed by James W. Horne.
Cast: Victor Jory (Lamont Cranston), Veda Ann Borg (Margo Lane),
Robert Moore (Vincent), Robert Fiske (Turner), J. Paul Jones (Mar-
shall), Jack Ingram (Flint), Charles Hamilton (Roberts), Edward
Piel, Sr. (Inspector Cardona), Frank LaRue (Commissioner Weston).

TERRY AND THE PIRATES (1940), 15 episodes. Directed by
James W. Horne. Cast: William Tracy (Terry Lee), Granville
Owen (Pat Ryan), Joyce Bryant (Normandie Drake), Allen Jung (Con-
nie), Victor De Camp (Big Stoop), Sheila Darcy (Dragon Lady), Dick
Curtis (Fang), J. Paul Jones (Dr. Lee), Forrest Taylor (Drake),
Jack Ingram (Stanton).

DEADWOOD DICK (1940), 15 episodes. Directed by James W.
Horne. Cast: Don Douglas (Deadwood Dick), Lorna Gray (Ann Butler), Harry Harvey (Dave), Marin Sais (Calamity Jane), Lane Chandler (Will Bill Hickok), Jack Ingram (Buzz), Charles King (Tex), Ed
Cassidy (Drew), Robert Fiske (Ashton), Lee Shumway (Bentley).

The GREEN ARCHER (1940), 15 episodes. Directed by James W.
Horne. Cast: Victor Jory (Spike Holland), Iris Meredith (Valerie
Howell), James Craven (Abel Bellamy), Robert Fiske (Savini), Dorothy
Fay (Elaine Bellamy), Forrest Taylor (Howett), Jack Ingram (Brad),
Joseph W. Girard (Inspector Ross), Fred Kelsey (Captain Thompson),
Kit Guard (Dinky).

WHITE EAGLE (1941), 15 episodes. Directed by James W. Horne.
Cast: Buck Jones (White Eagle), Raymond Hatton (Grizzly), Dorothy
Fay (Janet), James Craven (Darnell), Chief Yowlachie (Running Deer),
Jack Ingram (Cantro), Charles King (Brace).

The SPIDER RETURNS (1941), 15 episodes. Directed by James
W. Horne. Cast: Warren Hull (Richard Wentworth), Mary Ainslee
(Nina Van Sloan), Dave O'Brien (Jackson), Joe Girard (Commander
Kirk), Kenneth Duncan (Ram Singh), Corbet Harris (McLeod), Bry-
ant Washburn (Westfall), Charles Miller (Van Sloan).

The IRON CLAW (1941), 15 episodes. Directed by James W.
Horne. Cast: Charles Quigley (Bob Lane), Walter Sande (Jack
Strong), Joyce Bryant (Patricia Benson), Forrest Taylor (Anton Ben-
son), Alex Callam (James Benson), Norman Willis (Roy Benson),
Allen Doone (Simon Leach), Edythe Elliot (Milly Leach), John Beck
(Gyves), Charles King (Silk), James Morton (Casey), Hal Price
(O'Malley).

HOLT OF THE SECRET SERVICE (1941), 15 episodes. Directed
by James W. Horne. Cast: Jack Holt (himself), Evelyn Brent (Kay),

C. Montague Shaw (Malloy), Tristram Coffin (Valden), John Ward (Arnold), Ted Adams (Quist), Joe McGuinn (Crimp), Edward Hearn (Jim), Ray Parsons (Severn), Jack Cheatham (Frank).

CAPTAIN MIDNIGHT (1942), 15 episodes. Directed by James W. Horne. Cast: Dave O'Brien (Captain Midnight), Dorothy Short (Joyce), James Craven (Ivan Shark), Sam Edwards (Chuck), Guy Wilkerson (Ichabod Mudd), Bryant Washburn (Edwards), Luana Walters (Fury), Joe Girard (Major Steele), Ray Teal (Borgman), George Pembroke (Dr. Jordan), Charles Hamilton (Martel), Al Ferguson (Gardo).

PERILS OF THE ROYAL MOUNTED (1942), 15 episodes. Directed by James W. Horne. Cast: Robert Stevens (Sgt. MacLaine), Kenneth MacDonald, (Ransome), Herbert Rawlinson (Winton), Nell O'Day (Diana), John Elliott (Blake), Nick Thompson (Black Bear), Art Miles (Flying Cloud), Richard Fiske (Brady), Richard Vallin (Little Wolf) , Forrest Taylor (Hinsdale), Kermit Maynard (Collins), George Chesebro (Gaspard), Jack Ingram (Baptiste).

The SECRET CODE (1942), 15 episodes. Directed by Spencer Bennet. Cast: Paul Kelly (Dan Barton), Anne Nagel (Jean Ashley), Clancy Cooper (Pat), Alex Callam (Hogan), Trevor Bardette (Jensen), Robert O. Davis (Thyssen), Gregory Gay (Feldon), Louis Donath (Metzger), Beal Wong (Quito), Lester Dorr (Stahl), Jacqueline Dalya (Linda).

The VALLEY OF VANISHING MEN (1942), 15 episodes. Directed by Spencer Bennet. Cast: Bill Elliott (Bill), Slim Summerville (Missouri), Carmen Morales (Consuelo), Kenneth MacDonald (Kincaid), Jack Ingram (Butler), George Chesebro (Taggert), John Shay (Mullins), Tom London (Slater), Arno Frey (Engler), Julian Rivero (Jose), Roy Barcroft (Luke).

BATMAN (1943), 15 episodes. Re-issued as An Evening with Batman and Robin. Directed by Lambert Hillyer. Cast: Lewis Wilson (Batman), Douglas Croft (Robin), J. Carrol Naish (Daka), William Austin (Alfred), Shirley Patterson (Linda), Charles C. Wilson (Captain Arnold), Charles Middleton (Ken Colton), Robert Fiske (Foster), Michael Vallon (Preston), Gus Glassmire (Martin Warren).

The PHANTOM (1943), 15 episodes. Directed by B. Reeves Eason. Cast: Tom Tyler (The Phantom), Kenneth MacDonald (Dr. Bremmer), Frank Shannon (Professor Davidson), Jeanne Bates (Diana), Ace (Devil), Guy Kingsford (Byron Andrews), Joe Devlin (Singapore Smith), Ernie Adams (Rusty), John S. Bagni (Moku).

The DESERT HAWK (1944), 15 episodes. Directed by B. Reeves Eason. Cast: Gilbert Roland (The Hawk), Mona Maris (Princess Azala), Ben Welden (Omar), Kenneth MacDonald (Akbar), Frank Lackteen (Faud), I. Stanford Jolley (Saladin), Charles Middleton (Koda Bey), Egan Brecher (Grey Wizard).

Tom Tyler and Jeanne Bates in <u>The Phantom</u> (Columbia, 1943).

BLACK ARROW (1944), 15 episodes. Directed by B. Reeves Eason. Cast: Robert Scott (Black Arrow), Adele Jergens (Mary), Kenneth MacDonald (Jake Jackson), Robert Williams (Buck Sherman), Charles Middleton (Tom Whitney), Martin Garralaga (Pancho), George J. Lewis (Snake-That-Walks).

BRENDA STARR, REPORTER (1945), 13 episodes. Directed by Wallace W. Fox. Cast: Joan Woodbury (Brenda Starr), Kane Richmond (Lt. Larry Farrell), Syd Saylor (Chuck Allen), Joe Devlin (Tim), George Meeker (Frank Smith), Wheeler Oakman (Joe Heller), Cay Forester (Vera Harvey), Marion Burns (Zelda), Lotte Harrison (Abretha), Ernie Adams (Charlie), Jack Ingram (Kruger), Anthony Warde (Muller), John Merton (Schultz), Billy Benedict (Pesky).

The MONSTER AND THE APE (1945), 15 episodes. Directed by Howard Bretherton. Cast: Robert Lowery (Ken Morgan), George MacReady (Ernst), Ralph Morgan (Professor Arnold), Carole Matthews (Babs Arnold), Willie Best (Flash), Jack Ingram (Nordik), Anthony Warde (Flint), Ted Mapes (Butler), Eddie Parker (Blake), Stanley Price (Mead).

JUNGLE RAIDERS (1945), 15 episodes. Directed by Lesley Selander. Cast: Kane Richmond (Bob Moore), Eddie Quillan (Joe), Veda Ann Borg (Cora), Carol Hughes (Zara), Janet Shaw (Ann), John Elliott (Dr. Moore), Jack Ingram (Tom), Charles King (Jake Rayne), Ernie Adams (Charlie), I. Stanford Jolley (Brent), Kermit Maynard (Cragg), Bud Buster (Dr. Reed), George Turner (Carter), Nick Thompson (Chief), Jim Aubrey (Mark).

WHO'S GUILTY? (1945), 15 episodes. Directed by Wallace Grissell. Cast: Robert Kent (Bob Stewart), Amelita Ward (Ruth Allen), Tim Ryan (Duke Ellis), Jayne Hazard (Rita Royale), Minerva Urecal (Mrs. Dill), Belle Mitchell (Sara Caldwell), Charles Middleton (Patton), Davison Clark (Henry Calvert), Sam Flint (Horace Black), Bruce Donovan (Curt Bennett), Jack Ingram (Sgt. Smith), Milton Kibbee (Morgan Calvert), Nacho Galindo (Pancho), Roberto Tafur (Jose), Wheeler Oakman (Smiley), Charles King (Burk), Anthony Warde (Edwards).

HOP HARRIGAN (1946), 15 episodes. Directed by Derwin Abrahams. Cast: William Blakewell (Hop Harrigan), Jennifer Holt (Gail Nolan), Robert "Buzz" Henry (Jackie Nolan), Sumner Getchell (Tank Tinker), Emmett Vogan (Arnold), Claire James (Gwen Arnold), John Merton (Dr. Tobor), Wheeler Oakman (Ballard), Ernie Adams (Retner), Peter Michael (Craven), Terry Frost (Barry), Anthony Warde (Edwards), Jackie Moran (Fraser), Bobby Stone (Gray), Jack Buchanan (Deputy Sheriff), Jim Diehl (Carter).

CHICK CARTER, DETECTIVE (1946), 15 episodes. Directed by Derwin Abrahams. Cast: Lyle Talbot (Chick Carter), Douglas Fowley (Rusty Farrell), Julie Gibson (Sherry Marvin), Pamela Blake (Ellen Dale), Eddie Acuff (Spud), Robert Elliott (Dan Rankin), George Meeker (Nick Pollo), Leonard Penn (Vasky), Charles King (Joe Carney), Jack Ingram (Mack), Joel Friedkin (Jules Hoyt), Eddie Parker (Frank Sharp).

SON OF THE GUARDSMAN (1946), 15 episodes.   Directed by Derwin Abrahams.   Cast: Robert Shaw (David Trent), Daun Kennedy (Louise Markham), Robert "Buzz" Henry (Roger Mowbry), Jim Diehl (Allan Hawk), Hugh Prosser (Red Robert), Leonard Penn (Mark Crowell), Wheeler Oakman (Lord Markham), Charles King (Sir Edgar Bullard), John Merton (Lord Hampton), Ray Bennett (Duncan), I. Stanford Jolley (Sir William Pryor), Belle Mitchell (Dame Duncan), Frank Ellis (Morgan), Al Ferguson (Lynn).

JACK ARMSTRONG (1947), 15 episodes.   Directed by Wallace W. Fox.   Cast: John Hart (Jack Armstrong), Rosemary La Planche (Betty), Claire James (Alura), Joe Brown (Billy), Pierre Watkin (Uncle Jim), Charles Middleton (Grood), Professor Zorn (Wheeler Oakman), Jack Ingram (Blair), Eddie Parker (Slade), Hugh Prosser (Vic Hardy), John Merton (Gregory Pierce), Gene Stutenroth (Dr. Albour).

The VIGILANTE (1947), 15 episodes.   Directed by Wallace W. Fox.   Cast: Ralph Byrd (Greg Sanders), Ramsay Ames (Betty Winslow), Lyle Talbot (George Pierce), George Offerman, Jr. (Stuff), Robert Barron (Prince Amil), Hugh Prosser (Captain Reilly), Jack Ingram (Silver), Eddie Parker (Doc), George Chesebro (Walt), Eddie Cobb (Miller).

The SEA HOUND (1947), 15 episodes.   Directed by Walter B. Eason and Mack V. Wright.   Cast: Buster Crabbe (Captain Silver), Jimmy Lloyd (Tex), Pamela Blake (Ann Whitney), Ralph Hodges (Jerry), Robert Barron (Admiral), Hugh Prosser (Rand), Rick Vallin (Manila), Jack Ingram (Murdock), Spencer Chan (Kukal), Milton Kibbee (John Whitney), Al Baffert (Lon), Stanley Blystone (Black Mike), Robert Duncan (Sloan), Pierce Lyden (Vardmen), Rusty Wescoatt (Singapore).

BRICK BRADFORD (1947), 15 episodes.   Directed by Spencer Bennet.   Cast: Kane Richmond (Brick Bradford), Rick Vallin (Sandy Sanderson), Pierre Watkin (Professor Salisbury), Charles Quigle (Laydron), Jack Ingram (Albers), Fred Graham (Black), John Merton (Dr. Tymak), Leonard Penn (Byrus), Wheeler Oakman (Walthar), Carol Forman (Queen Khana), Charles King (Creed), John Hart (Dent), Helene Stanley (Carol Preston), Nelson Leigh (Prescott), Robert Barron (Zuntar), George De Normand (Meaker).

TEX GRANGER (1948), 15 episodes.   Directed by Derwin Abrahams.   Cast: Robert Kellard (Tex), Peggy Stewart (Helen), Buzz Henry (Tim), Smith Ballew (Blaze), Jack Ingram (Reno), I. Stanford Jolley (Carson), Terry Frost (Adams), Jim Diehl (Conroy), Britt Wood (Sandy).

SUPERMAN (1948), 15 episodes.   Directed by Spencer Bennet and Thomas Carr.   Cast: Kirk Alyn (Superman), Noel Neill (Lois

Lane), Tommy Bond (Jimmy Olsen), Carol Forman (The Spider Lady), George Meeker (Driller), Jack Ingram (Anton), Pierre Watkin (Perry White), Terry Frost (Brock), Charles King (Conrad), Charles Quigley (Dr. Hackett), Herbert Rawlinson (Dr. Graham), Forrest Taylor (Leeds), Stephen Carr (Morgan), Rusty Wescoatt (Elton).

CONGO BILL (1948), 15 episodes. Directed by Spencer Bennet and Thomas Carr. Cast: Don McGuire (Congo Bill), Cleo Moore (Lureena), Jack Ingram (Cameron), I. Stanford Jolley (Bernie McGraw), Leonard Penn (Andre Bocar), Nelson Leigh (Dr. Greenway), Charles King (Kleeg), Armida (Zalea), Hugh Prosser (Moreli), Neyle Morrow (Kahla), Fred Graham (Villabo), Rusty Wescoatt (Ivan), Anthony Warde (Rogan), Stephan Carr (Tom MacGraw).

BRUCE GENTRY, DAREDEVIL OF THE SKIES (1949), 15 episodes. Directed by Spencer Bennet and Thomas Carr. Cast: Tom Neal (Bruce Gentry), Judy Clark (Juanita Farrell), Ralph Hodges (Frank Farrell), Forrest Taylor (Dr. Benson), Hugh Prosser (Radcliffe), Tristram Coffin (Krendon), Jack Ingram (Allen), Terry Frost (Chandler), Eddie Parker (Gregg), Charles King (Ivor), Stephen Carr (Hill), Dale Van Sickel (Gregory).

BATMAN AND ROBIN (1949), 15 episodes. Directed by Spencer Bennet. Cast: Robert Lowery (Batman), John Duncan (Robin), Jane Adams (Vicki Vale), Lyle Talbot (Commissioner Gordon), Ralph Graves (Harrison), Don Harvey (Nolan), William Fawcett (Hammil), Leonard Penn (Carter), Rick Vallin (Brown), Michael Whalen (Dunne), Gregg McClure (Evans), House Peters, Jr. (Earl), Jim Diehl (Jason), Rusty Wescoatt (Ives).

ADVENTURES OF SIR GALAHAD (1949), 15 episodes. Directed by Spencer Bennet. Cast: George Reeves (Sir Galahad), Charles King (Bors), William Fawcett (Merlin), Pat Barton (Morgan Le Fay), Hugh Prosser (Sir Lancelot), Lois Hall (Lady of the Lake), Nelson Leigh (King Arthur), Jim Diehl (Kay), Don Harvey (Bartoc), Marjorie Stapp (Queen Guinevere), John Merton (Ulric), Pierce Lyden (Cawker).

CODY OF THE PONY EXPRESS (1950), 15 episodes. Directed by Spencer Bennet. Cast: Jock Mahoney (Archer), Dickie Moore (Cody), Peggy Stewart (Linda), William Fawcett (Ezra), Tom London (Doc), Helena Dare (Emma), George J. Lewis (Mort Black), Pierce Lyden (Slim), Jack Ingram (Pecos), Rick Vallin (Denver), Frank Ellis (Durk), Ross Elliott (Irv), Ben Corbett (Eric), Rusty Wescoatt (Chet).

ATOM MAN vs. SUPERMAN (1950), 15 episodes. Directed by Spencer Bennet. Cast: Kirk Alyn (Superman), Noel Neill (Lois Lane), Lyle Talbot (Luthor), Tommy Bond (Jimmy Olsen), Pierre Watkin (Perry White), Jack Ingram (Foster), Don Harvey (Albert), Rusty Wescoatt (Carl), Terry Frost (Beer), Wally West (Dorr), Paul Strader (Lawson), George Robotham (Earl).

PIRATES OF THE HIGH SEAS (1950), 15 episodes. Directed by
Spencer Bennet and Thomas Carr. Cast: Buster Crabbe (Jeff Drake),
Lois Hall (Carol Walsh), Gene Roth (Frederick Whitlock), Tristram
Coffin (Castell), Neyle Morgan (Kalana), Stanley Price (Lamar),
Hugh Prosser (Roper), Symona Boniface (Lotus Lady), William Faw-
cett (Wharton), Terry Frost (Carter), Lee Roberts (Barker), Rusty
Wescoatt (Adams), Pierce Lyden (Durk), I. Stanford Jolley (Turner),
Marshall Reed (Shark).

ROAR OF THE IRON HORSE (1951), 15 episodes. Directed by
Spencer Bennet and Thomas Carr. Cast: Jock Mahoney (Jim Grant),
Virginia Herrick (Carol Lane), William Fawcett (Rocky), Hal Landon
(Tom Lane), Jack Ingram (Homer Lathrop), Mickey Simpson (Cal),
George Eldredge (Karl Ulrich), Myron Healey (Ace), Rusty Wescoatt
(Scully), Frank Ellis (Bat), Pierce Lyden (Irv), Dick Curtis (Campo),
Hugh Prosser (Lefty).

MYSTERIOUS ISLAND (1951), 15 episodes. Directed by Spencer
Bennet. Cast: Richard Crane (Captain Harding), Marshall Reed
(Pencroft), Karen Randle (Rulu), Ralph Hodges (Bert), Gene Roth
(Shard), Hugh Prosser (Gideon), Leonard Penn (Captain Nemo), Terry
Frost (Ayrton), Rusty Wescoatt (Moley), Bernard Hamilton (Neb).

CAPTAIN VIDEO (1951), 15 episodes. Directed by Spencer Ben-
net and Wallace Grissell. Cast: Judd Holdren (Captain Video),
Larry Stewart (Ranger), George Eldredge (Tobor), Gene Roth (Vul-
tura), Don C. Harvey (Gallagher), William Fawcett (Alpha), Jack
Ingram (Aker), I. Stanford Jolley (Zarol), Skelton Knaggs (Retner),
Jimmy Stark (Rogers), Rusty Wescoatt (Beal), Oliver Cross (Pro-
fessor Markham), George Robotham (Drock), Bill Bailey (Professor
Dean).

KING OF THE KONGO (1952), 15 episodes. Directed by Spencer
Bennet and Wallace Grissell. Cast: Buster Crabbe (Thunda), Gloria
Dee (Pha), Leonard Penn (Boris), Jack Ingram (Clark), Rusty Wes-
coatt (Kor), Nick Stuart (Degar), Rick Vallin (Andreov), Neyle Mor-
row (Nahee), Bart Davidson (Alexis), Alex Montoya (Lipah), Bernie
Goizer (Zahila), William Fawcett (High Priest), Lee Roberts (Biake),
Frank Ellis (Ivan).

BLACKHAWK (1952), 15 episodes. Directed by Spencer Bennet.
Cast: Kirk Alyn (Blackhawk), Carol Forman (Laska), John Craw-
ford (Chuck), Michael Fox (Case), Don Harvey (Olaf), Rick Vallin
(Boris), Larry Stewart (Andre), Weaver Levy (Chop Chop), Zon
Murray (Bork), Nick Stuart (Cress), Marshall Reed (Aller), Pierce
Lyden (Dyre), William Fawcett (Dr. Ralph), Rory Mallinson (Hodge),
Frank Ellis (Hendrickson).

SON OF GERONIMO (1952), 15 episodes. Directed by Spencer
Bennet. Cast: Clayton Moore (Jim Scott), Bud Osborne (Tulsa),
Tommy Farrell (Frank Baker), Rodd Redwing (Porico), Marshall
Reed (Rance Rankin), Eileen Rowe (Ann Baker), John Crawford (Ace),
Zon Murray (Bat), Rick Vallin (Eadie), Lyle Talbot (Colonel Foster),
Chief Yowlachie (Geronimo).

Kirk Alyn (l.) and colleagues in Blackhawk (Columbia, 1952).

The LOST PLANET (1953), 15 episodes.   Directed by Spencer
Bennet.   Cast: Judd Holdren (Rex Barrow), Vivian Mason (Ella
Dorn), Ted Thorpe (Tim Johnson), Forrest Taylor (Professor Dorn),
Michael Fox (Grood), Gene Roth (Reckov), Karl Davis (Karlo), Leon-
ard Penn (Ken Wolper), John Cason (Hopper), Nick Stuart (Parl),
Joseph Mell (Lah), Jack George (Jarva), Frederick Berest (Alden),
I. Stanford Jolley (Robot #9), Pierre Watkin (Ned Hilton).

The GREAT ADVENTURES OF CAPTAIN KIDD (1953), 15 episodes.
Directed by Derwin Abbe and Charles Gould.   Cast: Richard Crane
(Richard Dale), David Bruce (Alan Duncan), John Crawford (Captain
Kidd), George Wallace (Buller), Lee Roberts (Denry), Paul Newlan
(Long Ben Avery), Nick Stuart (Dr. Brandt), Terry Frost (Moore),
John Hart (Jenkins), Marshall Reed (Captain Culliford), Eduardo
Cansino, Jr. (Native), Willetta Smith (Princess).

GUNFIGHTERS OF THE NORTHWEST (1954), 15 episodes.   Di-
rected by Spencer Bennet.   Cast: Jock Mahoney (Joe Ward), Clayton
Moore (Bram Nevin), Phyllis Coates (Rita), Don C. Harvey (Otis
Green), Marshall Reed (Lynch), Rodd Redwing (Bear Tooth), Lyle
Talbot (Inspector Wheeler), Tom Farrell (Arch Perry), Terry Frost
(Wildfoot), Lee Roberts (Arnold Reed), Joe Allen Jr. (Stone), Greg
Barton (Bridger), Chief Yowlachie (Running Elk).

RIDING WITH BUFFALO BILL (1954), 15 episodes.   Directed by
Spencer Bennet.   Cast: Marshall Reed (Bill Cody), Rick Vallin (Reb
Morgan), Joanne Rio (Maria Perez), Shirley Whitney (Ruth Morgan),

Jack Ingram (Ace), William Fawcett (Rocky Ford), Gregg Barton (Bart), Ed Coch (Jose Perez), Steve Ritch (Elko), Pierce Lyden (Darr), Michael Fox (King Carney), Lee Roberts (Zeke).

ADVENTURES OF CAPTAIN AFRICA (1955), 15 episodes. Directed by Spencer Bennet. Cast: John Hart (Captain Africa), Rick Vallin (Ted Arnold), Ben Welden (Omar), June Howard (Princess Rhoda), Bud Osborne (Nat Coleman), Paul Marion (Hamid), Lee Roberts (Borid), Terry Frost (Greg), Ed Coch (Balu), Michael Fox (Prime Minister).

PERILS OF THE WILDERNESS (1956), 15 episodes. Directed by Spencer Bennet. Cast: Dennis Moore (Laramie), Richard Emory (Sergeant Gray), Eve Anderson (Donna), Kenneth R. MacDonald (Randall), Rick Vallin (Little Bear), John Elliott (Homer Lynch), Don C. Harvey (Kruger), Terry Frost (Baptiste), Al Ferguson (Mike), Bud Osborne (Jake), Rex Lease (Sergeant Rodney), Pierce Lyden (Amby), John Mitchum (Brent).

BLAZING THE OVERLAND TRAIL (1956), 15 episodes. Directed by Spencer Bennet. Cast: Lee Roberts (Tom Bridger), Dennis Moore (Ed Marr), Norma Brooks (Lola Martin), Gregg Barton (Captain Carter), Don C. Harvey (Rance Devlin), Lee Morgan (Alby), Pierce Lyden (Bragg), Ed Coch (Carl).

THE SERIALS OF UNIVERSAL

FLASH GORDON (Universal Pictures, 1936), 13 episodes. Producer, Henry McRae. Director, Frederick Stephani. Screenplay, Frederick Stephani, Ella O'Neill, George Plympton and Basil Dickey; based on the comic strip written and drawn by Alex Raymond. Camera, Jerry Ash and Richard Fryer. Art Director, Ralph Berger. Music, Heinz Roemheld and Karl Hajos, incorporating classical compositions. With Buster Crabbe, Jean Rogers, Charles Middleton, Priscilla Lawson, Frank Shannon, Richard Alexander, John Lipson and Theodore Lorch.

To this day, Carl Laemmle, Jr. remains a relatively ignored figure in film history, and when he died in 1979, alone and forgotten at the age of 71, few newspapers took notice of his passing. Few people remembered that, for a while at least, he had once been a major force in the motion-picture industry, and few recalled that it was Laemmle who, at Universal Pictures in the 1930s, almost singlehandedly created the biggest explosion of quality horror and fantasy films that Hollywood was to produce until the release of Star Wars in 1977.

Universal Pictures was founded in 1912 by Carl Laemmle, Sr., a German immigrant and former motion-picture exhibitor who had been involved in film production since the earliest days of the industry. It was at Universal in the twenties that Irving Thalberg, only 21 years old, began his brief but remarkable career as a producer; and that directors like Erich von Stroheim helmed prestigious films like Foolish Wives (1922). Laemmle's studio continued to prosper and grow throughout the formative years of the silent period, offering a wide variety of movie products ranging from bread-and-butter westerns and serials to an occasional big-budget epic like The Hunchback of Notre Dame (1923).

Buster Crabbe and Jean Rogers in <u>Flash Gordon</u> (Universal, 1936), in which romance was a strong point.

It was in the late twenties that Laemmle, who had
long been the butt of industry jokes about his nepotistic hiring
practices, turned over a large measure of creative control
at Universal to his son Carl, Jr. Nevertheless, under the
younger Laemmle's supervision the studio saw its finest and
most artistically respectable period. In 1930, Laemmle, Jr.
produced director Lewis Milestone's highly-praised film version of Erich Maria Remarque's World War I pacifist novel,
All Quiet on the Western Front, which was followed in 1931
by Dracula and Frankenstein, the first noteworthy sound horror movies.

By 1931 Universal was already familiar with horror
and fantasy as film subject matter. They had produced the
original version of The Phantom of the Opera in 1925, and
the studio introduced a distinctly European flavor to films
by importing foreign directors like Paul Leni, who made The
Cat and the Canary in 1927. These and similar productions
had been successful, both creatively and financially, but it
was not until Dracula and Frankenstein that the continuing
marketability of the horror-fantasy genre was firmly established.

Dracula, which was based on a rather pedestrian but
successful Broadway stage adaptation of Bram Stoker's famous
novel, boasted a genuinely fine and unique performance by
Bela Lugosi in the title role, atmospheric camera work by
Karl Freund, and several very boring and tedious passages
after its excellent opening scenes. Had the film used some
of the more exciting passages in Stoker's novel, a more fluid
production would certainly have resulted. The picture was
criticized even in its day for Tod Browning's often madden-
ingly static direction; but Dracula is deservedly a classic,
and it is still a fascinating and entertaining film despite its
serious flaws. The film is historically important because
its acceptance by the public indicated a pronounced shift in
audience taste, for prior to Dracula, screen horror and fantasy (in America at least), had been presented only in a
historical context (in period stories such as The Phantom of
the Opera), or in "spoof" films like The Cat and the Canary,
in which the "supernatural" menaces were often intentionally
played for broad laughs and revealed in the closing scenes
to be either fakes or delusions. In Dracula, though, Lugosi's
supernatural vampire was real, and was readily accepted as
such by the audience.

Frankenstein, released later in 1931 and directed by

James Whale, was far superior to Dracula. Whale, an in-explicably neglected director who is just beginning to receive serious attention from film historians, had a fine visual sense and was that all-too-rare exception--a pictorialist able to in-fuse outrageous and flamboyant subject matter with genuine wit and style. Whale's unique abilities would probably have been out of place at any other Hollywood studio, but at Uni-versal, under Carl Laemmle, Jr.'s aegis, he flourished, and followed Frankenstein with three more fantasy pictures that have become permanent classics: The Old Dark House (1932), The Invisible Man (1933), and the great Bride of Franken-stein (1935), a direct sequel to Frankenstein that was even better than the original and represents the apex of Whale's career.

While Laemmle's popular horror films had earned large profits for Universal Pictures and initiated an industry-wide trend in the process, not all of the studio's ventures had been as economically sound. For all his incisive produc-tion acumen, Laemmle had demonstrated a disturbing pen-chant for financially risky gambles as early as 1930 with King of Jazz, which had been so expensive that it turned a profit with great difficulty, and by the mid-thirties big-budget duds like Sutter's Gold were still absorbing the earnings of box-office winners like Bride of Frankenstein. By 1936, the studio was in trouble, slowly but surely sinking in an eco-nomic mire, and the Laemmles were gradually losing their control to outside business interests. It was during this hec-tic period that Universal, perhaps suicidally clutching at straws, decided to attempt a revival of the fading serials by producing the most expensive chapter play ever made.

In 1934, Universal successfully negotiated the purchase of film rights to several newspaper comic strips published by King Features Syndicate, including such titles as Secret Agent X-9, Jungle Jim, Ace Drummond and Flash Gordon, among others, postulating that the already established popu-larity of the strip characters would practically guarantee the profits of any serial derived from them. It was a common-sense move that paid off; Tailspin Tommy was a successful serial in 1934, prompting a quick sequel, Tailspin Tommy and the Great Air Mystery, the following year.

At this time, Universal's serial department was under the supervision of Henry McRae, who had been alternately producing and directing serials at the studio since 1917. Since the sound revolution, McRae's unit had not been doing all that

well; Universal's (and the industry's) first all-talking serial,
The Indians Are Coming, was a listless failure about as inspired as its title, with the expected crudities of early sound
filming an inevitable fault, and things had pretty much evened
out from there.   Aware of the obvious visual possibilities of
the Flash Gordon comic strip, McRae and the studio decided
to gamble on reviving the petrified serial genre by investing
considerably more money than usual in the project.

The average budget for a Universal serial in the thirties
hovered around the $125,000 mark, and fell below that amount
as often as the studio front office could manage.   The final
negative cost on Flash Gordon was reportedly $350,000, a
budget far exceeding that allotted to most "A" features at the
time.   Despite this comparatively lavish funding, though,
some tight economizing was still brought into play.   There
was enough money for a few spacious, if noticeably empty
sets, such as Ming's throne room, but many of the film's
settings and props were lifted from other Universal features
of the period.   The huge tower set from James Whale's
Bride of Frankenstein pops up in Chapters 2 and 3, the crypt
set from the same film, minus the dust and cobwebs, is also
used, and the interior of the Transylvanian castle from Dracula's Daughter (1936), refurnished with electrical equipment,
became Ming's laboratory.   The "mad lab" electrical equipment, the only discernible function of which seems to be the
constant emission of photogenic showers of sparks, was designed and operated by Kenneth Strickfadden.   Strickfadden's
devices had appeared in both of the James Whale Frankenstein pictures (where the memorable "creation" scenes had
been inspired by a similar scene in Fritz Lang's silent epic,
Metropolis), as well as several other horror and fantasy films
of the thirties and forties, and the machines were still being
used as late as 1974 in Mel Brooks' spoof, Young Frankenstein.   The huge Egyptian idol seen in The Mummy (1932)
doubled for the god Tao in a couple of scenes, and even
Zarkov's rocketship itself was a second-hand prop, a miniature borrowed from the 1930 Fox feature, Just Imagine, a
unique musical-comedy with a futuristic setting that also
yielded some impressive footage of a huge leering idol worshipped by a horde of scantily-clad dancing girls.

This scene, along with some other incidental footage
from Just Imagine, was used to good advantage in Flash Gordon, providing the serial with some badly-needed scope, but
other attempts at integrating stock footage were obvious and
unintentionally ludicrous.   In chapter 3, Flash and Dale, ab-

ducted by King Kala's shark-men, are being transported to the underwater city in a submarine craft called a "hydrocycle" (an amazingly faithful reproduction of the vehicle drawn by Raymond in his strip). En route, their captors, forced to stop the hydrocycle in order to avoid destruction, stumble upon a battle between a giant shark and an "octosac." When we are shown this apocalyptic struggle, it turns out to be nothing more than ancient stock footage of a small shark and octopus desperately thrashing about in a cramped aquarium, the back walls of which are clearly visible. Grainy and shakily out of focus, this footage is glaringly unconvincing, and was even more so when it was resurrected for The Beast from 20,000 Fathoms in 1953.

While Flash Gordon's relatively opulent budget permitted many luxuries usually denied serials, such as glass paintings and some token matte and split-screen work, the film still has an inescapably "cheap" serial look about it, and this is probably attributable to producer Henry McRae. McRae, although a prolific and competent producer of serials, seemed to have difficulty extracting top screen value from his budgets, and a great deal of the money expended simply doesn't show on the screen; the result is some irritating crudities. There is a lot of over-dubbing on the soundtrack, employed to cover inconsistencies in the dialogue as it was originally written. Unfortunately, the same baritone voice is used to dub nearly every line, whether it is being read by Ming, Prince Barin, Zarkov or whomever, and this results in some unintentionally amusing scenes. In chapter 4, a distraught Zarkov, held captive by Ming, asks what has happened to Flash and Dale, who have been separated from him. "Do not worry, your friends are being cared for," replies Ming, and in the next instant Charles Middleton's voice, dubbed by another actor, rises in volume and picks up a trace of a Brooklyn accent as the explanatory tag "by Kala, king of the shark-men" is added!

Not all of the economies were detrimental to the finished picture. The musical score for Flash Gordon is a hodgepodge of compositions from other Universal films of the period, including Heinz Roemheld's scores for The In-

Opposite: At top, the excellent cast of Flash Gordon (Universal, 1936). L. to r.: Priscilla Lawson, Jean Rogers, Buster Crabbe, John Lipson and Charles Middleton. Below, clearly defined "bad girl" Priscilla Lawson, Buster Crabbe, and hapless victims of the mayhem in Flash Gordon.

visible Man (1933) and The Black Cat (1934), and Karl Hajo's music for Werewolf of London (1935). This "second-hand" score is surprisingly effective in Flash Gordon, and improved many scenes that were otherwise weak in style or content.

Flash Gordon's art director was Ralph Berger, who also designed the Bela Lugosi thriller White Zombie in 1932 and the 1935 serial The Lost City which, although a vastly inferior production, contains many visual similarities to Flash Gordon. The costumes worn by the actors in Flash Gordon, especially the incongruous Roman armor sported by Ming's guards, appear at first to have been hastily chosen, but they are in fact perfectly in tune with Raymond's drawings, and many of them, especially the costumes worn by Flash, Ming, Barin and Officer Torch, are exact reproductions of Raymond's designs. Ralph Berger's Mongo is a depressing world indeed; there is no vegetation on the planet, only bleak craggy mountains seared by harsh winds and inhabited by carnivorous dragons. Emperor Ming's palace is a maze of shadowy chambers and austere catacombs, and the only architectural beauty on Mongo (or rather, above it), seems to be the floating sky-city of the hawk-men, which is designed in art-deco style.

In recent times the Flash Gordon serials have endured largely undeserved mockery and criticism for their low-budget special effects sequences. One well-known special effects technician, currently practicing his craft on extravagant space-fantasy films, has even had the temerity to suggest rather condescendingly that the effects in these serials are indicative of the overall quality of special effects work in Hollywood at the time. Nothing could be further from the truth. It should be remembered that King Kong, with its highly regarded special effects work by Willis O'Brien, was released in 1933, three years before Flash Gordon; and that Alexander Korda's excellent production of Things to Come was released the very same year as the serial, 1936. The special effects in Flash Gordon are undeniably cut-rate in comparison with the technical work in features like King Kong and Things to Come, but this is mainly due to the fact that the technicians who shot them were on a rushed schedule. Although Flash Gordon's budget was relatively high, the film was after all only a serial, and the production had to be shot hurriedly in order to hold costs down.

The miniatures in Flash Gordon consisted of small-scale models of the rocketships, either manipulated by wires or suspended in a stationary position before a moving back-

A rare behind-the-scenes shot on the last day of filming
Flash Gordon, which coincided with Buster Crabbe's birthday.
Crabbe is seen here with Priscilla Lawson (l.) and Jean
Rogers. (Photo supplied and used with the kind permission
of Jean Rogers.)

ground depicting passing clouds. Due to the restrictive time
and cost factors involved, such badly-needed luxuries as
traveling mattes, stop-motion animation, rear-screen projection, and blue-screen work were unthinkable. Simple split-
screen photography was used in some very brief shots, but
almost all of the needed effects had to be achieved cheaply,
quickly, and in the camera, without expensive and time-
consuming lab work. Taking into account the conditions they
were required to work under, the technicians involved did
a commendable job, and the effects, though by no means convincing as reality, do work within the self-contained comic
strip context of the serial. Just as it never seemed to matter
that comic book characters are surrounded by black lines and
have dialogue ballons floating over their heads, so it never
really seemed to matter to movie audiences that serials like
Flash Gordon were much cheaper-looking than the "A" features with which they shared programs.

The only exceptions to this rule were the serials produced by Republic Pictures, justifiably famous for their excellent special effects work by Howard and Theodore Lydecker
--work of such high caliber that it was often superior to the
effects in much later multi-million dollar spectacles like
Ben-Hur. But Republic's product was just that--an exception.
At that studio, where the output was almost exclusively "B"
westerns and serials, the level of quality was almost homog-
enized, and even when Republic did make a top-notch grade
"A" picture, there really wasn't that much difference between
it and one of their serials. Unfortunately, Republic's artistry
stopped at its miniature department, and although the Republic serials have their devoted admirers, and the films
themselves are technically polished in almost every area,
creatively they are bland to the point of boredom, with competent but undistinguished direction, listless musical scores
and, with one or two notable exceptions, sexless heroines.
Even the very best of the Republic serials, The Adventures
of Captain Marvel and Spy Smasher, both released in 1942,
suffer from these flaws to varing degrees, and they are
noticeably lacking in the one great virtue of Flash Gordon--
characterization.

Flash Gordon is remarkable because it intertwines
characterization and plot into a solid whole. We aren't told
very much about the backgrounds of the characters in either
the serial or the newspaper strip, but in the film the actors
seem to flesh out their roles with their own personalities.
The happy result is that the characters seem to be much

more textured than they really are.   Add to this one of the
serial's most important ingredients, the sex appeal of Jean
Rogers and Priscilla Lawson (to Flash Gordon goes the distinction of being the sexiest serial ever made), and the sharp
contrast between this film and its peers becomes strikingly
evident.

Much of this élan is due to the chemistry of the leading actors, Buster Crabbe, Jean Rogers, Charles Middleton,
Priscilla Lawson, and Frank Shannon, but many of the serial's
good points can also be attributed to Frederick Stephani, the
production's director and head writer.   Stephani, whose first
directional assignment this was, brought real visual style to
the film, employing tilted camera angles à la Whale's Bride
of Frankenstein) and atmospheric photography that is as impressive as nearly anything seen in an "A" feature of the
period.   After Flash Gordon, Stephani left Universal, producing mostly nondescript films like Beg, Borrow or Steal
and Love Is a Headache for MGM, and he never had an opportunity to direct another film after his auspicious debut
with Flash Gordon.

Despite flaws, Flash Gordon's virtues were undeniable
in the wake of the flabby serials that preceded it, and upon
its release the 13-chapter epic proved so successful that it
played evening performances at first-run theaters and grew
to be one of the biggest box-office draws of 1936.   The show
business trade paper Variety felt that the picture was "An
unusually ambitious effort ... with feature production standards that have been maintained as to cast, direction and
background."   Carl Laemmle, Jr. and his studio had taken
a chance on Flash Gordon, and the resulting film, with its
richer characterizations, more detailed direction, and larger
budget, hinted at the possibility of renewed popularity for the
ailing serials.   Unfortunately, Flash Gordon's artistic and
commercial success was seen as a freak event by the industry, and the film's lessons went largely unheeded by Hollywood.   Ultimately the serials paid the price for their in-
ability to change with a changing society, but for a little
while, when Flash Gordon was released in 1936, it seemed
as though the serials had entered a second Golden Age, and
the road was paved for a sequel.

The 15-chapter sequel, Flash Gordon's Trip to Mars,
was released in 1938, with some important differences that
distinguish it from the first serial.   By 1937, the Laemmle
regime at Universal had finally succumbed to its disastrous

financial policies, and a new group of businessmen had gained power at the troubled studio. New and restrictive guidelines were promptly instituted at all levels of production and, even when the wildfire success of Flash Gordon made a sequel inevitable, the new power-brokers at Universal resolved that their studio would never again produce a $350,000 serial. Filmed at a cost of $175,000 (half the first serial's budget), Flash Gordon's Trip to Mars was still an expensive production by serial standards; but even though it was slicker, and in some ways even more entertaining than the previous film (this was the serial with the eerie Clay People), it seemed to lack force and cohesion. This was mainly due to the changing of key behind-the-scenes personnel; producer Henry McRae was replaced by Barney Sarecky, with Ford Beebe and Ray Taylor handling the joint directional chores, and perhaps even more importantly, art director Ralph Berger was replaced by Ralph Delacy, whose sets were essentially bright and cheerful three-dimensional comic strip environments, with little of the grim atmosphere found in Berger's designs. The cast, with the principals from the first picture repeating their roles, was once again in grand form, but Charles Middleton, whose flamboyant theatrical performance as Ming had done so much to enliven the first serial, was reduced almost to a supporting role in Trip to Mars, as he played second fiddle to the distaff villainy of Beatrice Roberts as the supernatural Azura, Queen of Magic. Also, the addition of unnecessary "comic relief" actor Donald Kerr as bumbling reporter "Happy" Hapgood was an irritation at times, even though Kerr was undeniably amusing in many scenes. As slick as it was, and even with the added novelty of some scenes being printed on color stock in order to produce a lurid tint, Flash Gordon's Trip to Mars looked noticeably tackier than its parent film. The fact that Jean Rogers was a brunette in this film and a blonde in the stock-footage flashbacks to the original that were edited into Trip to Mars didn't help the picture's occasional choppiness, either.

The third picture in the series, the 12-chapter Flash Gordon Conquers the Universe, although by far the cheapest and weakest of the trilogy, was nevertheless still more ef-

---

Opposite: Two scenes from Flash Gordon's Trip to Mars (Universal, 1938). Above, Donald Kerr and Frank Shannon lie unconscious as Buster Crabbe aids Jean Rogers. Below, l. to r., Richard Alexander, Jean Rogers, Frank Shannon, C. Montague Shaw and Donald Kerr watch as Beatrice Roberts prepares to disappear by supernatural means.

Charles Middleton as Emperor Ming in <u>Flash Gordon Conquers the Universe</u> (Universal, 1940).

fective than most of the contemporary serials, and boasts
what is probably the prettiest art direction ever to adorn a
chapter play.   The film's effectiveness was weakened by its
over-reliance on stock footage from the first serial, though,
and two of the early chapters seem to be almost entirely
composed of grainy stock footage lifted from the 1930 Leni
Riefenstahl documentary, White Hell of Pitz Palu.   In Flash
Gordon Conquers the Universe, different actors essayed the
roles of Barin, Dale, and Aura, and the continuity of the
story line, which had been ignored in Trip to Mars, was con-
fused even further in the third film.   In spite of these flaws
and its noticeably lower budget, Flash Gordon Conquers the
Universe was successful, and a few years after its release
in 1940 there was even discussion of filming a fourth Flash
Gordon serial, but these plans never materialized.

L. to r. : Frank Shannon, Buster Crabbe, Carol Hughes and
Roland Drew in Flash Gordon Conquers the Universe (Universal, 1940).

Seen today, the three Universal Flash Gordon serials are rarely shown in their original form. In 1936, a feature version of Flash Gordon was prepared for exhibition in theaters whose managers had no desire to book a serial for the necessary extended running time. This feature, although very well edited, is very curious because the music and sound effects heard in the feature version are not the same sound tracks used in the serial itself, and this changes and reduces the impact of many scenes. The same was true of the 1938 feature version of the second serial, titled Mars Attacks the World in order to exploit the then-current War of the Worlds radio braodcast by Orson Welles. The editing of Mars Attacks the World was abysmal, though, and rendered the plot almost incomprehensible. In the late thirties, when both feature versions were released on a double-bill, Flash Gordon was retitled Rocketship, and it is this title that appears on all current prints of the feature.

In the late sixties, different feature versions were edited from the serials for television use. Flash Gordon gave birth to Spaceship to the Unknown and Perils from the Planet Mongo; Flash Gordon's Trip to Mars produced The Deadly Ray from Mars; and Flash Gordon Conquers the Universe, which never appeared in theatrical feature form, yielded The Purple Death from Outer Space. Unfortunately, it is always these choppily-edited feature versions that are shown on television, and when the original serial chapters are shown, even these prints have been slightly bowdlerized, and the main titles have been inexplicably changed to Space Soldiers, Space Soldiers' Trip to Mars, and Space Soldiers Conquer the Universe. Along with these ludicrous title changes, current prints of the serials include spoken narration over the printed titles that recap the plot line from each previous chapter. This narration never appeared in the theatrical prints, and was added to the sound track by the television distributors, presumably on the theory that TV viewers can't read.

The less said about the atrocious 1980 remake, Flash Gordon, the better. This astronomically budgeted, multi-million dollar excrescence was produced with contempt by Dino Di Laurentiis, scripted in ham-handed "camp" fashion by Lorenzo Semple, Jr. , and assaulted film-goers with some of the ugliest art direction and one of the most raucous musical scores (by the rock band Queen) ever presented in a major production. Even with a production schedule spanning years and over thirty-million dollars at their disposal, the film-makers involved failed to surpass the original serial, shot for $350,000 on a six-week schedule! The remake, an inept and artless product of talentless cynics, is already nearly forgotten by the public, and should suffice as the ultimate proof of how good those old serials really were, and still are.

BUCK ROGERS (Universal, 1939), 12 episodes. Associate producer, Barney Sarecky. Directors, Ford Beebe and Saul A. Goodkind. Screenplay, Norman S. Hall and Ray Trampe; from the newspaper comic strip by Philip Nowlan and Dick Calkins. Camera, Jerry Ash. Art Direction, Jack Otterson and Ralph DeLacy.
With Buster Crabbe, Constance Moore, Jackie Moran, Jack Mulhall, Anthony Warde, C. Montague Shaw and Philson Ahn.

Surprisingly, the Flash Gordon comic stip had been created by King Features newspaper syndicate as competition for the rival Buck Rogers strip, and not the reverse, as most people assume. This is a real tribute to Flash Gordon artist-writer Alex Raymond's imagination and skill as an illustrator, for his creation wasn't derivative of its competitor at all, and looking at those old strips today it is Raymond's work that remains far more inspired and memorable, easily surpassing the charming but juvenile Buck Rogers. In the mid-thirties, the film rights for Buck Rogers were purchased by Universal Pictures, and when the first two Flash Gordon serials proved to be such huge successes, Buck Rogers was also seen as a natural for serial treatment.

Although Buck Rogers and Flash Gordon differed greatly in their newspaper comic strip incarnations, Universal wasn't very resourceful in translating Buck Rogers to the screen, and what finally emerged in 1939 was, ironically enough, a veritable clone of Flash Gordon but without that serial's strong points of characterization and tight plotting. Not that Buck Rogers didn't have very real possibilities. The plot relates how pilot Rogers and young assistant Buddy Wade, flying an experimental dirigible on a test mission, are imprisoned in a state of suspended animation when they crash land and are exposed to their cargo of "Nirvano" gas. Unconscious for five-hundred years, Buck and Buddy are finally discovered and revived by a team of future scientists. They are taken to the Hidden City, a concealed research outpost and military base, and learn that the world of the future is

ruled by the despotic Killer Kane and his horde of super-
gangsters. The inhabitants of the Hidden City, led by Dr.
Huer, are the last defenders of freedom, and forming an
alliance with their forces and the natives of the planet Saturn,
Buck eventually defeats Kane and his evil mob.

It's fun to imagine an entire world ruled by swagger-
ing Cagney and Bogart types, enforcing their dictatorship
with rocket ships and the latest in ray-gun technology, but
the writers assigned to Buck Rogers either couldn't or wouldn't
exploit the obvious humor of this idea. The results are flat,
prosaic, and curiously inadequate. The art direction and
special effects are very similar to the Flash Gordon serials
(with a slight improvement in the handling of the rocket ship
miniatures) and, with the addition of the same music tracks
used in the previous serials, Buck Rogers seemed very much
like stale goods. Buster Crabbe also, always underrated
and every bit as competent here as he was in the Flash Gordon serials, generates too much déjà vu. To its further det-
riment, the film gives leading lady Constance Moore little
to do, and the writers even fell back on the time-worn gimmick of saddling the hero with a juvenile sidekick, presumably for the purpose of providing "identification" for the
younger members of the audience.

The direction is competent, but neither outstanding
nor creative, and the relative overall weakness of concept
and execution is perhaps best illustrated by the scene on the
planet Saturn in which Buck and his companions are placed
on trial in the "Chamber of Judges." The huge set used for
this sequence, seemingly carved from the solid rock of a
cavern and sprawling across one of the immense Universal
sound stages, was extended to even larger proportions through
the use of a meticulous glass painting. It is one of the largest sets ever built for a serial, impressive by any standards.
But because the serial's plot is not very involving, that set
just doesn't make an impression, and for all it accomplishes
the scene could have probably been filmed to equal effect
with far more modest surroundings.

On the plus side (and admittedly this is an extraneous,
superficial "virtue" that the film has acquired only with the
passage of years), Buck Rogers, far more so than Flash
Gordon, is an excellent example of 1930s science-fiction.
Indeed, this serial is virtually a nostalgic catalog of early
SF pulp magazine concepts, with suspended animation, mind
control, space travel, anti-gravity devices, and invisibility

Buster Crabbe (l.), on the dusty plains of Saturn, in Buck Rogers (Universal, 1939).

rays proliferating. Because Buck Rogers is more firmly grounded in "science" than the more romantic Flash Gordon, though, the pseudo-scientific "transgressions" of the serial's writers are far more irritating than the similar flights of fancy in Flash Gordon. In one chapter, for example, Buck and Buddy speed towards Saturn in their rocket ship, and Buck casually offers the pithy observation that Saturn's gravity is many times greater than Earth's; however, when they finally land on the ringed planet, Buck and company seem to have very little trouble moving about in a normal manner!

Buck Rogers was profitable, but its success was only

marginal, and a sequel was never made. Although hardly a bad serial (it remains, in spite of itself, one of the best ever produced), Buck Rogers simply didn't jell, and failed to draw the huge audiences that the Flash Gordon pictures had, perhaps because those two previous films had so thoroughly milked the same basic gimmicks, situations and paraphernalia. Buck Rogers certainly pulled in enough money to justify a sequel, but considering its relatively mediocre box-office performance, Universal eventually decided to produce a follow-up to Flash Gordon's Trip to Mars instead, and released Flash Gordon Conquers the Universe in 1940.

Buck Rogers (like Flash Gordon), inspired an unbelievably cheap and very short-lived TV series in the fifties, the deficiencies of which were made more apparent by the eventual release of the original serial to television. The recent NBC network series, starring Gil Gerard and Erin Gray in the original Buster Crabbe and Constance Moore roles (with Crabbe even making a guest appearance in one episode), was so bland that it was comparatively inoffensive. Hopelessly awash in a cesspool of distressingly similar Star Wars copies, and economically using many of the costly special effects filmed for ABC's obscenely expensive flop Battlestar Galactica, the series was redeemed only by the presence of the provocative Erin Gray, who filled out her spandex jumpsuit nicely and proved to be considerably more eye-catching than the show's glittering and impersonal wall-to-wall hardware.

SILENT FILMS

LUCILLE LOVE, GIRL OF MYSTERY (1914), 15 episodes. Directed by Francis Ford. Cast: Francis Ford, Grace Cunard, Harry Rattebury, Ernest Shields.

The TREY O' HEARTS (1914), 15 episodes. Directed by Wilfred Lucas. Cast: Leo Madison, George Larkin, Edward Sloman, Tom Walsh, Roy Hanford.

The MASTER KEY (1914), 15 episodes. Directed by Robert Leonard. Cast: Florence LaBadie, Marguerite Snow, James Cruze, Frank Farrington, Sidney Bracy, Creighton Hale, Mitchell Lewis, Irving Cummings.

The BLACK BOX (1915), 15 episodes. Directed by Otis Turner. Cast: Herbert Rawlinson, Anna Little, William Worthington, Mark Fenton, Laura Oakley, Frank MacQuarrie, Frank Lloyd, Helen Wright, Beatrice Van.

UNDER THE CRESCENT (1915), 6 episodes. Directed by Burton King. Cast: Ola Humphrey, Edward Sloman, William Dowlan, Carmen Phillips, Helen Wright, Edna Mason.

The BROKEN COIN (1915), 22 episodes. Directed by Francis Ford. Cast: Francis Ford, Grace Cunard, Harry Mann, Eddie Polo, John Ford, Mina Cunard, Harry Schumm, Ernest Shields.

GRAFT (1915), 20 episodes. Directed by Richard Stanton. Cast: Hobart Henley, Harry D. Carey, Nanine Wright, Richard Stanton, Hayward Mack, Jane Novak, Glen White, L. M. Wells, W. Horne, Mary Ruby, Edward Brown.

The ADVENTURES OF PEG O' THE RING (1916), 15 episodes. Directed by Francis Ford and Jacques Jaccard. Cast: Francis Ford, Grace Cunard, Ruth Stonehouse, Peter Gerald, Charles Munn, G. Raymond Nye, Eddie Polo, Mark Fenton, Jean Hathaway.

LIBERTY, A DAUGHTER OF THE U.S.A. (1916), 20 episodes. Directed by Jacques Jaccard and Henry McRae. Cast: Marie Walcamp, Jack Holt, Neal Hart, G. Raymond Nye, L. M. Wells, Eddie Polo, Hazel Buckham, Roy Stewart, Maude Emory, Bertram Grassby.

The PURPLE MASK (1916), 16 episodes.   Directed by Francis Ford.   Cast: Francis Ford, Grace Cunard, Jean Hathaway, Peter Gerald, Jerry Ash, Mario Bianchi, John Featherstone, John Duffy.

The VOICE ON THE WIRE (1917), 15 episodes.   Directed by Stuart Paton.   Cast: Neva Gerber, Ben Wilson, Francis McDonald, Ernest Shields, Joseph W. Girard, Frank Tokonaga, Howard Crampton.

The GRAY GHOST (1917), 16 episodes.   Directed by Stuart Paton. Cast: Harry Carter, Priscilla Dean, Emory Johnson, Eddie Polo, Howard Crampton, Sidney Dean, Lou Short, Gypsy Hart, Gertrude Astor, T. D. Crittenden, J. Morris Foster, Richard la Reno, John Cook.

The RED ACE (1917), 16 episodes.   Directed by Jacques Jaccard. Cast: Marie Walcamp, Larry Peyton, Yvette Mitchell, Bobby Mack, L. M. Wells, Charles Brindley, Miriam Shelby, Noble Johnson, Harry Archer.

The MYSTERY SHIP (1917), 18 episodes.   Directed by Harry Harvey and Henry McRae.   Cast: Ben Wilson, Neva Gerber, Kingsley Benedict, Duke Worne.

BULL'S EYE (1918), 18 episodes.   Directed by James W. Horne. Cast: Eddie Polo, Vivian Reed, Hal Cooley, Roy Hanford, Frank Lanning, William Welsh, Noble Johnson.

The LION'S CLAW (1918), 18 episodes.   Directed by Jacques Jaccard and Harry Harvey.   Cast: Marie Walcamp, Thomas Lingham, Gertrude Astor, Alfred Allen, Edwin August, Leonard Chapman, Harry Von Meter, Frank Lanning, Roy Hanford.

The BRASS BULLET (1918), 18 episodes.   Directed by Ben Wilson.   Cast: Juanita Hansen, Jack Mulhall, Charles Hill Mailes, Joseph W. Girard, Harry Dunkinson, Helen Wright, Ashton Dearholt.

LURE OF THE CIRCUS (1918), 18 episodes.   Directed by J. P. McGowan.   Cast: Eddie Polo, Josie Sedgwick, Eileen Sedgwick.

ELMO, THE MIGHTY (1919), 18 episodes.   Directed by Henry McRae.   Cast: Elmo Lincoln, Grace Cunard, Fred Starr, Virginia Craft, Ivor McFadden, James Cole.

The GREAT RADIUM MYSTERY (1919), 18 episodes.   Directed by Robert Broadwell and Robert F. Hill.   Cast: Cleo Madison, Robert Reeves, Eileen Sedgwick, Bob Kortman, Ed Brady.

The LION MAN (1919), 18 episodes. Directed by Albert Russell and Jack Wells. Cast: Kathleen O'Connor, Jack Perrin, Mack V. Wright, J. Barney Sherry, Gertrude Astor, Henry Barrows, Leonard Chapman, Robert Walker.

The RED GLOVE (1919), 18 episodes. Directed by J. P. McGowan. Cast: Marie Walcamp, Pal O'Malley, Truman Van Dyke, Evelyn Selbie, Alfred Allen, Andrew Waldron, Thomas Lingham, Leon de la Mothe.

The MIDNIGHT MAN (1919), 18 episodes. Directed by James W. Horne. Cast: James J. Corbett, Orral Humphrey, Sam Polo, Kathleen O'Connor, Joseph W. Girard, Frank Jonasson, Noble Johnson, William Sauter, Georgia Woodthorpe, Joseph Singleton.

ELMO, THE FEARLESS (1920), 18 episodes. Directed by J. P. McGowan. Cast: Elmo Lincoln, Louise Lorraine, William Chapman, Ray Watson, Frank Ellis, V. L. Barnes, Gordon McGregor.

The MOON RIDERS (1920), 18 episodes. Directed by B. Reeves Eason and Albert Russell. Cast: Art Acord, Mildred Moore, George Field, Beatrice Dominguez, Charles Mewton, Tote Decrow.

The VANISHING DAGGER (1920), 18 episodes. Directed by Edward Kull and Eddie Polo. Cast: Eddie Polo, Thelma Percy, Leach Cross, Laura Oakley, G. Normand Hammond, Arthur Jerris, Ray Ripley, Thomas Lingham, Ruth Royce, Peggy O'Dare.

The DRAGON'S NET (1920), 12 episodes. Directed by Henry McRae. Cast: Marie Walcamp, Harlan Tucker, Otto Lederer, Wadsworth Harris.

The FLAMING DISC (1920), 18 episodes. Directed by Robert F. Hill. Cast: Elmo Lincoln, Louise Lorraine, Lee Kohlmar, Ray Watson, George Williams, Monty Montague, Jenks Harris.

KING OF THE CIRCUS (1920), 18 episodes. Directed by J. P. McGowan. Cast: Eddie Polo, Corrine Porter, Harry Madison, Kittoria Beveridge, Charles Fortune.

The WHITE HORSEMAN (1921), 18 episodes. Directed by Albert Russell. Cast: Art Acord, Eva Forrestor, Beatrice Dominguez.

DO OR DIE (1921), 18 episodes. Directed by J. P. McGowan. Cast: Eddie Polo, J. P. McGowan, Inez McDonald, Magda Lane, Jay Marchant, Jean Perkins.

TERROR TRAIL (1921), 18 episodes. Directed by Edward Kull. Cast: Eileen Sedgwick, George Larkin, Albert J. Smith, Barney Furey.

WINNERS OF THE WEST (1921), 18 episodes. Directed by Ed

Laemmle. Cast: Art Acord, Burton C. Law, Percy Pembroke, Jim Corey, Burt Wilson, Myrtle Lind.

The SECRET FOUR (1921), 15 episodes. Directed by Albert Russell and Perry Vekroff. Cast: Eddie Polo, Kathleen Myers, Doris Dean, Hal Wilson.

The DIAMOND QUEEN (1921), 18 episodes. Directed by Edward Kull. Cast: Eileen Sedgwick, George Chesebro, Al Smith, Frank Clarke, Lou Short, Josephine Scott.

WITH STANLEY IN AFRICA (1922), 18 episodes. Directed by William Craft and Edward Kull. Cast: George Walsh, Louise Lorraine, Charles Mason, William Welsh, Gordon Sackville.

The ADVENTURES OF ROBINSON CRUSOE (1922), 18 episodes. Directed by Robert F. Hill. Cast: Harry Myers, Noble Johnson, Gertrude Olmstead, Percy Pembroke, Aaron Edwards, Josef Swickard, Gertrude Claire, Emmet King.

PERILS OF THE YUKON (1922), 15 episodes. Directed by Perry Vekroff, Jay Marchant and J. P. McGowan. Cast: William Desmond, Laura La Plante, Ruth Royce, Clarke Comstock, Joseph W. Girard, Fred R. Stanton, Joe McDermott, George A. Williams, Mack V. Wright, Princess Neela, Chief Harris.

IN THE DAYS OF BUFFALO BILL (1922), 18 episodes. Directed by Ed Laemmle. Cast: Art Acord, Dorothy Woods, Duke R. Lee.

The RADIO KING (1922), 10 episodes. Directed by Robert F. Hill. Cast: Roy Stewart, Louise Lorraine, Al Smith, Sidney Bracey, Clark Comstock, Ernest Butterworth, Jr.

The SOCIAL BUCCANEER (1923), 10 episodes. Directed by Robert F. Hill. Cast: Jack Mulhall, Margaret Livingstone, Robert Anderson, Sidney Bracy, Percy Pembroke, Fontaine LaRue, Tote Ducrow, Wade Boteler, Lucille Ricksen.

The OREGON TRAIL (1923), 18 episodes. Directed by Ed Laemmle. Cast: Art Acord, Louise Lorraine, Duke R. Lee, Jim Corey, Burton C. Law, Sidney DeGray.

The PHANTOM FORTUNE (1923), 12 episodes. Directed by Robert F. Hill. Cast: William Desmond, Esther Ralston.

AROUND THE WORLD IN 18 DAYS (1923), 12 episodes. Directed by B. Reeves Eason and Robert F. Hill. Cast: William Desmond, Laura La Plante, Spottiswoode Aiken, William P. DeVaul, Wade Boteler, William Welsh.

IN THE DAYS OF DANIEL BOONE (1923), 15 episodes. Directed by William Craft. Cast: Jack Mower, Eileen Sedgwick, Duke R. Lee, Charles Brinley, Albert J. Smith, Ruth Royce.

The EAGLE'S TALONS (1923), 15 episodes. Directed by Duke Worne. Cast: Fred Thomson, Ann Little, Al Wilson, Joe Bonomo.

BEASTS OF PARADISE (1923), 15 episodes. Directed by William Craft. Cast: William Desmond, Eileen Sedgwick, William N. Gould, Ruth Royce, Margaret Morris, Jim Welsh, Clarke Comstock, Joe Bonomo, Slim Cole.

GHOST CITY (1923), 15 episodes. Directed by Jay Marchant. Cast: Pete Morrison, Margaret Morris, Al Wilson.

The STEEL TRAIL (1923), 15 episodes. Directed by William Duncan. Cast: William Duncan, Edith Johnson, Harry Carter, John Cossar, Harry Woods, Mabel Randall.

The FAST EXPRESS (1924), 15 episodes. Directed by William Duncan. Cast: William Duncan, Edith Johnson, Albert J. Smith, Harry Woods, John Cossar, Harry Carter.

The IRON MAN (1924), 15 episodes. Directed by Jay Marchant. Cast: Lucien Albertini, Joe Bonomo, Margaret Morris, Jack Daugherty, Lola Todd, Jean DeBriac.

WOLVES OF THE NORTH (1924), 10 episodes. Directed by William Duncan. Cast: William Duncan, Edith Johnson, Esther Ralston, Joseph W. Girard, Frank Rice, Joe Bonomo, Clarke Comstock, Edward Cecil, Harry Woods.

The RIDDLE RIDER (1924), 15 episodes. Directed by William Craft. Cast: William Desmond, Eileen Sedgwick, Helen Holmes, Claude Payton, William N. Gould, Ben Corbett, Hughie Mack.

The GREAT CIRCUS MYSTERY (1925), 15 episodes. Directed by Jay Marchant. Cast: Joe Bonomo, Louise Lorraine.

FIGHTING RANGER (1925), 18 episodes. Directed by Jay Marchant. Cast: Jack Daugherty, Eileen Sedgwick, Al Wilson, William Welsh, Bud Osborne, Charles Avery, Frank Lanning, Sam Polo, Slim Cole, Gladys Roy.

PERILS OF THE WILD (1925), 15 episodes. Directed by Francis Ford. Cast: Joe Bonomo, Margaret Quimby, Jack Mower.

ACE OF SPADES (1925), 15 episodes. Directed by Henry McRae. Cast: William Desmond, Mary McAllister, Jack Pratt, Albert J. Smith.

The SCARLET STREAK (1926), 10 episodes. Directed by Henry McRae. Cast: Jack Daugherty, Lola Todd, Virginia Ainsworth, Albert J. Smith, Al Prisco.

The WINKING IDOL (1926), 10 episodes. Directed by Francis Ford. Cast: William Desmond, Eileen Sedgwick, Grace Cunard,

Herbert Sutch, Jack Richardson, Helen Broneau, Les Sailor, Art Ortego.

The RADIO DETECTIVE (1926), 10 episodes. Directed by William Crinley and William Craft. Cast: Jack Daugherty, Margaret Quimby, Jack Mower, Florence Allen, John T. Prince, Sammy Gervon, Wallace Baldwin, Howard Enstedt and the Boy Scouts.

STRINGS OF STEEL (1926), 10 episodes. Directed by Henry McRae. Cast: William Desmond, Eileen Sedgwick, Albert J. Smith, George Ovey, Ted Duncan, Alphonse Martel.

FIGHTING WITH BUFFALO BILL (1926), 10 episodes. Directed by Ray Taylor. Cast: Wallace MacDonald, Elsa Beham, Grace Cunard, Howard Truesdell, Robert E. Homans, Edmund Cobb, Cuyler Supplee.

The SILENT FLYER (1926), 10 episodes. Directed by William Craft. Cast: Silver Streak, Malcolm MacGregor, Louise Lorraine, Thur Fairfax, Hughie Mack, Anders Rudolph, Edithe Yorke.

The FIRE FIGHTERS (1927), 10 episodes. Directed by Jacques Jaccard. Cast: Jack Daugherty, Helen Ferguson, Wilbur McGaugh, Lafe McKee, Albert Hart.

The RETURN OF THE RIDDLE RIDER (1927), 10 episodes. Directed by Robert F. Hill. Cast: William Desmond, Lola Todd, Grace Cunard, Tom London, Henry Barrows, Scotty Mattraw, Lewis Dayton, Norbert Myles, Howard Davies.

WHISPERING SMITH RIDES (1927), 10 episodes. Directed by Ray Taylor. Cast: Wallace MacDonald, Rose Blossom, J. P. McGowan, Clarke Comstock, Henry Herbert, W. M. McCormick.

BLAKE OF SCOTLAND YARD (1927), 12 episodes. Directed by Robert F. Hill. Cast: Hayden Stevenson, Gloria Gray, Monty Montague, Grace Cunard, Albert Hart.

TRAIL OF THE TIGER (1927), 10 episodes. Directed by Henry McRae. Cast: Jack Daugherty, Frances Teague, Jack Mower.

The VANISHING RIDER (1928), 10 episodes. Directed by Ray Taylor. Cast: William Desmond, Ethlyne Clair, Bud Osborne, Nelson McDowell.

HAUNTED ISLAND (1928), 10 episodes. Directed by Robert F. Hill. Cast: Jack Daugherty, Helen Foster, Al Ferguson, Grace Cunard, Myrtis Grinley, Carl Miller, Scotty Mattraw, John T. Price.

The SCARLET ARROW (1928), 10 episodes. Directed by Ray Taylor. Cast: Francis X. Bushman, Jr., Bess Flowers, Hazel Keener, Al Ferguson, Aileen Goodwin, Clarke Comstock.

TARZAN, THE MIGHTY (1928), 15 episodes. Directed by Jack Nelson. Cast: Frank Merrill, Natalie Kingston, Al Ferguson, Robert Nelson, Lorimer Johnston.

The MYSTERY RIDER (1928), 10 episodes. Directed by Jack Nelson. Cast: William Desmond, Derelys Perdue, Sid Saylor, Walter Shumway, Tom London, Bud Osborne, Red Basset, Ben Corbett.

The DIAMOND MASTER (1929), 10 episodes. Directed by Jack Nelson. Cast: Hayden Stevenson, Louise Lorraine, Al Hart, Monty Montague, Louis Stern, Walter Maly.

A FINAL RECKONING (1929), 12 episodes. Directed by Ray Taylor. Cast: Newton House, Louise Lorraine, Jay Wilsey, Edmund Cobb.

PIRATE OF PANAMA (1929), 12 episodes. Directed by Ray Taylor. Cast: Jay Wilsey, Natalie Kingston.

SOUND FILMS

The ACE OF SCOTLAND YARD (1929), 10 episodes. Directed by Ray Taylor. Cast: Crauford Kent (Inspector Blake), Florence Allen (Lady Diana), Herbert Pior (Lord Blanton), Albert Priscoe (Prince Darius), Monte Montague (Jarvis), Grace Cunard (Queen of Diamonds).

TARZAN THE TIGER (1929), 15 episodes. Directed by Henry McRae. Cast: Frank Merrill (Tarzan), Natalie Kingston (Jane Porter), Lillian Worth (Queen La), Al Ferguson (Bobby Nelson).

The JADE BOX (1930), 10 episodes. Directed by Ray Taylor. Cast: Jack Perrin (Jack Lamar), Louise Lorraine (Helen Morgan), Francis Ford (Martin Morgan), Wilbur S. Mack (Edward Haines), Leo White (Percy Winslow), Monroe Salebury (John Lamar).

The LIGHTNING EXPRESS (1930), 10 episodes. Directed by Henry McRae. Cast: Lane Chandler (Jack Venable), Louise Lorraine (Bobbie Van Tyme), Al Ferguson (Whispering Smith), Greta Granstedt (Kate), J. Gordon Russell (Frank Sanger), John Oscar (Bill Lewellyn), Martin Clichy (Hank Pardelow), with Floyd Criswell, Jim Pierce, Robert Kelly.

TERRY OF THE TIMES (1930), 10 episodes. Directed by Henry McRae. Cast: Reed Howes (Terry), Lotus Thompson (Eileen), Sheldon Lewis (Macy), John Oscar (Rastus), Will Hays (Patch Dugan), Mary Grant (Moll), Norman Thompson (Blind Man), Kingsley Benedict (Hunchback).

The INDIANS ARE COMING (1930), 12 episodes. Directed by Henry McRae. Cast: Tim McCoy (Jack Manning), Ailene Ray (Mary

Woods), Charles Royal (Amos), Edmund Cobb (George Woods), Francis Ford (Rance Carter), Don Francis (Bill Williams), Ring (Dynamite).

FINGER PRINTS (1931), 10 episodes. Directed by Ray Taylor. Cast: Kenneth Harlan (Gary Gordon), Edna Murphy (Lois Mackey), Gayne Whitman (Kent Martin), Gertrude Astor (Jane Madden), William Worthington (John Mackey), William Thorne (Joe Burke), Monte Montague (Rooney).

HEROES OF THE FLAMES (1931), 12 episodes. Directed by Ray Taylor. Cast: Tim McCoy.

DANGER ISLAND (1931), 12 episodes. Directed by Ray Taylor. Cast: Kenneth Harlan (Harry Drake), Lucile Brown (Bonnie Adams), Tom Rickells (Professor Adams), Walter Miller (Ben Arnold), W. L. Thorne (Bull Black), Beulah Hutton (Aileen Chandos), Andy Devine (Briny), George Regan (Lascara), Everett Brown (Cebu).

BATTLING WITH BUFFALO BILL (1931), 12 episodes. Directed by Ray Taylor. Cast: Tom Tyler (Buffalo Bill), Rex Bell (Dave Archer), Lucile Brown (Miss Archer), Francis Ford (Jim Rodney), William Desmond (John Mills), Jim Thorpe (Swift Arrow), Yakima Canutt (Jack Brady), Chief Thunderbird (himself), Bud Osborne (Joe Tempas).

SPELL OF THE CIRCUS (1931), 10 episodes. Directed by Robert F. Hill. Cast: Francis X. Bushman, Jr. (Jack Grant), Alberta Vaughn (Marie Wallace), Tom London (Butte Morgan), Walter Shumway (George Wallace), with Monte Montague, Bobby Nelson.

DETECTIVE LLOYD (1932), 12 episodes. Directed by Ray Taylor. Cast: Jack Lloyd (Inspector Lloyd), Wallace Geoffrey (Giles Wade), Muriel Angelus (Sybil Craig), Lewis Dayton (Randall Hale), Janice Adair (Dion Brooks), Tracy Holmes (Chester Dunn), Emily Fitzroy (The Ghost), Humberstone Wright (Lodgekeeper), John Turnbull (Barclay), Shale Gardner (Walters), Clifford Buckton (Sherwood), Vic Kaley (Charwoman), Fewlass Llewillyn (Curator), Ethel Ramsey (Housekeeper).

The AIRMAIL MYSTERY (1932), 12 episodes. Directed by Ray Taylor. Cast: James Flavin (Bob Lee), Lucile Brown (Mary Ross), Wheeler Oakman (Judson Ward), Frank S. Hagney (Mason), Sidney Bracey (Driscoll), Nelson McDowell (Sims), Walter Brennan (Holly), Al Wilson (Jimmy Ross), Bruce Mitchell (Captain Grant), Jack Holley (Andy).

HEROES OF THE WEST (1932), 12 episodes. Directed by Ray Taylor. Cast: Noah Beery, Jr. (Noah Blaine), Diane Duval (Ann Blaine), Onslow Stevens (Tom Crosby), William Desmond (John Blaine), Martha Mattex (Martha Blaine), Philo McCullough (Rance Judd), Harry Tenbrook (Butch Gole), Frank Lackteen (Buckskin Joe), Edmund Cobb (Bart Eaton), Jules Cowles (Missouri), Francis Ford (Captain Donovan), Thunderbird (himself).

The JUNGLE MYSTERY (1932), 12 episodes. Directed by Ray Taylor. Cast: Tom Tyler (Kirk Montgomery), Cecilia Parker (Barbara Morgan), William Desmond (Mr. Morgan), Philo McCullough (Shillow), Noah Beery, Jr. (Fred Oakes), Carmelita Geraghty (Belle Waldron), Sam Baker (Zungu).

The LOST SPECIAL (1932), 12 episodes. Directed by Henry Mc-Rae. Cast: Frank Albertson (Tom Hood), Cecilia Parker (Betty Moore), Ernie Nevers (Bob Collins), Caryl Lincoln (Kate Bland), Francis Ford (Botter Hood), Frank Glendon (Sam Slater), Tom London (Dink), Al Ferguson (Gavin), Edmund Cobb (Spike), George Magrill (Lefty), Joe Bonomo (Joe), Harold Nelson (Professor Wilson), Jack Clifford (Doran).

CLANCY OF THE MOUNTED (1933), 12 episodes. Directed by Ray Taylor. Cast: Tom Tyler (Sergeant Tom Clancy), Jacqueline Wells (Ann Louise), Earl McCarthy (Steve Clancy), Rosalie Roy (Maureen Clancy), W. L. Thomas ("Black" MacDougal), Leon Duval (Pierre LaRue), Francis Ford (Cabot), Tom London (Constable Mac-Gregor), Edmund Cobb (Constable McIntosh).

The PHANTOM OF THE AIR (1933), 12 episodes. Directed by Ray Taylor. Cast: Tom Tyler (Bob Raymond), Gloria Shea (Mary Edmunds), LeRoy Mason (Mort Crome), Hugh Enfield (Blade), Willian Desmond (Mr. Edmunds), Sidney Bracey (Munsa), Walter Brennan ("Skid"), Jennie Cramer (Marie), Cecil Kellog (Joe).

GORDON OF GHOST CITY (1933), 12 episodes. Directed by Ray Taylor. Cast: Buck Jones (Buck Gordon), Madge Bellamy (Mary Gray), Walter Miller (Rance Radigan), Hugh Enfield (Ed), William Desmond (John), Tom Rickett (Amos Gray), Francis Ford (Jim Carmody), Dick Rush (Sheriff), Ed Cobb (Scotty), William Steele (Bob), Bob Kerrick (Tom), Ethan Laidlaw (Pete), Jim Corey (Jeff), Bud Osborne (Frank), Silver (himself).

The PERILS OF PAULINE (1934), 12 episodes. Directed by Ray Taylor. Cast: Evelyn Knapp (Pauline Hargrave), Robert Allen (Robert Ward), James Durkin (Professor Hargrave), John Davidson (Dr. Bashan), Sonny Ray (Willie Dodge), Frank Lackteen (Fang), Pat O'Malley (Aviator), William Desmond (Professor Thompson), Adolph Muller (Captain), Josef Swickard (Foreign Consul), William Worthington (American Consul).

PIRATE TREASURE (1934), 12 episodes. Directed by Ray Taylor. Cast: Richard Talmadge (Dick Moreland), Lucille Lund (Dorothy Craig), Walter Miller (Stanley Brasset), Pat O'Malley (John Craig), William Desmond (Captain Carson), William E. Thorne (Drake), Del Lawrence (Robert Moreland), Ethan Laidlaw (Curt), George De Normand (Jed), Al Ferguson (Tony), Beulah Hutton (Marge).

The VANISHING SHADOW (1934), 12 episodes. Directed by Louis Freidlander. Cast: Onslow Stevens (Stanley Stanfield), Ada Ince (Gloria), Walter Miller (Ward Barnett), James Durkin (Carl Van

Dorn), William Desmond (MacDonald), Richard Cramer (Dorgan),
Sidney Bracey (Denny), Eddie Cobb (Kent).

The RED RIDER (1934), 15 episodes. Directed by Louis Fried-
lander. Cast: Buck Jones (Red Davidson), Grant Withers (Silent
Slade), Marion Shilling (Marie Maxwell), Walter Miller (Jim Breen),
Richard Cramer (John Portos), Margaret LaMarr (Joan McKee),
Charles French (Robert Maxwell), Edmund Cobb (Johnny Snow),
J. P. McGowan (Scotty McKee), William Desmond (Sheriff).

TAILSPIN TOMMY (1934), 12 episodes. Directed by Louis Fried-
lander. Cast: Maurice Murphy (Tailspin Tommy), Patricia Farr
(Betty Lou Barnes), Noah Beery, Jr. (Skeeter), Belle Daube (Mrs.
Tompkins), Lee Beggs (Deacon Grimes), Grant Withers (Milt Howe),
Walter Miller (Bruce Hoyt), Charles A. Browne (Paul Smith), Ed-
mund Cobb (Speed Walton), John Davidson (Tiger Taggart), Monte
Montague (Cliff), Jack Leonard (Al), Bud Osborne (Grease Rowle),
William Desmond (Sloane).

RUSTLERS OF RED DOG (1935), 12 episodes. Directed by Louis
Friedlander. Cast: Johnny Mack Brown (Jack Woods), Joyce Comp-
ton (Mary Lee), Walter Miller (Deacon), Raymond Hatton (Laramie),
H. L. Woods (Rocky), Fredric McKaye (Snakey), Charles K. French
(Tom Lee), Lafe McKee (Bob Lee), William Desmond (Ira Dale),
J. P. McGowan (Captain Trent), Edmund Cobb (Buck), Bud Osborne
(Jake), Monty Montague (Kruger).

The CALL OF THE SAVAGE (1935), 12 episodes. Directed by
Louis Friedlander. Cast: Noah Beery, Jr. (Jan), Dorothy Short
(Mona Andrews), H. L. Woods (Borno), Bryant Washburn (Dr. Harry
Trevor), Walter Miller (Dr. Frank Bracken), Fredric McKaye (Dr.
Charles Phillips), Russ Powell (Andrews), John Davidson (Emperor).

The ROARING WEST (1935), 15 episodes. Directed by Ray Tay-
lor. Cast: Buck Jones (Montana Larkin), Muriel Evans (Mary
Parker), Walter Miller (Gil Gillespie), Frank McGlynn, Sr. (Jingle-
bob Morgan), Harlan Knight (Clem Morgan), William Desmond (Jim
Parker), William Thorne (Marco Brett), Eole Galli (Ann Hardy),
Pat O'Brien (Steve).

TAILSPIN TOMMY AND THE GREAT AIR MYSTERY (1935), 12
episodes. Directed by Ray Taylor. Cast: Clark Williams (Tailspin Tommy), Noah Beery, Jr. (Skeeter), Jean Rogers (Betty Lou),
Delphine Drew (Inez Casmetto), Bryant Washburn (Ned Curtis),
Helen Brown (Mrs. Tompkins).

The ADVENTURES OF FRANK MERRIWELL (1936), 12 episodes.
Directed by Cliff Smith. Cast: Don Briggs (Frank Merriwell),
Jean Rogers (Elsie Bellwood), John King (Bruce Browning), Carla
Laemmle (Carla Rogers), Summer Getchell (Harry Rattletown), Wal-
lace Reid, Jr. (himself), House Peters, Jr. (himself), Allan Her-
sholt (himself), Bentley Hewett, (Daggett), Allen Bridge (Black),
Monte Montague (Monte), Bud Osborne (Gorman).

FLASH GORDON (1936), 13 episodes. Feature versions: Rocketship, Spaceship to the Unknown and Perils from the Planet Mongo. Directed by Frederick Stephani. Cast: Buster Crabbe (Flash Gordon), Jean Rogers (Dale Arden), Charles Middleton (Ming), Priscilla Lawson (Aura), John Lipson (Vultan), Richard Alexander (Prince Barin), Duke York, Jr. (King Kala), Earl Askam (Officer Torch), Theodore Lorch (High Priest), James Pierce (King Thun), Muriel Goodspeed (Zona), Richard Tucker (Professor Gordon), Glenn Strange (Fire Monster), Constantine Romanoff (Ape-Man), Bull Montana (Ape-Man).

The PHANTOM RIDER (1936), 15 episodes. Directed by Ray Taylor. Cast: Buck Jones (Buck Grant), Maria Shelton (Mary Grayson), Diana Gibson (Helen Moore), Joel Ray (Steve), Harry Woods (Harvey DeLaney), Frank LaRue (Judge Holmes), George Cooper (Spooky), Eddie Gribbon (Sheriff Mark), Helen Shipman (Lizzie), James Mason (Dirk), Charles Lemoyne (Roscoe).

ACE DRUMMOND (1936), 13 episodes. Directed by Ford Beebe and Cliff Smith. Cast: John King (Ace Drummond), Jean Rogers (Peggy Trainor), Noah Beery, Jr. (Jerry), Guy Bates Post (Grand Lama), Arthur Loft (Chang-Ho), Chester Gan (Kai-Chek), Jackie Morrow (Billy Merdith), James B. Leong (Henry Kee), James Eagle (Johnny Wong), Selmer Jackson (Meredith), Robert Warwick (Winston), C. Montague Shaw (Trainor), Fredrick Vogedine (Bauer), Al Bridge (Wyckoff), Lon Chaney, Jr. (Ivan), Stanley Blystone (Sergei), Ed Cobb (Nicolai), Richard Wessel (Boris), Louis Vinzinot (Lotan), Sam Ash (Le Page).

JUNGLE JIM (1937), 12 episodes. Directed by Ford Beebe and Cliff Smith. Cast: Grant Withers (Jungle Jim), Betty Jane Rhodes (Joan), Raymond Hatton (Malay Mike), Henry Brandon (The Cobra), Evelyn Brent (Shanghai Lil), Bryant Washburn (Bruce Redmond), Selmer Jackson (Tyler), Al Bridge (Slade), Paul Sutton (LaBat), Al Duvall (Kolu), William Royale (Hawks).

SECRET AGENT X-9 (1937), 12 episodes. Directed by Ford Beebe and Cliff Smith. Cast: Scott Kolk (Secret Agent X-9), Jean Rogers (Shara Graustark), Henry Hunter (Tommy Dawson), David Oliver (Pidge), Larry Blake (Wheeler), Monte Blue (Baron Karsten), Henry Brandon (Blackstone), Lon Chaney, Jr. (Maroni), Max Hoffman, Jr. (Marker), Bentley Hewlett (Scarlett), George Shelley (Packard), Robert Dalton (Thurston), Leonard Lord (Ransom), Bob Kortman (Delaney), Edward Piel, Sr. (The Fence), Lynn Gilbert (Rose).

WILD WEST DAYS (1937), 13 episodes. Directed by Ford Beebe and Cliff Smith. Cast: Johnny Mack Brown (Kentucky), George Shelly (Dude), Bob Kortman (Trigger), Frank Yaconelli (Mike), Lynn Gilbert (Lucy), Frank McGlynn (Larry), Russell Simpson (Keefer), Francis McDonald (Purvis), Walter Miller (Doc Hardy), Chief Thunderbird (Red Hatchet), Al Bridge (Steve).

RADIO PATROL (1937), 12 episodes. Directed by Ford Beebe

Grant Withers (l.), Betty Jane Rhodes and Raymond Hatton
in <u>Jungle Jim</u> (Universal, 1937).

and Cliff Smith. Cast: Grant Withers (Pat O'Hara), Catherine
Hughes (Molly), Mickey Rentschler (Pinky Adams), Adrian Morris
(Sam), Max Hoffman, Jr. (Selkirk), Frank Lackteen (Thata), Leonard
Lord (Franklin), Monte Montague (Pollard), Dick Botiller (Zutta),
Silver Wolf (Irish).

TIM TYLER'S LUCK (1937), 12 episodes. Directed by Ford
Beebe. Cast: Frankie Thomas (Tim Tyler), Frances Robinson
(Lora Lacey), Al Shean (Professor Tyler), Norman Willis (Spider
Webb), Earl Douglas (Lazarre).

FLASH GORDON'S TRIP TO MARS (1938), 15 episodes. Feature
versions: Mars Attacks the World and The Deadly Ray from Mars.
Directed by Ford Beebe and Robert F. Hill. Cast: Buster Crabbe

(Flash Gordon), Jean Rogers (Dale Arden), Charles Middleton (Ming), Frank Shannon (Dr. Zarkov), Beatrice Roberts (Queen Azura), Richard Alexander (Prince Barin), C. Montague Shaw (King of the Clay People), Donald Kerr (Happy Hapgood), Wheeler Oakman (Tarnak).

FLAMING FRONTIERS (1938), 15 episodes. Directed by Ray Taylor and Alan James. Cast: Johnny Mack Brown (Tex Houston), Eleanor Hansen (Mary Grant), Charles Middleton (Ace Daggett), James Blaine (Bart Eaton), Charles Stevens (Breed), William Royle (Tom Crosby), Horace Murphy (Sheriff), Michael Slade (Postmaster), John Rutherford (Buffalo Bill), Chief Thunder Cloud (himself).

RED BARRY (1938), 13 episodes. Directed by Ford Beebe and Alan James. Cast: Buster Crabbe (Red Barry), Frances Robinson (Mississippi), Edna Sedgewick (Natacha), Cyril Delevanti (Wing Fu), Frank Lackteen (Quong Lee), Wade Boteler (Inspector Scott), Hugh Huntley (Vane), Philip Ahn (Cholly), William Ruhl (Mannix), William Gould (Commissioner), Wheeler Oakman (Weaver), Stanley Price (Petrov), Earle Douglas (Igor), Charles Stevens (Captain Moy).

SCOUTS TO THE RESCUE (1939), 12 episodes. Directed by Ray Taylor and Alan James. Cast: Jackie Cooper (Bruce Scott), Vondell Darr (Mary Scanlon), Edwin Stanley (Pat Scanlon), William Ruhl (Hal Marvin), Bill Cody, Jr. (Skeets Scanlon), David Durand (Rip Dawson), Ralph Dunn (Pug O'Toole), Jason Robards (Doc), Frank Coghlan, Jr. (Ken), Ivan Miller (Turk Mortenson), Victor Adams (Hurst), Sidney Miller (Hermie), Richard Botiller (Leeka).

BUCK ROGERS (1939), 12 episodes. Feature versions: Planet Outlaws and Destination Saturn. Directed by Ford Beebe and Saul A. Goodkind. Cast: Buster Crabbe (Buck Rogers), Constance Moore (Wilma Deering), Jackie Moran (Buddy Wade), Anthony Warde (Killer Kane), C. Montague Shaw (Dr. Huer), Guy Usher (Aldar), William Gould (Marshall Kragg), Philson Ahn (Prince Tallen), Henry Brandon (Captain Lasca), Wheeler Oakman (Patten), Kenneth Duncan (Lieutenant Lacy), Carleton Young (Scott), Reed Howes (Roberts).

The PHANTOM CREEPS (1939), 12 episodes. Directed by Ford Beebe and Saul A. Goodkind. Cast: Bela Lugosi (Dr. Alex Zorka), Robert Kent (Captain Bob West), Regis Toomey (Jim Daley), Dorothy Arnold (Jean Drew), Edward Van Sloan (Chief Davis), Eddie Acuff (Mac), Anthony Averill (Rankin), Jack C. Smith (Monk), Roy Barcroft (Parker), Forrest Taylor (Black).

The OREGON TRAIL (1939), 15 episodes. Directed by Ford Beebe. Johnny Mack Brown (Jeff Scott), Louise Stanley (Margaret Mason), Bill Cody, Jr. (Jimmie Clark), Fuzzy Knight (Deadwood Hawkins), Ed LeSaint (John Mason), James Blaine (Sam Morgan), Jack C. Smith (Bragg), Roy Barcroft (Colonel Custer), Colin Kenny (Slade).

The GREEN HORNET (1940), 13 episodes. Directed by Ford Beebe and Ray Taylor. Cast: Gordon Jones (Britt Reid), Wade

Boteler (Michael Oxford), Keye Luke (Kato), Anne Nagel (Lenore Case), Philip Trent (Jasper Jenks), Walter McGrail (Dean), John Kelly (Hawks), Gene Rizzi (Carney), Douglas Evans (Mortinson), Ralph Dunn (Andy), Arthur Loft (Joe Ogden), Edward Earle (Felix Grant), Cy Kendall (Monroe).

FLASH GORDON CONQUERS THE UNIVERSE (1940), 12 episodes. Feature version: Purple Death from Outer Space. Directed by Ford Beebe and Ray Taylor. Cast: Buster Crabbe (Flash Gordon), Carol Hughes (Dale Arden), Charles Middleton (Ming), Frank Shannon (Dr. Zarkov), Anne Gwynne (Sonja), Roland Drew (Prince Barin), Shirley Deane (Princess Aura), Victor Zimmerman (Thong), Don Rowan (Officer Torch), Michael Mark (Karm), Sigmund Nillson (Korro), Lee Powell (Roka), Edgar Edwards (Turan), Ben Taggart (General Lupi), Harry C. Bradley (Keedish).

WINNERS OF THE WEST (1940), 12 episodes. Directed by Ford Beebe and Ray Taylor. Cast: Dick Foran (Jeff Ramsay), Anne Nagel (Claire Hartford), James Craig (Jim Jackson), Tom Fadden (Tex Houston), Charles Stevens (Snakeye), Trevor Bardette (Raven), Harry Woods (King Carter), Chief Yowlatchie (Chief War Eagle), Edward Keane (John Hartford), William Desmond (Brine), Edmund Cobb (Maddox).

JUNIOR G-MEN (1940), 12 episodes. Directed by Ford Beebe and John Rawlins. Cast: Billy Halop (Billy Barton), Huntz Hall (Gyp), Gabriel Dell (Terry), Bernard Punsley (Lug), Roger Daniels (Midge), Philip Terry (Jim Bradford), Kenneth Lundy (Buck), Russell Hicks (Colonel Barton), Cy Kendall (Brand), Kenneth Howell (Harry Trent).

The GREEN HORNET STRIKES AGAIN (1940), 15 episodes. Directed by Ford Beebe and John Rawlins. Cast: Warren Hull (Britt Reid), Kaye Luke (Kato), Wade Boteler (Michael Oxford), Anne Nagel (Lenore Case), Eddie Acuff (Lowery), Pierre Watkin (Grogan), Joe A. Devlin (Dolan), William Hall (Don DeLuca), Dorothy Lovett (Frances Grayson), Jay Michael (Foranti), C. Montague Shaw (Weaver).

SEA RAIDERS (1941), 12 episodes. Directed by Ford Beebe and Ray Taylor. Cast: Billy Halop (Billy Adams), Huntz Hall (Toby Nelson), Gabriel Dell (Bilge), Bernard Punsley (Butch), Hally Chester (Swab), Joe Recht (Lug), William Hall (Brack Warren), John McGuire (Tom Adams), Mary Field (Aggie Nelson), Edward Keane (Elliott Carlton), Marcia Ralston (Leah Carlton), Reed Hadley (Carl Tonjes), Stanley Blystone (Captain Nelson), Richard Alexander (Jenkins).

SKY RAIDERS (1941), 12 episodes. Directed by Ford Beebe and Ray Taylor. Cast: Donald Woods (Captain Robert Dayton), Billy Halop (Tim Bryant), Robert Armstrong (Lieutenant Ed Carey), Edward Cianelli (Felix Lynx), Kathryn Adams (Mary Blake), Jacqueline Dalya (Innis Clair), Jean Fenwick (Countess Irene), Reed Hadley (Caddens), Irving Mitchell (Hinchfield), Edgar Edwards (Teal), John

Holland (Hess), Roy Gordon (Major General Fletcher), Alex Callam (Captain Long), Bill Cody, Jr. (Hurd).

RIDERS OF DEATH VALLEY (1941), 15 episodes.   Directed by Ford Beebe and Ray Taylor.   Cast: Dick Foran (Jim Benton), Leo Carillo (Pancho), Buck Jones (Tombstone), Charles Bickford (Wolf Reade), Lon Chaney, Jr. (Butch), Noah Berry, Jr. (Smokey), Guinn "Big Boy" Williams (Borax Bill), Jeanne Kelly (Mary Morgan), James Blaine (Joseph Kirby), Monte Blue (Rance Davis), Glenn Strange (Tex).

DON WINSLOW OF THE NAVY (1942), 12 episodes.   Directed by Ford Beebe and Ray Taylor.   Cast: Don Terry (Don Winslow), Walter Sande (Lieutenant Red Pennington), Wade Boteler (Mike Splendor), Paul Scott (Captain Farfield), John Litel (Menlin), Peter Leeds (Chapman), Anne Nagel (Misty), Claire Dodd (Mercedes), Frank Lackteen (Koloki).

GANG BUSTERS (1942), 13 episodes.   Directed by Ray Taylor and Noel Smith.   Cast: Kent Taylor (Bill Banister), Irene Hervey (Vicky Logan), Ralph Morgan (Professor Mortis), Robert Armstrong (Tim Nolan), Richard Davies (Happy Haskins), Joseph Crehan (Chief O'Brien), George Watts (Mayor Hansen) , Ralph Harolde (Halliger), John Gallaudet (Wilkinson), Victor Zimmerman (Barnard), George Lewis (Mason).

JUNIOR G-MEN OF THE AIR (1942), 12 episodes.   Directed by Ray Taylor and Noel Smith.   Cast: Billy Halop ("Ace" Holden), Gene Reynolds (Eddie Holden), Lionel Atwill (The Baron), Frank Albertson (Jerry Markham), Richard Lane (Don Ames), Huntz Hall ("Bolts" Larsen), Bernard Punsley ("Greaseball" Plunkett), Frankie Darro (Jack), Turhan Bey (Araka), John Bleifer (Beal), Noel Cravat (Monk), Edward Foster (Comora).

OVERLAND MAIL (1942), 15 episodes.   Directed by Ford Beebe and John Rawlins.   Cast: Lon Chaney, Jr. (Jim Lane), Helen Parrish (Barbara Gilbert), Noah Beery, Jr. (Sierra Pete), Don Terry (Buckskin Billy Burke), Bob Baker (Young Bill Cody), Noah Beery, Sr. (Frank Chadwick), Tom Chatterton (Tom Gilbert), Charles Stevens (Puma), Robert Barrow (Charles Darson), Harry Cording (Sam Gregg).

ADVENTURES OF SMILIN' JACK (1943), 13 episodes.   Directed by Ray Taylor and Lewis D. Collins.   Cast: Tom Brown (Smilin' Jack), Marjorie Lord (Janet), Philip Ahn (Wu Tan), Jay Novello (Kushimi), Nigel de Brulier (Lo San), Edgar Barrier (Tommy), Turhan Bey (Kageyama), Rose Hobart (Frauline Von Teufel), Keye Luke (Captain Wing), Sidney Toler (General Kai Ling), Cyril Delavanti (Mah Ling).

DON WINSLOW OF THE COAST GUARD (1943), 13 episodes.   Directed by Ray Taylor and Lewis D. Collins.   Cast: Don Terry (Don Winslow).

ADVENTURES OF THE FLYING CADETS (1943), 13 episides.

Directed by Ray Taylor and Lewis D. Collins. Cast: Johnny Downs
(Danny Collins), Bobby Jordan (Jinx Roberts), Ward Wood (Scrapper
MacKay), Billy Benedict (Zombie Parker), Eduardo Cianelli (Karl
Von Heiger), Regis Toomey (Captain Ralph Carson), Robert Arm-
strong (Arthur Galt), Selmer Jackson (Professor Mason), Jennifer
Holt (Andre Mason).

The GREAT ALASKAN MYSTERY (1944), 13 episodes. Directed
by Ray Taylor and Lewis D. Collins. Cast: Milburn Stone (Jim
Hudson), Marjorie Weaver (Ruth Miller), Edgar Kennedy (Bosun),
Samuel S. Hinds (Herman Brock), Martin Kosleck (Dr. Hauss),
Ralph Morgan (Dr. Miller), Joseph Crehan (Bill Hudson), Fuzzy
Knight ("Grit" Hartman), Harry Cording (Captain Greeder), Anthony
Warde (Brandon).

RAIDERS OF GHOST CITY (1944), 13 episodes. Directed by Ray
Taylor and Lewis D. Collins. Cast: Dennis Moore (Captain Steve
Clark), Wanda McKay (Cathy Haines), Lionel Atwill (Alex Morel),
Joe Sawyer (Idaho Jones), Regis Toomey (Captain Clay Randolph),
Virginia Christine (Trina Dessard), Eddy C. Waller (Doc Blair),
Emmett Vogan (Carl Lawton), Addison Richards (Colonel Sewell),
Charles Wagerheim (Abel Rackerby).

MYSTERY OF THE RIVERBOAT (1944), 13 episodes. Directed
by Ray Taylor and Lewis D. Collins. Cast: Robert Lowery (Steve
Langtry), Eddie Quillan ("Jug" Jenks), Marion Martin (Celeste El-
tree), Marjorie Clements (Jenny Perrin), Lyle Talbot (Rudolph Tol-
ler), Arthur Hohl (Clayton), Oscar O'Shea (Captain Perrin), Mantan
Moreland (Napolean), Isn Wolfe (Herman Einreich), Jay Novello
(Pierre), Francis Macdonald (Batiste).

JUNGLE QUEEN (1945), 13 episodes. Directed by Ray Taylor
and Lewis D. Collins. Cast: Edward Norris (Bob Elliott), Eddie
Quillan (Chuck Kelly), Douglass Dumbrille (Lang), Lois Collier
(Pamela Courtney), Ruth Roman (Lothel), Tala Birell (Dr. Elise
Bork), Clarence Muse (Kyba), Napolean Simpson (Maati), Cy Kendall
(Tambosa Tim), Clinton Rosemond (Godac).

The MASTER KEY (1945), 13 episodes. Directed by Ray Taylor
and Lewis D. Collins. Cast: Milburn Stone (Tom Brant), Jan Wiley
(Janet Lowe), Dennis Moore (Jack Ryan), Addison Richards (Garret
Donohue), Byron Foulger (Professor Henderson), Maria Wrixon
(Dorothy Newton), Sarah Padden (Aggie), Russell Hicks (Chief O'Brien),
Alfred La Rue (Migsy), George Lynn (Herman).

SECRET AGENT X-9 (1945), 13 episodes. Directed by Ray Tay-
lor and Lewis D. Collins. Cast: Lloyd Bridges (Secret Agent X-9),
Keye Luke (Ah Fong), Jan Wiley (Lynn Moore), Victoria Horne
(Nabura), Samuel S. Hinds (Solo), Cy Kendall (Lucky Number), Jack
Overman (Marker), George Lynn (Bach), Clarence Lane (Takahari),
Benson Fong (Hakahima), Arno Frey (Kapitan Graf), Gene Stuten-
roth (Yogel), Ann Codee (Mama Pierre), Edward M. Howard (Dor-
gan), Edmund Cobb (Bartender).

The ROYAL MOUNTED RIDES AGAIN (1945), 13 episodes. Directed by Ray Taylor and Lewis D. Collins. Cast: George Dolenz (Frenchy), Bill Kennedy (Wayne Decker), Daun Kennedy (June Bailey), Paul E. Burns (Bucket), Milburn Stone (Taggart), Robert Armstrong (Price), Danny Morton (Dancer), Addison Richards (Jackson Decker), Tom Fadden (Lode MacKenzie), Joseph Haworth (Bunker), Helen Bennett (Madame Mysterioso), Joseph Crehan (Sgt. Nelson), Selmer Jackson (MacDonald), Daral Hudson (Ladue), George Lloyd (Kent), George Eldredge (Grail).

The SCARLET HORSEMAN (1946), 13 episodes. Directed by Ray Taylor and Lewis D. Collins. Cast: Paul Guilfoyle (Jim Bannion), Peter Cookson (Kirk Norris), Virginia Christine (Carla), Victoria Horne (Loma), Danny Morton (Ballou), Fred Coby (Tioga), Janet Shaw (Elise Halliday), Jack Ingram (Tragg), Edward M. Howard (Zero Quick), Harold Goodwin (Idaho), Ralph Lewis (Pecos), Edmund Cobb (Kyle), Cy Kendall (Amigo).

LOST CITY OF THE JUNGLE (1946), 13 episodes. Directed by Ray Taylor and Lewis D. Collins. Cast: Russell Hayden (Rod Stanton), Jane Adams (Marjorie Elmore), Lionel Atwill (Sir Eric Hazarias), Keye Luke (Tal Shan), Helen Bennett (Indra), Ted Hecht (Doc Harris), John Eldredge (Dr. Elmore), John Miljan (Caffron), John Gallaudet (Grebb), Ralph Lewis (Kurtz).

The MYSTERIOUS MR. M (1946), 13 episodes. Directed by Lewis D. Collins and Vernon Keays. Cast: Richard Martin (Kirby Walsh), Pamela Blake (Shirley Clinton), Dennis Moore (Grant Farrell), Jane Randolph (Marina Lamont), Danny Norton (Derek Lamont), Virginia Brissac (Grandma Waldron), Edmund MacDonald (Anthony Waldron), Byron Foulger (Wetherby), Joseph Crehan (Captain Blair), Jack Ingram (Shrak).

FEATURE VERSION AND RE-ISSUE TITLE
CROSS-REFERENCE LISTING

(Listed chronologically by year of original serial release)

Feature versions

California in '49: from Days of '49 (1924--Arrow)

Desert Command: from The Three Musketeers (1933--Mascot)

Chandu on the Magic Isle: from The Return of Chandu (1934--Mascot)

Radio Ranch and Men With Steel Faces: from The Phantom Empire (1935--Mascot)

Tarzan and the Green Goddess: from The New Adventures of Tarzan (1935--Burroughs-Tarzan)

Batmen of Africa: from Darkest Africa (1936--Republic)

Sharad of Atlantis: from Undersea Kingdom (1936--Republic)

Robinson Crusoe of Mystery Island: from Robinson Crusoe of Clipper Island (1936--Republic)

Rocketship, Spaceship to the Unknown and Perils From the Planet Mongo: from Flash Gordon (1936--Universal)

The Torpedo of Doom: from Fighting Devil Dogs (1938--Republic)

Mars Attacks the World and The Deadly Ray From Mars: from Flash Gordon's Trip to Mars (1938--Universal)

Lost Island of Kioga: from Hawk of the Wilderness (1938--Republic)

Planet Outlaws and Destination Saturn: from Buck Rogers (1939--Universal)

Purple Death From Outer Space: from Flash Gordon Conquers the Universe (1940--Universal)

Doctor Satan's Robot: from The Mysterious Doctor Satan (1940--Republic)

Spy Smasher Returns: from Spy Smasher (1942--Republic)

Nyoka and the Lost Secrets of Hippocrates: from The Perils of Nyoka (1942--Republic)

Black Dragon of Manzanar: from G-Men vs. the Black Dragon (1943--Republic)

Sakima and the Masked Marvel: from The Masked Marvel (1943--Republic)

Jungle Gold: from The Tiger Woman (1944--Republic)

Captain Mephisto and the Transformation Machine: from Manhunt of Mystery Island (1945--Republic)

FBI 99: from Federal Operator 99 (1945--Republic)

D-Day on Mars: from The Purple Monster Strikes (1945--Republic)

Cyclotrode X: from The Crimson Ghost (1946--Republic)

Sombra, the Spider Woman: from The Black Widow (1947--Republic)

Code 645: from G-Men Never Forget (1948--Republic)

R. C. M. P. and the Treasure of Genghis Kahn: from Dangers of the Canadian Mounted (1948--Republic)

Golden Hands of Kurigal: from Federal Agents vs. Underworld, Inc. (1949--Republic)

Lost Planet Airmen: from King of the Rocketmen (1949--Republic)

Slaves of the Invisible Monster: from The Invisible Monster (1950--Republic)

Retik, the Moon Menace: from Radar Men From the Moon (1952--Republic)

U-238 and the Witch Doctor: from Jungle Drums of Africa (1953--Republic)

Missile Base at Taniak: from Canadian Mounties vs. Atomic Invaders (1953--Republic)

Target: Sea of China: from Trader Tom of the China Seas (1954--Republic)

The Claw Monsters: from Panther Girl of the Kongo (1955--Republic)

Re-Issue Titles

King of Jungleland: originally Darkest Africa (1936--Republic)

Return of Captain Marvel: originally Adventures of Captain Marvel
(1941--Republic)

Dick Tracy vs. the Phantom Empire: originally Dick Tracy vs.
Crime, Inc. (1941--Republic)

Nyoka and the Tigermen: originally The Perils of Nyoka (1942--
Republic)

Manhunt In the African Jungle: originally Secret Service in Darkest
Africa (1943--Republic)

An Evening With Batman and Robin: originally Batman (1943--Colum-
bia)

Return of Captain America: originally Captain America (1944--Re-
public)

Perils of the Darkest Jungle: originally The Tiger Woman (1944--
Republic)

Ghost Riders of the West: originally The Phantom Rider (1946--
Republic)

INTERVIEWS

1. Buster Crabbe

Buster Crabbe is a show-business rarity, an athlete turned actor who actually exhibited some genuine talent as a performer. As an actor, Crabbe wasn't in the same league as Claude Rains, but he could certainly hold his own in serials and "B" pictures, lending a solid presence to his roles and reciting even the most outrageous dialogue with believability and conviction. He was far more versatile than Johnny Weismuller, who, although effective in his early appearances as Tarzan at MGM, was never more than a one-role performer. Crabbe played Tarzan, too, in a dismal low-budget 1933 serial, but he branched out far beyond that type of role, playing everything from cowboys to big-city gangsters, and he deserves more respect than he has received from most film critics and historians.

Born in Oakland, California on February 7, 1908, Clarence Linden Crabbe (he was nicknamed "Buster" by his father) spent his early years in Hawaii, where he participated in high school sporting events. By 1928, he had won a bronze medal in the 1500-meter freestyle event at the Olympics, and went on to win a gold medal by breaking Johnny Weismuller's 400-meter record in a time of 4 minutes and 48 seconds at the 1932 Olympics. While attending law school at the University of Southern California, Crabbe entered films in 1932, starring in King of the Jungle for Paramount, his first and only "A" feature. In 1933 he married Adah Virginia Held, and the couple later had two children, Susan Ann and Cullen Held.

Crabbe's career was mired in "B" pictures and serials throughout the thirties, largely due to mismanagement by Paramount Pictures, where he was under contract. The Flash Gordon serials brought Crabbe a certain degree of fame,

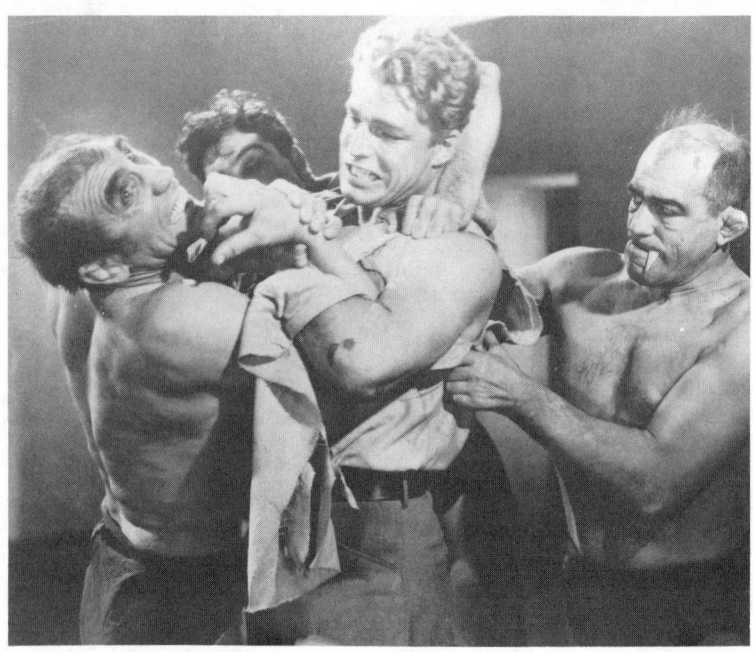

A harassed Buster Crabbe (c.) battles Emperor Ming's killer
ape-men in Flash Gordon (Universal, 1936).

but they did little to advance his career, and by the forties
he was under contract to Producer's Releasing Corporation,
an economy-minded "poverty row" outfit, where he appeared
in a long line of cheap, action-filled westerns. One of these,
Frontier Outlaws (1944), was so low-budgeted that in one
scene Crabbe backs out of a window while holding a gun on
his opponent--and cracks his head on the window frame.
PRC was too cheap even to reshoot the scene, and the flub
remained in the finished picture. The PRC westerns might
not have won any awards, but they served their purpose at
the time, and they provided Crabbe with star billing.

Crabbe, continuing to appear in films on an intermit-
tent basis, moved east with his family in the fifties, where
he hosted a New York children's TV show and went into business with Cascade Industries. In the seventies, Crabbe was
still in the news, setting three records in swimming for men
aged 60 to 64 in 1971, and in 1976 he was officially made a

member of The World Bodybuilding Guild Hall of Fame at its annual testimonial dinner in New York. Buster Crabbe died on April 23, 1983.

The following interview was conducted on May 2, 1981.

Q: How did you get the lead role in the Flash Gordon serials?

A: We made three of those, in '36, '38, and '40; there are forty episodes involved. I got interested in the thing through the Alex Raymond comic strip. When I went home in the evening I'd pick up the paper to find out what old Flash had gotten himself into with Ming or whatever.

Inadvertently, back in August of 1935, I picked up a copy of The Hollywood Reporter, and noticed a blurb at the bottom of the page announcing that Universal Studios was going to do a serial of Alex Raymond's comic strip, and in those days I thought "it's too fantastic," it was just too crazy to be doing, having these three people get in a rocketship, and going off to Mongo and getting involved in all sorts of things.... The announcement also said that if you wanted to try out for the part, to check into the Universal casting office, and if they thought you were likely, they would have a test the following week.

Now, I had done a couple of things at Universal, and the people at the casting office knew me, so I called up a man there by the name of Miller, and told him that I'd read the announcement in The Hollywood Reporter, and he said, "Do you want to test for the part, Buster?" and I said "Hell no--but I would like to get on the set and see who's crazy enough to try out for this thing," so he said "Well, come on out, and I'll get you on the set."

So I went out to the studio the next day; it was a Wednesday or a Thursday. In those days they had just 12 shooting stages at Universal, and they have about 42 now. They told me that they were testing on stage 7 or 8, and I wandered on out there and stood off to the side. There were fifteen or sixteen actors there testing; two I noticed right away who I thought were possibilities, and the others I thought didn't qualify. One of the guys that I thought had a chance was an actor by the name of George Bergaman, a nice-looking young man who was into body-building and that kind of thing. He was a bit actor in Hollywood, and I had been in a couple of films he'd worked on. I thought he'd be perfect for the part, they'd just have to bleach his hair. The other guy, it was lucky for him that he didn't get the part, because a

couple of months later John Ford picked him to play the
juvenile lead in a picture he was going to do called Hurricane.
The actor's name, of course, was Jon Hall, and Hurricane
made him a star.

Somebody on the set pointed me out to the producer,
Henry McRae, and I found out later that he'd been producing
serials at Universal since 1927. He came over and introduced himself, and asked me, naturally, why I was there.
I explained that it was just curiosity on my part, so we talked
a little while, and he said, "Well, how would you like to do
the part?," and I said, "I really don't know."

So we talked a little further, and he finally said, "You
have the part if you want it," and I started to tell him that
I was under contract with another studio when he said, "I
know, Buster, you're under contract to Paramount ... We'll
borrow you." My automatic answer was "Well, if I'm borrowed, then I'll have to do what the bosses at Paramount
tell me to do," but privately I was thinking, "I hope the studio
tells them I'm not available." So I shook hands with McRae
and turned to go. I think you know the rest of the story....

Q: What memories do you have about the production
of the first serial?

A: They started in October of '35, and to bring it in
on the six-week schedule, we had to average 85 set-ups a
day; that means moving and rearranging the heavy equipment we had, the arc lights and everything, 85 times a day.
We had to be in makeup every morning at 7:00, and on the
set at 8:00 ready to go. They'd knock off for lunch, and
then we always worked after dinner; they'd give us a break
of a half-hour or 45 minutes, and then we'd go back on the
set and work until about 10:30 every night. It wasn't fun,
it was a lot of work. We finished just before the six weeks
were up, around Christmas I think, and I kind of brushed my
hands together and thought, "Well, we put that turkey to bed!"

Q: Do you have any comments to make on the surprising success of the first serial?

A: It was released in February of '36, and the biggest money-maker that year at Universal was a Deanna Dur-
bin picture called Three Smart Girls; and it was a surprise
to me, and, I think to Universal as well, that this serial we
made was the second biggest money-maker for the studio that
year. What they didn't realize, I think, was that if we could
get the youngsters started with us on the first or second epi-

sode, then we'd have them right back in the same seat week after week; and that's exactly what happened. This was at a time when the best seat in the house was 50 or 55 cents; so you figure, 13 episodes all strung together at an average of 10 cents for every admission ... that's $1. 30 that each youngster would put into the till.

Q: What, specifically, do you think was responsible for the success of Flash Gordon?

A: There are three factors, I think, behind the success of the series. Alex Raymond was one: he originated the idea; Charlie Middleton as the "heavy" was another factor; and the third factor, I think, was the special effects ... they had nothing to go on as far as what the rocketships would look like, except what Raymond had drawn.

Q: Did you see any of the special effects in the process of being filmed?

A: Well, a lot of it was done in the laboratory ... the action of the ray gun, what they did there was scrape the emulsion off each individual frame of film to produce the effect. The most amazing thing to me that the special effects department did was when Ming had strapped me down into this chair, and conveniently, alongside the chair was this statue, a Buddha kind of statue, and Ming comes in and says something like "I've got you in my power again, and now I'm going to show you the strength of my ray," and he aims the ray at the statue and it melts before your eyes. I had read this in the script the night before, and I thought to myself, "Now how is special effects going to do that? ," So before checking into makeup the next day I went directly to see Eddie Keys over in special effects and asked him how he was going to do that one, and he said, "I'll show you." What he did was make a cast of that statue, and put steel dust inside of it. Then he magnetized it, took the form away, and painted the "statue," and when he broke the electrical current of the magnet, it just "melted" into a heap.

Q: You used a lot of sets from other pictures....

A: We stole a lot of sets from The Phantom of the Opera and that sort of thing, any set that we thought would be appropriate to the action we had to film. They'd let us go in and grab a shot or two, then we'd get out....

Q: Did Frederick Stephani take more time in planning action and lining up shots than the directors of the two sequels, Ford Beebe and Ray Taylor?

A: Yes, I think he did. I don't think that Stephani was basically a serial director. I wondered why they had picked him to do the first one, because they had Ray Taylor out there, and Ford Beebe, who were both excellent; they had done a lot of serials, but they didn't go to work until the second one. The reason they had the two of them working was because they got smart; they would have one of them come in and shoot while the other guy would prepare, and that way they would know exactly how they were going to set up the scenes they were involved in. It speeded up production.

Q: Why did Universal make three Flash Gordon serials and only one Buck Rogers?

A: Well, it was a toss-up whether they were going to do a third Flash Gordon or a second Buck Rogers, and I think they went for the third Flash Gordon because they had more stock footage. I thought this was kind of cheating, because we brought the third one in after five weeks of shooting as opposed to six weeks for the other two.

Q: Did you ever see the syndicated Flash Gordon TV series made in the fifties?

A: I can't remember where I saw it, but I saw about half of one ... God it was terrible! They made it in the south of France or somewhere. I'll tell you who made it, a man named Matty Fox. He was connected with Universal, and because he worked there he knew that the studio's rights on Flash Gordon were ready to expire and the property was going to revert to King Features. He went in and made a deal with King Features to use the title, and he blew it. The thing didn't go at all....

Q: As an actor, how do you approach a role like Flash Gordon?

A: Well I certainly didn't approach it tongue-in-cheek, because I feel if you're not going to be serious about the thing, forget it, because nobody else is going to be serious. That's one of the faults I found with the new Flash Gordon; I don't blame Sam Jones for this; I think it was the direction....

Q: Did you like anything about the remake?

A: Well, I liked the special effects--that shot in particular when all the Hawkmen are flying to attack Ming's palace, I thought that was the best shot in the picture....
I thought the fight scene that Flash and Barin had on the platform with the spikes was for the birds.

Q: Speaking of fight scenes, you had an excellent one in the first chapter of Flash Gordon....

A: That's a funny thing ... it was a hard place to fight, no furniture to jump over, no walls to climb or anything. They let these three wild men out, and they had fangs and everything. It took a day and a half to get this scene, because we had to rehearse, and I had to get rid of one guy before the other guy hit me and so on, and we'd make mistakes and have to repeat. Well, the second afternoon there was just one more guy to throw and I thought, "Well, we finally got it in the can at last," when all of a sudden one of the wild men stood up and said, "cut, cut!," and Stephani came out of his chair like he was shot out of a cannon, saying, "What the hell's the matter?," and the actor says, "Mr. Stephani, I'm sorry, but I lost my fangs!" It really didn't matter. He could have finished the scene without them, turned his back to the camera or something, but we had to go around and look for the fangs, and we finally found them and completed the scene. It was an exciting scene, a good way to start the serial off.

Q: How about the scene in chapter three, where Flash fought the shark men?

A: It's too bad about that, the water got dirty, with everyone diving in and out, and the scene was kind of smoky looking. It was shot through the window of a round tank on the back lot at Universal.

Q: Did you use a stunt double in the serials?

A: No, I did all my own stuff at first, until about the time my first son came along. I took a hell of a bump sometimes; it wasn't an enjoyable thing to do. Then when they had a couple of accidents on The Charge of the Light Brigade, the insurance rates went up and they wouldn't let an actor walk down a steep flight of stairs. It was good for the stuntmen, though, because it gave them a job and made some money for them.

Q: You worked with W. C. Fields in You're Telling
Me. Do you have any memories of him? What was he like?

A: Like he was, the same way you saw him on screen.
He'd go to a water cooler, and of course there would be no
water in there, it'd be gin ... you never saw the guy drunk,
though. He was a funny guy ... if he blew a line, he'd say
something that was a lot funnier than what he was supposed
to say.... He wasn't an outgoing person, he was always
kind of by himself....

Q: Do you have any comments to make on your career
as a leading man in westerns?

A: I made a lot of westerns, around 80 in all. I
made 40 Billy the Kid westerns, and I was a second lead to
Randolph Scott in the Zane Grey things he was doing. That
was right after I first got started, and he went to the front
office one day and told them that he wasn't going to do any
more westerns, he wanted to do the romantic leading man
type of thing. He was just getting to be a star, so they
went along with him, and the films that had been earmarked
for him, I got 'em.

Q: Do you have a favorite director of the ones you
worked with?

A: No, not really. I always wanted to work with a
good one, but I never got the chance. The only "A" picture
I ever made was King of the Jungle back in 1932; it took
fourteen weeks to make that film; it was a good picture....

Q: You had a TV show in New York in the fifties.
What was that like?

A: When I got into television and started at WOR-TV
in New York with a five-days-a-week kid's show, I ran serials
and westerns, and whatever I thought would interest the kids.
Not only my serials and westerns, but whatever we could get
hold of at the right price and run on the program.

Q: Do you have a favorite co-star among the actors
and actresses you've worked with?

A: I liked Charlie Middleton. He was the greatest;
he was one of the really good things we had in the Flash
Gordon series. Jean Rogers made a good Dale; she was a
nice girl to work with.

Q: Your career in serials spanned two decades. Towards the end, in the fifties, were you aware of the deteriorating production values?

A: Oh, yes. We would make a serial for $100,000 or $175,000, in through there.

Q: Of all the films you've appeared in, do you have a personal favorite?

A: Well, of course, the Captain Gallant of the Foreign Legion TV series, and the reason for that was because I had my son in it with me; I didn't play his father in it, though. The premise of the series was that his father had been a captain in the Foreign Legion like I was, and his dad had been killed in Indochina, so he played my ward in the series. He called me Uncle Mike....

BUSTER CRABBE: A FILMOGRAPHY

The following are all full-length feature films unless identified as serials.

King of the Jungle (Paramount, 1933)

Man of the Forest (Paramount, 1933)

Tarzan the Fearless (Principal, 1933)--SERIAL

To the Last Man (Paramount, 1933)

The Sweetheart of Sigma Chi (Monogram, 1933)

The Thundering Herd (Paramount, 1933)

The Search for Beauty (Paramount, 1934)

You're Telling Me (Paramount, 1934)

Badge of Honor (Mayfair, 1934)

We're Rich Again (RKO, 1934)

The Oil Raider (Mayfair, 1934)

She Had to Choose (Mayfair, 1934)

Hold 'em Yale (Paramount, 1935)

The Wanderer of the Wasteland (Paramount, 1935)

Nevada (Paramount, 1935)

Drift Fence (Paramount, 1936)

Desert Gold (Paramount, 1936)

Flash Gordon (Universal, 1936)--SERIAL

The Arizona Raiders (Paramount, 1936)

Lady Be Careful (Paramount, 1936)

Rose Bowl (Paramount, 1936)

Arizona Mahoney (Paramount, 1936)

Murder Goes to College (Paramount, 1937)

King of the Gamblers (Paramount, 1937)

Forlorn River (Paramount, 1937)

Sophie Lang Goes West (Paramount, 1937)

Daughter of Shanghai (Paramount, 1937)

Thrill of a Lifetime (Paramount, 1937)

Flash Gordon's Trip to Mars (Universal, 1938)--SERIAL

Tip-off Girls (Paramount, 1938)

Hunted Men (Paramount, 1938)

Red Barry (Universal, 1938)--SERIAL

Illegal Traffic (Paramount, 1938)

Buck Rogers (Universal, 1939)--SERIAL

Unmarried (Paramount, 1939)

Million Dollar Legs (Paramount, 1939)

Colorado Sunset (Republic, 1939)

Call a Messenger (Universal, 1939)

Flash Gordon Conquers the Universe (Universal, 1940)--
    SERIAL

Sailor's Lady (20th Century-Fox, 1940)

Jungle Man (PRC, 1941)

Billy the Kid, Wanted (PRC, 1941)

Billy the Kid's Roundup (PRC, 1941)

Billy the Kid Trapped (PRC, 1942)

Smoking Guns (PRC, 1942)

Jungle Siren (PRC, 1942)

Wildcat (Paramount, 1942)

Law and Order (PRC, 1942)

Mysterious Rider (PRC, 1942)

Sheriff of Sage Valley (PRC, 1942)

Queen of Broadway (PRC, 1943)

The Kid Rides Again (PRC, 1943)

Fugitive of the Plains (PRC, 1943)

Western Cyclone (PRC, 1943)

The Renegade (PRC, 1943)

Cattle Stampede (PRC, 1943)

Blazing Frontier (PRC, 1943)

Devil Riders (PRC, 1943)

The Drifter (PRC, 1943)

Nabonga (PRC, 1944)

Frontier Outlaws (PRC, 1944)

Thundering Gunslingers (PRC, 1944)

Valley of Vengeance (PRC, 1944)

The Contender (PRC, 1944)

Fuzzy Settles Down (PRC, 1944)

Rustler's Hideout (PRC, 1944)

Wild Horse Phantom (PRC, 1944)

Oath of Vengeance (PRC, 1944)

His Brother's Ghost (PRC, 1945)

Shadows of Death (PRC, 1945)

Gangster's Den (PRC, 1945)

Stagecoach Outlaws (PRC, 1945)

Border Badmen (PRC, 1945)

Fighting Bill Carson (PRC, 1945)

Prairie Rustlers (PRC, 1945)

Lightning Raiders (PRC, 1945)

Gentlemen with Guns (PRC, 1946)

Ghost of Hidden Valley (PRC, 1946)

Prairie Badmen (PRC, 1946)

Terrors on Horseback (PRC, 1946)

Overland Raiders (PRC, 1946)

Outlaw of the Plains (PRC, 1946)

Swamp Fire (Paramount, 1946)

The Last of the Redmen (Columbia, 1947)

The Sea Hound (Columbia, 1947)--SERIAL

Caged Fury (Paramount, 1948)

Captive Girl (Columbia, 1950)

Pirates of the High Seas (Columbia, 1950)--SERIAL

The Lawless Eighties (Republic, 1951)

King of the Congo (Columbia, 1952)--SERIAL

Gun Brothers (United Artists, 1956)

Badman's Country (Warner Brothers, 1958)

Gunfighters of Abilene (United Artists, 1960)

The Bounty Killer (Embassy, 1965)

Arizona Raiders (Columbia, 1965)

The Comeback Trail (Entity Productions, 1972)

2. Jean Rogers

Jean Rogers was born of Swedish parents on March 25, 1916 in Watertown, Massachusetts. Eleanor Dorothy Lovegren changed her name to Jean Rogers after winning a trip to Hollywood and a screen test in a local talent contest. She was cast in a small role in the film Eight Girls in a Boat, produced by Charles Rogers, and from there she went on to a short, unproductive stint at Warner Brothers before graduating to a role in Stormy at Universal Pictures in 1935. She was promptly signed to a contract, and appeared in several features and serials before producer Henry MacRae chose her for the role of Dale Arden in Flash Gordon. She repeated the role in the sequel, Flash Gordon's Trip to Mars, in 1938, but by that time she had grown tired of her reign as Universal's "serial queen," and moved on to Twentieth Century-Fox.

Jean Rogers and Buster Crabbe return to Earth at the con-
clusion of Flash Gordon (Universal, 1936).

Jean married talent agent Dan Winkler in 1939. They
were divorced a couple of years later, but remarried in
1943, and a daughter, Ellen, was born in 1944. Jean left
Twentieth Century-Fox for a contract at Metro, but ultimately
decided to neglect her career in order to devote more time
to her marriage and care for her ailing mother. She continued to appear in an occasional film and her last appearance was in a Robert Young mystery, The Second Woman,
in 1951. In 1952 Jean was tested for the second lead in the
Joan Crawford film, Sudden Fear, but Gloria Grahame finally
won the role. Jean Rogers earned a permanent niche in film

history with her role as Dale Arden in the Flash Gordon
serials, a role that rewarded her with the same sort of pop
immortality that Fay Wray achieved with her appearance in
King Kong.

The following interview was conducted on March 21,
1981.

Q: The first Flash Gordon serial you did in 1936 has
a very distinctive atmosphere; visually it is reminiscent of
Universal's classic horror pictures. In your opinion, did
the director, Frederick Stephani, take more interest in Flash
Gordon than a serial director normally would?

A: I think that Frederick Stephani did take more time.
I don't know what Frederick Stephani's background is, and I
don't know what happened to him; I haven't heard anything
about him since Flash Gordon. Ford Beebe did a lot of westerns and things before Flash Gordon's Trip To Mars, and
to him it was just kind of another job. Frederick Stephani
seemed to show more interest in making and directing the
first picture, but maybe I'm prejudiced because everybody
seems to like the first one better than the second one.

Q: Did Carl Laemmle, Jr. , the head of Universal
and the executive producer of most of their horror films,
take any personal interest in the production of the first Flash
Gordon serial?

A: I wouldn't know that, because that was the front
office, but he must have, otherwise why would they make a
second one? Buster and I and the rest of the cast thought
making the first one was crazy, because the story was so
fantastic. Laemmle must have thought that it was just exciting enough as a serial to make a second one.

Q: Did you have any personal contact with Universal
producer Henry McRae?

A: Yes. He was the producer of all the serials I
did. A jolly, plump guy; very nice; I liked him. Richard
Fryer was his favorite cameraman.

Q: Do you have any memories of Charles Middleton,
who played Ming?

A: When he was in his cloak, and made up like Ming, he strutted around like Ming; he really did strut! He was a very nice guy, but he had to stay in character, so he strutted around, but the minute he got out of his street clothes, he was a different person ... it was really quite amusing!

Q: Were you friendly at all with Priscilla Lawson, who played Princess Aura?

A: Yes, we were good friends, and everyone's found a different story for what's happened to her. I heard that she died from tuberculosis in a sanitarium years ago, and Buster heard that she was running a floral shop in Los Angeles and had lost one leg in a car accident. Nobody really knows, but I think that if she was still around someplace, I think that she would have come forward and we'd know about it. A lot of people have tried to track her down and couldn't find her.

Q: What about Richard Alexander, who was Prince Barin in the serials?

A: Buster and I visited him just recently. We had heard that he wasn't doing very well, and we were surprised to learn that he is well. Mentally he's fine, he had some old photos to show us, and he was in a wheel chair, but he was all dressed up with a shirt and a tie. In Flash Gordon he was kind of plump with curly hair. He's still attractive, but now there's not much hair and he's very thin. A lot of years have gone by.

Q: There are a couple of scenes in the first Flash Gordon serial that look as though they might have been rather unpleasant to shoot. For instance, in chapter three, Flash and Dale are attacked by shark men in a pool of water....

A: Oh, the water was dirty and cold; it was horrible, it was just awful! That was done on the Universal back lot, which I understand is now part of the Universal tour.

Q: In chapter five of the same serial, you're involved in a scene where you're chased by a bear across the throne room of the hawk-men. Was that dangerous?

A: Yes, because I had to be on the stage with him. Before we did the scene, there was this horrible commotion in back of the scenery, and we all wondered what in the world it was. The poor bear had been there for just hours and hours waiting to do his scene, and apparently he was not very happy about the whole thing, and he became very ugly with his trainer. So then they said, "Now he's going to chase you across the set," and I was really scared to death because he had just tried to attack his trainer! I wasn't very happy about doing that scene!

Q: Was the production schedule on serials hectic?

A: They didn't have any such thing as an eight-hour day; gosh, you worked until midnight and then had to be back in make-up in the morning. Believe me, Sunday was welcome, because I think I spent the whole day sleeping, but it wasn't so bad, because we were so young.

Q: Did the director use more than one camera during the filming of a serial?

A: They had more than one. Most of the time just one, for certain scenes, as I recall, more than one.

Q: In the first Flash Gordon serial you're a blonde, and in the second serial you're a brunette. Why did Universal change your hair color for the second serial?

A: I think according to the comic strip, Dale's a brunette, so why they had me a blonde in the first place, I don't know ... they probably didn't even think about it, and then all of a sudden someone probably said, "Well, you know, she really is a brunette," and they decided to make me a brunette! That long blonde hair was really a fall, it was bleached the same color as mine, and they would just pin it on up underneath my real hair.

Q: In the second serial, Flash Gordon's Trip to Mars, they have flashbacks which are stock footage from the first serial, and of course, you're a blonde in those....

A: I know, I've heard that; isn't that horrible? I don't know the reason for that!

Q: Did you happen to see any of the Flash Gordon special effects in the process of being filmed?

A: I didn't, I really didn't, because I just wasn't involved in that part of the production, and I never had a chance to.

Q: Do you recall any specific details about the Flash Gordon serials as far as production techniques are concerned?

A: They used to spend so much money on clothes; and even though it was in black and white, they had to have the colors bright and so forth. Ming's costume was real fur, and that was a red velvet cloak he wore ... and that white dress (if you can call it a dress) that I wore, with the gold trim, that was beautiful material. They used very expensive material for the dresses and things in Flash Gordon; they were very beautifully made; and they were made for the movie.

Q: Do you still keep in touch with any of the Flash Gordon production crew?

A: Yes, Eddie Keys, who was head of props at Universal, and as a matter of fact I heard that he just retired about a year ago, and he's been at Universal all these years. He stopped by to see me about three years ago, and we had a nice visit. Whether he was head of the prop department when he did Flash Gordon, I'm not sure. A very nice guy.

Q: You weren't in the third serial of the group, Flash Gordon Conquers the Universe; Carol Hughes took over your role of Dale Arden. Did Universal make any attempt at all to cast you in the third serial?

A: Yes. I left Universal because they wouldn't raise my salary and I wanted to go on; I felt that was the thing to do. They tried to borrow me from 20th Century-Fox to do the third one, but Fox had plans for me and they wouldn't let me go, so that's how Carol Hughes ended up with the role.

Q: Have you seen the 1980 remake of Flash Gordon?

A: I've gotten a lot of fan mail on it, fans writing to tell me what they thought of the new Flash Gordon, and actually the response is not good, but I didn't think it was that bad. My biggest complaint about it was that I didn't think the music went with it. I just felt that the music didn't help the picture, that's my opinion. I liked the two girls, but I have to agree with Buster, they kind of looked too much alike. I did not like Ming, I thought our Ming was much better; I didn't like Dr. Zarkov; I liked our Dr. Zarkov very much. Vultan was OK in the new film. I didn't like Sam

Jones as Flash, but, I think I'm prejudiced. Most of the
fans say that as corny as the old one is, it's much better.

Q: Do you have any comments to make on the other
Universal serials you appeared in?

A: Tailspin Tommy and the Great Air Mystery was
an interesting serial to make. The head of the studio then
was a man named Fred Myers, and his daughter Delphine
Drew and I became very good friends. We were such good
friends that Fred Myers used to say, "Now I've got two
daughters, a blonde and a brunette." I liked the whole family,
and it was such a pleasant movie to do, because we had such
a good time making it together. I did see her a while after
that, but I don't know where she is now.

Q: Do you have any memories of Boris Karloff, who
co-starred with you in the film Night Key?

A: He helped me a great deal; I was new to acting.
In Flash Gordon there wasn't very much acting, you know.
"Where did you go, Flash, where are you?" It was that
kind of thing, not much dialogue. Karloff was a kind man,
really. He played these awful monsters, but he was very
sweet. He helped me a great deal, coaching me every time
I had to do a scene, if I asked him; he would never butt in,
though. If I played a scene and I asked, "Well, is that al-
right?" he'd either say, "That's fine" or "Well, I have a
suggestion to make." He was a sweet guy, and I learned
a lot from him.

Q: What about Whistling in Brooklyn with Red Skelton?

A: Oh, that was a fun picture to make. Red Skelton
was so much fun to work with. The only trouble was that
he knew the script, but he didn't quite keep the dialogue the
way it's supposed to go, so you kind of have to go along,
and I understand he still does the same thing. It's hard to
keep up with him.

Q: How about Let's Make Music?

A: They borrowed me from Fox; my husband was one
of the executives at RKO. I would assume he had something
to do with it. I don't think he really had that much influence,
but there was nobody under contract at the time that they
thought could play the part who was right for it.

Q: Do you recall Edmund Lowe in The Strange Mr. Gregory?

A: He was fine, but he was very hammy; he had to be the whole scene and make sure his face was shown, and he wasn't very cooperative as far as feeling, "Well, she's a young actress, and I've had more experience than she has." It wasn't one of those things; it was going to be Edmund Lowe or else! But he was nice; he was pleasant; but I can't say one of my favorite actors to work with.

Q: How about Hotel for Women?

A: That was with Linda Darnell and Ann Southern ... a good cast. Gregory Ratoff was the director, and he was so funny to work for, because it was a girl's story, and if he didn't like the way you were playing a scene, instead of telling you how, he would act it out himself. He had a very thick accent, and when he would show us how to do a scene, we all thought he was hilarious! We liked him so much ... he was delightful to work for.

Q: Are there any other films that you have fond memories of?

A: Another picture that was enjoyable to do was Always in Trouble with Jane Withers. Oh, she was just a child, and so chubby, and her mother was always on the set, trying to keep her away from candy. She would always go around and try to get a nickel from the crew so she could sneak a candy bar for herself! Sometimes she got away with it, but most of them said, "No," because they knew her mother was trying to keep her weight down.

Q: Do you have a favorite film, or a favorite type of role?

A: No, I don't have a favorite. I think my favorite type of part was when I had a chance to do something other than leads, character-type parts like in Whistling in Brooklyn, which was comedy, and then in Swing Shift Maisie. I played a "heavy" in that. Then at Fox I did a movie called Inside Story, where I had a chance to do something other than just a plain ingenue. I enjoyed those roles; I can't say I really had a favorite part, though.

Q: How about a favorite co-star?

A: Buster comes first. I liked working with Glenn Ford; I enjoyed working with Red Skelton, too. John Wayne I enjoyed working with in <u>Conflict</u>. He was one of my favorite people; he was a <u>very</u> nice person.

Q: How about a favorite director?

A: Gregory Ratoff. He was a good director; I liked him. When they take their job <u>too</u> seriously, they take it out on the actor or actress. <u>That</u> isn't very fair. Ricardo Cortez was the <u>outstanding</u> one. The first picture I made for him was <u>Heaven with a Barbed Wire Fence</u>, with Glenn Ford. Neither Glenn nor I liked him. He was awful to work for, so it wasn't a pleasant picture to do because he was so ugly. I think he was under contract to them as a director, and I went to the front office, and I said, "Look, I will never work for that man again ... he's <u>impossible</u>," so along came <u>Inside Story</u>, and he was to direct that, and I said, "No, I'm not going to do it," and they said, "We'll put you on suspension, then," so I got to thinking about <u>that</u>, and then they told me he had calmed down, he would be much nicer, and I have to say he was--still impossible, but a little nicer.

Q: During your film career, you worked at most of the major Hollywood studios. Did you have a favorite studio?

A: Yes, Metro. That was my ambition--to be under contract there; and I got my wish. They were the top, the quality of their pictures was considered to be the best.

Q: Your last picture was <u>The Second Woman</u> in 1951, but your role was rather small. <u>Was it originally</u> more prominent?

A: They cut it a great deal. It was much bigger, but they cut it.

Q: What have you been doing in recent years?

A: I've been in the newspaper business; I enjoyed it. I did a little bit of everything--the complaint department, answering phones, and marketing surveys. It was a little of this and a little of that, no specific thing. I tried for a couple of commercials, but I didn't make it. It's not like it used to be, because my agent used to take me up to the studios for an interview, and now they just line you up in an office. There can be 20 or 30 others there for the same commercial, and you have to wait for hours sometimes. It's just an unhappy experience.

Q: Over the years, your Flash Gordon serials have become extremely popular on television, and they've developed quite a following.   Do you enjoy hearing from your fans?

A: I get some of the craziest letters, you just wouldn't believe them.   But then I get an awful lot that make sense that I've been corresponding with.   I enjoy that.

CONCLUSION

Generally ignored in most film histories and surveys, the serial was nearly forgotten after its demise in 1956, aside from an occasional novelty re-issue or television showing. Then Star Wars was released in the middle of 1977. This highly profitable film, directed by George Lucas for 20th Century-Fox, caused a sensation with its seemingly welcome return to entertainment for entertainment's sake, and went on, in the modern world of inflated ticket prices, to become the highest-grossing movie in history.

Star Wars, diverting though it may have been, was highly overrated by some; those with good memories (or a sense of history) and an acquaintance with the sleazier vestiges of popular culture immediately recognized the film's roots in the loam of old movie serials and comic books. Set, as everyone knows by now, "a long time ago in a galaxy far, far away," Star Wars, with its fantastic costumes, swashbuckling music, frenetic action, and simplistic dialogue, recalled the better serials of yore. Even the opening expository titles (identical in style to those used at the beginning of every chapter in Flash Gordon Conquers the Universe) and the old-fashioned transitional optical wipes echoed movies of the thirties and early forties, the cliffhangers in particular. For better or worse, Lucas had drawn a clear historical line from Flash Gordon, The Phantom Empire and others to the modern cinema.

Considering these shallow origins, it was only natural that Star Wars would suffer from limitations; the basic concept was puerile, the editing forced and desperate at times, and much of the acting contemptible. Few seemed to notice, or care, that the inert Harrison Ford was on the same dramatic level with Judd Holdren in Republic's Zombies of the Stratosphere, and the consensus among devotees of Star Wars was that if Lucas was hardly original in concocting such a

celluloid pastiche, then at least his heart seemed to be in
the right place. Certainly the picture's dazzling special effects, convincing, expensively detailed and achieved through
the combination of tried-and-true methods reinforced with the
latest in computer-controlled camera technology, were the
prime factor behind its success, serving to conceal, and perhaps even partially compensate for, the film's many flaws.
But as the profits from the box office and attendant toy and
game merchandising grew to immense proportions (and cheap
imitations of the movie proliferated), several facts became
painfully clear. What had originally seemed to be appealing
naiveté on Lucas' part was eventually revealed as shrewd
marketing strategy in disguise; Lucas, well aware of the
hitherto largely unexploited, shadowy sub-culture of comic
book and science-fiction fans, had pushed all the right psy-
chological buttons with Star Wars, right down to the film's
quasi-religious undertone, personified by that sage apostle
of the mystic "Force," Alec Guinness (just about the only
decent actor in the cast).

As the resulting science-fiction boom took off with
the subsequent release of director Steven Spielberg's Close
Encounters of the Third Kind later the same year, it grew
increasingly obvious that Hollywood's largest crop of quality
fantasy pictures since the 1930s would result in a few stunning moments of technical proficiency, but very little else
of lasting worth. These movies were, from Star Wars, to
Alien, to the Star Wars sequel, The Empire Strikes Back,
all tailored from the same threadbare fabric--expensive,
over-designed, manipulative and, finally, artless. Even the
special effects in these films, for all their modern technical
aptitude, have none of the strange, unforgettable allure seen
in the miniature shots created for fantasy pictures in the
twenties and thirties; inevitably, Star Wars appears to have
had its greatest influence not on other movies (except in the
form of blatant imitation), but in the field of ad graphics and
in the design of facile video games. None of these movies
was based on or inspired by great or even good novels or
plays; their impetus stems from the third-rate: Star Wars
and The Empire Strikes Back both emanate from the serials,
as does Raiders of the Lost Ark, the plot of which appears
to have been lifted from Republic's The Perils of Nyoka; and
Alien is actually an unofficial remake of a 1958 "B" picture,
It, the Terror from Beyond Space.

The cliffhangers and "B" pictures, cheap and unobtru-
sive, served their purpose in their day, but as enjoyable as

the modern, souped-up descendants of the old serials may be to the general public, their style and content is symptomatic of all that is wrong with the modern film industry. The great movies of the past, pictures like King Kong, Citizen Kane, and The Adventures of Robin Hood, were created by diverse talents trained in a wide variety of fields--men who arrived in Hollywood and applied to the art of movie-making what they had learned in stage-direction, scenic design, writing, sculpture, and even the filming of documentaries. They found that motion pictures, in combining all those fields, could be a hundred times more effective than any one of them alone; but they also sensed that in this consolidation of the other arts the movies would seldom result in great art themselves. Consequently, they had few pretensions about their work, and in their passion to entertain a nation they created many enduring classics.

Clearly, as Star Wars and its progeny demonstrate, the modern film industry's directors have learned nearly everything there is to know about how the greatest films of the past were made, but very little about why they were made that way in the first place. For those perceptive enough to realize it, every great movie points the way down a cultural road leading to something greater (usually to the original art forms that led to its creation); but the road from Star Wars, paved with gold though it may be over the remains of old serials, leads only to a cultural dead end. That is the tragedy, and the sad failure, of the New Hollywood.

TITLE INDEX

Titles of feature-length films are designated "(F)". Pages containing illustrations are underlined.

NAME INDEX

Creative and Technical Personnel